A bible for atheists

A bible for atheists

Thomas Wright Sulcer

Copyright © 2023 by Thomas Wright Sulcer
All Rights Reserved
The moral rights of the author have been asserted

ISBN: 9798386786175 (paperback)

All rights reserved. No part of this book may be reproduced in any form or by an electronic or mechanical means, including information storage and retrieval systems, without permission in writing from the author, except by a reviewer who may quote brief passages in a review. Except for historical figures and quoted authorities, names used in the text do not bear any resemblance to actual persons, living or dead, and any apparent resemblances are purely accidental.

Second edition: April 2023

Interior formatting by Vidya and Jason of ebookpbook.com

Cover: *Young Lady in a Boat* by James Tissot (1836-1902)

Table of Contents

Introduction ix

Beginnings 1
    Genesis 1
    The engine of creation 6
    Living creatures 10
    Cause and effect 12

An individual human 15
    Human dominance 15
    The human mind 17
    The Principle of Association 20
    The mind-body problem 22
    Basics of thinking 23
    Edifices of knowledge 26
    The process of thinking 27
    Fluidity of thought 29
    Executive function 32
    The puzzle of fate and free will 34
    Free will properly understood 38
    The Basic Principle of Ethics 43
    The Principle of Accountability 49
    Types of learning 50
    The structure of knowledge 53
    Systems of life 55
    Goldilocks transformations 59
    Human agency 61
    Why we die 61

TABLE OF CONTENTS

Religion	65
Essence of religion	65
Benefits of religion	72
Drawbacks of religion	75
Atheism	79
Why we won't meet aliens	80
A human with other humans	**84**
Emotions	84
The power of emotions	84
Dual perspectives	87
Classifying the emotions	90
Pleasure-based emotions	93
Pain-based emotions	97
Desires	101
Emotional management	107
Ethics with others	113
Humans in larger systems	115
Character	117
The Binding Principle	120
Friends and enemies	123
Human reproduction	131
Evolutionary realities	131
Different roles	132
Beauty in objects	134
Human beauty	137
Biological realities	140
Romantic relationships	143
Expansion of knowledge	149
Economy	153
Estimating value	153
Fair transactions	156
Creating value	157
Systems of employment	162

How nations create value	164
Humans as creators	172
The artist	172
The process of creation	174
Creations	177
Fighting	181
Wisdom	186
Humans and the environment	194
A human in a state	197
Political structures	197
Autocrats and dictators	201
Hybrid structures	203
Rights and laws and freedom and liberty	206
Criteria for good laws	210
Principles of a good state	212
Citizenship	218
The rights of states	225
Regulatory issues	226
Violence	230
How to fight violence	234
Preventing violence	235
War	238
Meaning in our lives	242

Introduction

A bible for atheists is about how to be a good human. It was written by an atheist for other atheists. While most religions have a written text to set forth their major beliefs, there is no such text for atheists. This book is an attempt to meet such a need. While atheists are often defined by what we *don't* believe, this book tries to assert in a positive way what many atheists *do* believe. It tries to answer the big questions in a coherent and systematic way. It is not intended as a vehicle to convert believers into non-believers. It is not a definitive guide to atheism but only one approach; hence the title is ***A** bible for atheists and not **The** bible for atheists*.

A bible for atheists is in many respects the opposite of the traditional Judeo-Christian Bible. The traditional Bible is fixed and finished, with much of it written two thousand years ago, although it has undergone numerous translations; in contrast, *a bible for atheists* is a work-in-progress that may inspire knowledgeable thinkers to write improved versions. The Bible is believed to have been written by God or by humans with divine inspiration; in contrast, the *bible* is the work of an imperfect and flawed human. The Bible is presumed to be perfect; the *bible* has no such presumptions. The Bible has stories about deities and the supernatural and miracles that often violate the laws of nature; in contrast, the laws of nature hold in the *bible*. The Bible is supposed to be trusted on faith, while the *bible* encourages readers to be skeptical. The Bible sometimes offers commandments of the do-this and don't-do-that variety, while the *bible* is more advice-oriented. The Bible is often fantastical while the *bible* strives to be based on reason and science and common sense. The Bible is a combination of a history and poetry

INTRODUCTION

book with parables and stories and letters intertwined in a roughly historical order, while the *bible* is ordered from small to large, from simple to complex, starting with basic biochemistry and moving to an individual human, to groups of humans, and to humans in nations.

A bible for atheists brings in thinking from two main pathways: philosophy and science and secular humanism, and religious wisdom shorn of its supernatural aspects. What emerges is a consensus about the underlying rules of life. The book is in some respects a product of, and an extension to, the Enlightenment. It begins with generally accepted notions regarding evolution and time and human history, and weaves these ideas together to offer sometimes radical conclusions about free will and ethics. It strives to be comprehensive, covering such topics as proper thinking, management of the emotions, freedom and liberty and rights and politics, how to live a fulfilled life, the nature of happiness and wisdom, and the meaning of life. Since readers may already know or agree with parts of this text, it is organized in sections to allow skipping.

A few of the many topics covered, in no particular order or importance, are as follows: Why the sun spins. How life sprang from chemicals. The puzzle of fate and free will, solved. The best governments. Why humans dominate the Earth. How to prevent crime. How Da Vinci created the *Mona Lisa*. The rules of life. Goldilocks transformations. Why we die. Why humans believe in religion. How to rein in our emotions. Why we won't meet aliens. The goodness formula. Citizenship defined. How bonds can free us. Rights defined. Why sunsets are beautiful. Benefits of atheism. The pros and cons of religion. How to cultivate wisdom. Why autocrats in power don't last. How marriage resolves opposing sexual agendas. How the idea of lifting an arm lifts an arm. The flirting formula. Why symmetrical faces are beautiful. Strategies to prevent violence. Love or limerence? Criteria for good laws. How exchanges benefit buyers and sellers. How top performers practice. Layers of complexity. How to thwart procrastination. Keys to career success. How a business firm thinks. Why humans fight. The engine of creation. The meaning of life. And much more.

In sum, this text addresses the mysteries of life and the big questions in an internally consistent structure.

So let's begin.

Beginnings

Genesis

The universe was, is, and always will be.

There was no beginning and there will be no ending.

This idea may be difficult to accept since humans think in terms of birth and life and death, of things entering and leaving, of a story having a beginning and a middle and an end, and so when we think about the universe, we think that it too has a beginning and a middle and an end, just like us. If we imagine a vast void of nothingness, and if we try to imagine anything emerging from this nothingness, then it seems impossible. A magician can not make a rabbit spontaneously spring from an empty hat. Similarly, a universe can not spring from an empty void.

Simply, something can not emerge from nothing.

If we think about any point in time in which there was something, and ask, what existed before that, and what existed before that, then we can do this endlessly until we can persuade ourselves that the universe has always existed.

Further, the universe stretches outward in all directions, endlessly, infinitely.

If we could build a faster-than-light spaceship and travel throughout the universe, then the idea that we would bump into a wall at the outermost edge of the universe does not seem right. How could such a hypothetical wall have been built? And what lies beyond it? The idea of cordoning off the universe into a *something-ness* and a *nothing-ness* does not make sense, and if we think that way, we will be using our finite-only human-type thinking instead of our logical common-sense type thinking. We will be thinking as if the universe is a finite structure with boundaries such as a house or a planet, but this is not the case. The universe extends outward, forever, in all directions, and any spaceship that we build in search of any such boundary will be traveling forever.

While the universe is infinite, our human world is finite, and it is important for us, as living creatures with finite life spans, to understand our place in the universe. Accordingly, it is important to understand our origins partly because many of the patterns of creation are continuing today. But understanding our beginnings is difficult because there were no scientists or journalists or historians to record what happened. While we do not understand the complete sequence of events, we can see specific points in our past, and our understanding becomes clearer as we learn more.

Scientists speculate about how life began. At present, they can not speculate about what happened before the *Big Bang* about fourteen billion years ago. Although new information and tools become available to help them piece together the sequence of events, the transition from inanimate chemicals to living beings remains murky and unclear. What follows is a guess about what happened, with the caveat that what follows is highly speculative and subject to revision.

About four billion years ago our sun and the Earth were created. While the sun with its powerful gravity absorbed almost all of the gaseous cloud, some particles did not get drawn in, and these became the planets and moons as well as some asteroids and space dust. Because particles inside the sun were unevenly distributed, and because each particle exerted a pull on nearby particles, it happened that, over time, some pulls were stronger than others, causing the sun to spin. Something similar happened in the solar system, so planets spin around the sun, and each planet spins on its own axis. All spinning is in roughly the same direction on a rather flat two dimensional platter in our galaxy, except for Uranus and Venus with backwards orbits, probably because of hits from large asteroids.

Most likely, the early Earth was a "hellish fiery wasteland" bombarded by meteors and asteroids according to Neal deGrasse Tyson. But our planet was well suited for life. It was just the right distance from the sun so that it was neither too hot nor too cold, and it was just the right size so its gravity was strong enough to keep it together, but not so strong that nothing could move on the surface. Earth benefitted from having much larger planets even further out on the solar platter that could attract asteroids and other space debris. Jupiter acts like a giant bodyguard to yank in almost all planet-shattering life-destroying asteroids before they can collide with the Earth.

Earth had the elements of life ready for assembly: oxygen and hydrogen and phosphorus and nitrogen and especially carbon, which was highly important because of its unique structure. Carbon atoms have six electrons organized into an inner ring of two electrons and an outer ring of four electrons, enabling the outer electrons to bind easily with other elements such as oxygen and hydrogen and nitrogen and phosphorus. Carbon can share electrons with other atoms like neighbors who share a common driveway. It binds them together, but the bond is not so strong that it can't be broken, but it is strong enough to form stable complex molecules. Carbon is so versatile that it can make ten million unique compounds. It can bind with itself to make molecules necessary for life, such as amino acids and DNA and proteins. Some carbon-based molecules can make molecules that store energy, such as glucose. In addition, these molecular arrangements can store information, so that a particular ordering of them, in a particular sequence, can serve as an instruction for how to do some other process. For many reasons, carbon is the molecule of life.

Earth has one more lucky molecule that enables life: water. It is unclear at this time whether the original Earth had water, but over time, hydrogen and oxygen atoms came together to make water molecules. Water is an ideal medium for bringing atoms together in new arrangements because it lets atoms touch each other, and bind together or split apart. Water is like a county fair that brings buyers and sellers together in new ways. Water is a better medium for bringing elements together than rocks which hold atoms in fixed arrangements. Water is a better medium than a gas because atoms move too quickly in it to bind.

So, the stage is set for life to spring forth. There's Earth. There are the right elements. There is water for them to slosh about in. There is time, lots of time, millions and millions of years for new combinations of atoms and molecules to form and reform, to experiment with new arrangements. There is energy from the inner Earth, from lightning, and from the sun to jiggle molecules into new arrangements. Sometimes the molecules would shuffle into long chains, sometimes looping back on themselves, forming a circle or a spherical shape, with an inside and an outside.

Then, some structures got the ability to self-replicate. By random chance and fluke experimentation, they made more of themselves. It is not clear how this happened, but it is likely that this did, indeed, happen. These self-replicating structures became abundant, and they served as a springboard for the creation of other types of self-replicating structures.

During millions of years, the process of evolution began working on these new self-replicating structures. They adapted to new environments like living creatures do, in what scientists call chemical evolution. One theory maintains that the earliest life originated deep in ocean vents, with the energy from the Earth's core forming self-replicating bacteria or other primitive single-celled creatures. Energy shuffled them into new combinations. By trial-and-error, structures that were best suited, or the most fit, survived and thrived. Successful adaptations got locked in, and they became, in turn, the basis for further adaptations. In such a way, slowly, inexorably, life sprung from simple atoms to more complex structures, and from these, to even more complex structures. Life could build on life. As Richard Dawkins explained, "Darwinian natural selection is so stunningly elegant because it solves the problem of explaining complexity in terms of nothing but simplicity, by providing a smooth ramp of gradual, step-by-step increment."

If one thinks in terms of living beings springing to life, instantaneously, then it seems impossible, leading one to think that such a transformation would require a creator deity with the power to instantly create complex beings such as ourselves. But life did not happen instantly. It took billions of years to figure out how things work, trillions and trillions of experiments, almost all of them fruitless which resulted in nothing in particular. But occasionally, rarely and randomly, things clicked, and when they clicked, a new structure would get locked in place to become the basis for more complex structures. These new structures were more complex than those that existed before. They could affect and be affected by more things. They had a transformative power. A simple pebble would just sit there, forever, affecting nothing. But a more complex living being, moving about, taking in things and excreting out things, could move the pebble.

For the first few billion years of Earth's history, there were probably only simple single-celled creatures called prokaryotes. It took another billion years to spawn larger single-celled creatures with a nucleus, called eukaryotes. According to one estimate, about five hundred million years ago, the first multicellular creatures were created. This transformation may have happened when one single-cell creature ate another single-cell creature, but the digestion was not complete, so that both creatures worked together to sustain life; over time, the half-digested creature may have evolved into a specialized organ for the outer creature.

This speculation is based on evidence from fossils and the radiometric dating of rocks and bones. The current thinking is that our particular human species is approximately 250,000 years old and originated in Africa as hunter-gatherer bands. They adapted to live on every continent except Antarctica, and learned how to grow crops and domesticate livestock perhaps 10,000 years ago.

In the present era, these changes continue. Humans build

spaceships to fly to the moon and back, and submarines to explore the ocean depths. We have permanent bases on the treacherously cold continent of Antarctica.

While it may seem implausible that living things could spring forth from random chemicals, consider a virus. It is not like a living thing that eats or drinks or breathes or walks, yet it exists. It is a mere string of chemicals sitting on a door handle, tiny and unseen. It was not created by a deity or by humans but it emerged through random mutation and chemical evolution. It is picked up by a hand which rubs a nose to get inside the human body. Its particular chemical pattern tricks cells into letting it inside, where it hijacks the cellular machinery to make copies of itself. The human gets a cold, then sneezes out the offspring of the virus, including some slightly different copies of itself, to lie in wait on future door handles to infect new humans. That is how it reproduces. If a mutated version of the virus is better adapted to promulgate itself within humans, then it flourishes. The point is that happenstance chemical combinations might have reproduced like a virus, since the patterns are similar.

So, this is probably how we came to be. If this is the case, it suggests that we are extremely lucky to be alive, to have been the beneficiaries of trillions and trillions of lucky experiments, to exist on the only planet among millions that was suitable for life, and to be alive at this time when we continue to reap the fruits of creation.

The engine of creation

The early transition from inanimate chemicals to living structures was one example of a repeating pattern that we might call the **engine of creation**. It is important to understand this pattern because it has implications for human creativity. The pattern has been happening repeatedly during the past fourteen billion years.

The pattern follows a three stage trajectory.

At an initial starting point, there is an intense concentration, extremely hot, loaded with energy, simple, surrounded by a huge empty area that is spread out and devoid of energy.

Then there is a transition such that the concentrated thing bursts outward, cooling as it radiates, making diverse things that are dispersed unevenly. Forces of attraction among the diverse things cause some of the scattered parts to clump together into new structures that never existed before, that are fresh and original and unique. While the rest remains simple and boring, these new clumped arrangements are relatively complex. They have new patterns of order and hierarchy. They are governed by new rules and they have new properties. They compete with other such structures to see what, if anything, works best. The simpler things within a clump essentially remain simple, but their interactions with other simple things cause them to act differently than they did before, as functioning members of the more complex structure. The change from simpler things to more complex things gets locked into the system, so that the new things hold their complexity and don't revert to their earlier simpler state. They have less total energy than the initial starting point, but their relative concentration of energy is higher than the initial starting point. Scientists use the term *emergence* to describe how complex things spring forth in this manner. The mechanism of evolution operates on these new creations, as they adapt to try to maintain their new arrangements. During the later stages of the transition, the pace of concentration speeds up considerably.

Last, the pattern resolves into an ending point. What emerges are structures which are smaller than the initial starting point but that are more complex and concentrated. While the amount of bundled energy at the initial starting point is considerable, the energy flows within the new complex things are even greater in a relative sense. While they are somewhat stable, they are fragile, and they can not exist indefinitely. Then, the pattern repeats, so that the ending point becomes the starting point for a whole new transformation, so that the engine of creation keeps cranking out amazing new things. The system as a whole doesn't become more complex, but mostly it stays the same, and only a few small parts become more complex. That's why the universe is mostly boring and simple and empty and cold and still and lifeless, with only a tiny fraction of it being interesting and complex and full and hot and action packed and lively.

If this seems abstract, we can examine the transformation from farming to cities about ten thousand years ago.

At an initial starting point, humans were farming in the Fertile Crescent area of Mesopotamia. Most humans were still living the simpler nomadic lifestyle of hunter-gatherer bands. The initial extent of the complexity was in the farms. These had energy flows in the form of sunlight and work by farmers to till the soil and plant the seeds and so forth, resulting in stored food energy. By farming, humans were able to capture more energy by staying in one place, rather than moving regularly to hunt for game and to search for berries.

Then, there's a transition. Since farmers needed tools and seeds, villages formed where such transactions could take place, often centrally located. The farms were not spaced evenly but were dispersed over a geographic area, so that some farms were closer together in clumps while others were farther apart. As time passed, the clumps of farms became larger villages which then grew into small cities. Forces of attraction pulled workers in, to become specialists working together in a more densely packed space, with greater relative energy in the form of food and wealth than on the individual farms. A city seems to emerge magically on its own, as if one might not have guessed beforehand that the simple farms would bring about the more complex city. It has tall buildings. Its workers specialize in banking and insurance and policing and buying and selling. It is governed by new rules. It competes with other cities to attract workers and businesses by adapting and evolving. The city is somewhat fragile in the sense that it depends on complex energy flows to maintain its structure. Many things have to work properly for it to continue to exist. The city draws food from the surrounding farms, and it supplies tools and services in return. Like an individual farm, the city is a finite thing that will not endure forever.

Then, the city serves as an ending point which will become, in turn, the starting point for subsequent transformations. This engine of creation repeats to bring about even more complex structures, such as city-states and empires.

While this is one example, this pattern has been repeating again and again. It is how amazing new things are created out of simpler materials. It is how stars emerged, and from stars, planets and new elements like uranium and carbon, and from these, life. The engine is operating today as humans create new technologies such as satellites and smartphones.

The pattern describes the beginning of our particular section of the universe. At that time, about fourteen billion years ago, everything was squeezed into an incredibly hot and concentrated space, which we can think of as the initial starting point. Then it burst apart in a gigantic explosion called the *Big Bang.* During this transition stage, particles spewed forth in all directions, cooling, forming hydrogen and helium atoms, which were relatively more complex than what existed before. These atoms were new creations, made of different parts, namely, protons and neutrons and electrons, governed by new rules. They were relatively stable in that they did not degenerate back into the relatively simpler parts that comprised the beginning of the *Big Bang*, that is, this change got locked into the system. Since atoms were not dispersed uniformly but unevenly, forces of attraction between them caused some to clump into gaseous clouds, and these, in turn, sometimes became stars. It is as if the atoms were struggling to adapt to the new arrangement, and they *evolved* into stars. The atoms were so tightly packed within the star that the extremely high temperatures caused the stars to emit light and heat. The star had a relatively greater concentration of energy than the initial phase of the *Big Bang*. We could describe stars as the ending point.

Then, the pattern repeated. Some stars would explode in spectacular supernovas, with even more intense heat, fusing protons and neutrons in new combinations, creating new elements such as carbon and uranium and gold, which were catapulted throughout the universe. These new elements had greater complexity than simple hydrogen or helium, with more protons and neutrons and electrons. They *emerged,* as if by magic.

While the engine of creation keeps repeating as a pattern, the pace of creation is speeding up. The *Big Bang* was 13.8 billion years ago. Our sun was created 4.6 billion years ago. Life on Earth happened about 3.5 billion years ago. Multicellular creatures happened 0.5 billion years ago. Humans were created about 250,000 years ago. They created agriculture about 10,000 years ago. The Industrial Revolution started 270 years ago. The overall trend is that new creations are emerging faster and faster.

Living creatures

The universe is almost entirely empty, a massively expansive dark void, cold and lifeless, with matter being just a small part of it, and living creatures being a tiny fraction of that. If the universe is a giant multi-tiered wedding cake, life is a tiny sliver of icing at the top.

While living beings are made of inanimate things, they are qualitatively different and tend to share these basic properties:

- **Desire.** It is a powerful motivating force to get nourishment, water, air, sunlight, minerals and so forth, whatever is needed to survive, as well as to reproduce. In a human, desire is a complex rearranging of the basic attractions between particles, so the same forces which join quarks or atoms prompt a human to seek an apple or a sexual partner, except that these forces are arranged in a more complex way.
- **Border.** There is an inside and an outside, with the internal area being more predictable and constant than the external

area. Humans need an internal watery environment with a fairly constant temperature for our cells to carry out vital chemical reactions.
- **Structure.** Creatures need a fixed shape that includes such things as bones or cartilage, skin, membranes, and cell walls. The parts must work together in harmony to preserve a constancy in the internal environment. Forces keep the parts together so that a body doesn't disperse in every direction.
- **Metabolism.** Creatures must take in enough energy to move chemicals internally. Plants get this energy from the sun by photosynthesis, while animals eat plants or other animals to get their stored energy. Viruses do not have their own metabolism but hijack energy from the host cells.
- **Reproduction.** They make copies of themselves so that the species can continue after particular creatures die.
- **Adaptation.** Since the environment can change, from hot to cold, from wet to dry, or from light to dark, creatures must adapt to these changes. This is true for the creature as an individual as well as for the species in its entirety.

Many animals have a front-to-back orientation, with their forward-area holding a brain and perceptual apparatus, which is oriented toward gathering energy and food and finding mates and avoiding danger, while their backward-area is where waste is released. Larger creatures generally live longer than smaller ones.

Creatures are interconnected to each other in complex ever-changing food chains. The tiniest creatures serve as food for larger creatures, which serve as food for even larger ones. Tiny creatures tend to be more numerous than larger ones. But even the largest creatures can be eaten by smaller ones. The waste products of some creatures serve as food and nutrients for others. So life-supporting elements including nitrogen and oxygen and carbon dioxide are not lost after being used but are constantly being recycled in a sprawling ecosystem. The Earth is a giant recycling station for life, with a relatively constant resupply of energy from the sun.

The basic characteristics of life are found in simple things like cells and in complex things like humans. For example, cells have a cell membrane; humans have skin. Cells need nutrients; humans need food. Higher-order living things like humans are more complex, with more working parts, so they can do things that lower-order creatures can not do. For example, a human can think while a cell can not.

Cause and effect

A basic law of the universe is **cause-and-effect**. It operates everywhere, all the time. It is a simple idea, easily understood, in that a cause *causes* an effect, and an effect is caused by a cause. The cause happens before the effect, and the effect happens after the cause. If we describe a cause-and-effect relation on a timeline, with time moving from left to right, the cause happens to the left and the effect happens to the right, and the arrow between them denotes the relation between the cause and the effect. It can happen that multiple causes can have one effect, or that one cause can have multiple effects. The idea of cause-and-effect is accepted widely, and it is recognized by almost all religious traditions; for example, in the Bhagavad Gita, the notion of karma is that every event is both a cause and an effect, and that every act has consequences which in turn cause further consequences.

Cause-and-effect is not something mysterious that we have to take on faith but rather it is observable directly from our experience. When we see a flash of lightning and then hear the crash of thunder, we think that the lightning *caused* the thunder.

Cause-and-effect is how humans think. When we try to understand how things happen, we think in terms of *this* causing *that*, or *these things* causing *those things*. It is our default way of interpreting our world. These determinations are guesses which may be wrong or right. We value correct guesses since they are a key to our survival in an uncertain world.

While cause-and-effect is visible everywhere, it may be impossible to prove. If we look at one billiard ball striking another, for example, then we might think that the first ball caused the second ball to move. However, if we focus a microscope at the space between those balls, magnifying the image as much as we can, we still could not say with certainty why one ball caused the other ball to move. It may be the case that there is an unseen mysterious power which controls the movement of both the first ball and the second ball, such that the unseen power made it seem like the first ball caused the second to move, but in actuality, the unseen third power did the moving. But cause-and-effect relations are so prevalent everywhere we look, and are valuable in helping humans stay alive, that it makes sense to accept the idea that cause-and-effect is an essential property of the universe.

At subatomic levels, there appears to be an essential randomness. Numerous experiments suggest that the way that electrons move is impossible to predict. If scientists know the speed of an electron, they can't know its position, or if they know its position, they can't know its speed. But at higher levels of matter, there is no measurable randomness, so the laws of nature apply consistently. If we stand at sea level and throw a ball in the air, it will always come down. Gravity holds. How things behave is predictable, and this predictability enables humans to exist and for living beings to thrive.

We think of time as having a past, a present, and a future. The past is what happened before, the present is what is happening now, and the future is what will happen later. We can see something in the present and make a guess about what happened in the past, such as when scientists find a fossil and speculate about a creature that once lived. We think not only in terms of the past and the present but we can imagine time extending into the future, and we can imagine what the future might be like. This enables planning. The rule is that time always moves forward and not backward. We can neither return to the past nor stop the progression of time.

BEGINNINGS

Everything is changing, all the time, and it has always been this way and it will always be this way. Nothing is fixed and everything is moving and this is good because it enables life. If nothing moved, life would come to a terrifying halt. Acrobats in a circus and butterflies flying across a prairie are obviously moving but even cold and hard things like the marble in a statue are made of atoms which have spinning electrons. Even the statue is subjected to wind and rain and freezing cold which can affect its outer layers over time and cause it to crumble. Colder things move more slowly than warmer things.

An individual human

Human dominance

This is our world from which we evolved. From the Big Bang fourteen billion years ago, to our sun and Earth four billion years ago, by the luck of having a Goldilocks planet that is neither too hot nor too cold, with energy sources to mix chemicals in random ways in a liquid stew, life blossomed. During several billion years, living creatures evolved from tiny single-celled creatures reproducing asexually to complex multicellular creatures reproducing sexually. Plants developed ways to extract energy directly from sunlight by photosynthesis using chlorophyll. Animals learned to eat plants. The traits of creatures varied considerably, such that the best adapted creatures survived and reproduced.

Scientists currently believe that humans first appeared on the planet approximately 250,000 years ago. A combination of powerful adaptations helped our ancestors. Our brains were large in relation to our body size. Our upright posture left our hands free to grasp objects, along with the helpful adaptation of opposable thumbs. We could communicate complex thoughts with other humans by passing air through our vocal cords to make unique recognizable sounds. No other species had this particular combination of adaptations.

Today, we are Earth's dominant creature. Our activity can cause entire species to either prosper or become extinct. We inhabit every continent. We can change the course of rivers, tunnel through mountains, raise the Earth's average temperature or take actions to prevent this. We can invent new chemical elements. We can trap tigers and keep them in zoos. We can teach killer whales to perform

AN INDIVIDUAL HUMAN

tricks in theme parks. We create medicines to subdue microscopic attackers such as smallpox and diphtheria.

The force behind human dominance is that we adapt extremely rapidly. Most species adapt slowly. For example, birds in the Galapagos might, by random genetic variation, develop a refined beak to help them eat a worm particular to that island. The improved beak is an adaptive trick, but that is its one trick, and it took decades to evolve. Further, an individual animal might learn a new trick by trial and error, such as a new food source or means of opening a coconut, but that knowledge is lost when the animal dies, and must be re-learned by successive generations.

But our human ability to communicate with symbolic language lets us teach future generations what was learned. It is more efficient than requiring each generation to relearn everything on their own. Further, the technology of writing furthers the efficiency, bypassing the need for a teacher. Humans are continually improving ways of transmitting information, from stone tablets to paper scrolls and books, and more recently by the Internet.

The result is that our storehouse of adaptive tricks grows with extreme rapidity. Anthropologists describe this advantage with the term *collective learning*. Unlike birds in the Galapagos that learn a new trick every few generations by random mutations and adaptation, humans are learning new tricks every day. It enables humans to make smart phones and scuba gear and satellites. Young humans can acquire important knowledge early in their lives, avoiding mistakes made by their ancestors. Each new generation is collectively smarter than the last one. While the knowledge of any particular human is not that impressive, the total knowledge of our entire species is awesome.

Another human advantage is that we can sometimes function as an individual and other times as a member of a group. By communicating, we can coordinate our actions when this is beneficial, and at other times we can work as isolated individuals. For instance, if a tiger approaches, humans can form a group to scare it away, and when it ambles away, we can resume individual activity. Some types of problems are better solved by a group while others are better solved by an individual. So we get the best of both worlds. In contrast, most species are stuck either as solitary creatures such as spiders or as group creatures such as bees.

Life consists of a wide diversity of beings, from microscopic single-celled creatures to complex animals with billions of cells working in a coordinated system. Every living thing has ways of dealing with its changing environment. Plants adjust their leaves toward the sun. Animals evolved an entire organ for thinking.

The human mind

Through the miracle of evolution, through the happenstance of trillions of lucky transformations, the marvelous human brain emerged. It is a spectacular and powerful organ. A human brain has a hundred billion neurons, connected in zillions of ways with baffling complexity. It can take in countless photons in a nanosecond and almost instantly recognize a human face—*one particular face* out of the eight billion faces on the planet—even though it may never have seen that particular face from that angle or with that lighting. We can recognize a song in seconds after only a few notes are played. We can sense vibrations from the vocal cords of another human to interpret human speech. Our brains use an incredible amount of energy. Even though it only occupies about five percent of the human body mass, it uses about twenty percent of the body's energy. Cranial nerves need a steady supply of oxygen and food and water, and if they are deprived of them for even a few minutes, the cells begin to die.

The mind directs our activity. It tells us what to do. It chooses our goals. It helps us make sense of our world. Hopefully it works to keep us alive, to overcome obstacles and to solve problems. But it is an imperfect organ. Sometimes it can be its own worst enemy, hindering us, distracting us, preventing us from getting what we want. So it is important for humans to understand our minds, to think about how we think, since it is vital for human freedom and happiness.

Generally we have the two fairly distinct mental states of being awake or being asleep, although there are in-between states such as falling asleep or waking up, or semi-awake states such as daydreaming or sleepwalking or hallucinating or being inebriated.

Consciousness can be thought of as an awareness of our awareness. We have a sense of things happening directly in front of us in the immediate present. It is an instantaneous-seeming sense of our body in relation to itself and in relation to other bodies and to the world in general. It is as if our brains have one set of neurons perceiving and feeling and thinking, and a second set of neurons aware of the first set, with both sets functioning simultaneously.

Mental states vary. We can be thinking actively about solving a problem, or listening to a train whistle, or thinking of nothing in particular as if our minds are wandering with no specific destination. Mental states impose different requirements for the brain; each state uses different neural circuits. Some states, such as sleeping, are necessary for other states to function properly at a later time. Our mental state should help us do what we should do. For example, if we are trying to solve a problem, we should not daydream; if we are trying to listen to a lesson from a teacher, we should not sleep.

Humans gather information through sense organs which take physical stimuli, such as photons and sonic vibrations and physical pressure and airborne chemicals, and convert these stimuli into chemical pulses which are processed by our brains. This activity helps us form a coherent mental picture of what is happening. Our brains sift through the bewildering rush of stimuli to focus on what's most important. We look for patterns such as a face or a figure walking on a landscape. Much mental processing happens before the impulses reach the deeper levels of our conscious thought. For example, the initial layer of nerves in the eye detect photons, while a slightly deeper layer detects that they're in a line, and an even deeper level detects the shape of a triangle, which gets relayed to even deeper levels. Our brains try to extract meaning from a torrent of mostly irrelevant stimuli.

Generally most of our senses are focused on what happens outside of us and not what happens within us. That way we can adjust to what happens in the external world. We have less need of an awareness of our internal bodily processes because they happen automatically without thinking. An exception is that there are sensors for pain inside our bodies, and sensors along our digestive system, which is like an external highway running through our bodies.

In addition to seeing and hearing and touching and smelling and tasting, we can sense:

- **time**—helpful for making music, dancing, walking
- **pain**—without this sense, we could not learn to avoid damaging ourselves
- **our bodily movements**—we can feel how far we've lifted an arm, for example
- **temperature**—so we can avoid hot or cold things
- **pressure**—helps us roll over periodically while sleeping
- **balance**—three circular canals inside our ears, at right angles to each other, help us stand on two feet without falling

It is how we comprehend the world around us. We can act intelligently to avoid pain and seek pleasure.

Generally we perceive things which we can do something about. We generally do not perceive things beyond our control such as small or large things. We can not see microscopic organisms like viruses or bacteria. These creatures are so small that it is not practical for a human to devote perceptual machinery to deal with them. We can not see extremely large things like the Earth itself unless we are far away in a spacecraft orbiting the moon. But we can see creatures within a range of about a few centimeters in length like a mosquito to large creatures such as a rhinoceros, since we are equipped to do something about each, whether to swat the mosquito or run from the rhinoceros.

Our senses are considerable although limited. Some creatures have better sensory capabilities, such as eagles with terrific eyesight, dogs with excellent senses of smell, and butterflies with a greater ability to differentiate color. Humans have created tools to enhance our perceptual powers; with a microscope, we can see an amoeba swimming in a dish; with a telescope, we can see distant planets such as Neptune.

Thinking is important. We are creatures of action. Our actions are based on thinking. It is how we can get what we want. Our minds have various states of activity, sometimes feverish, sometimes controlled and logical. Sometimes unrelated ideas seem to pop in out of nowhere, as if our minds saunter about like a teenager with time to burn. We always seem to be thinking about something. It is almost impossible to think about nothing.

It seems to us as if there are two worlds: one physical and one mental. The physical world is our bodies, things we can touch and see such as furniture and trees and water sloshing in a garden pond. And there is a mental world of the *ideas* of our bodies, ideas of furniture and ideas of trees and ideas of sloshing water. Both realms are subject to the laws of cause-and-effect. If we turn a cup upside down, the coffee spills; similarly, if we have an idea of turning a cup upside down, then we can have the idea of the spill. In essence, we can have physical things causing other physical things to happen, like our physical hands turning a physical coffee cup upside down, spilling the coffee, and we can have ideas *causing* other ideas, such as the idea of overturning the cup *causing* the idea of the spill.

The Principle of Association

An underlying basis of thinking is as follows.

The ***Principle of Association*** is when two or more things happen simultaneously or in close succession, our brains learn to associate them.

The things being linked can be perceptions such as auditory or visual signals, as well as ideas, words, people, and pretty much anything that can be conceived. We learn to associate the sound of our name with our person, so our minds link the sound with the concept of us as a person. We link the sound of the word *four* with the image of four fingers. We associate lightning with thunder. Somewhere in our brains, our neurons and synapses align to give us the idea that *lightning causes thunder*.

Association is a building block of thinking. We link simple ideas into more complex ideas. We link symbols of things with actual things, such as the word *tree* with the idea of a multistory shrubbery with a trunk and branches and leaves. From this, we can build more complex thoughts, such as the idea that trees provide shade in the summer, and from this the idea that having trees around one's house may lower the cost of summer air conditioning. It enables higher-order thinking.

Association is a key means of determining cause-and-effect. One thing happens. A second thing happens. We remember the first thing happening and then the second thing happening. We associate the two events happening in close succession, which may lead us to think that the first thing *caused* the second thing to happen. For example, a baby cries, the mother feeds it, then the baby stops crying. We think that the baby crying caused the mother to feed the baby, and that the mother feeding the baby caused the baby to stop crying.

We associate not only past events but possible future events. We can imagine a series of cause-and-effect actions that we might take that might get us what we want. For example, we know from memory that a specific shop has ice cream and we remember its hours of operation. We can imagine walking a specific route to the shop and buying a peppermint chip cone. This sequence of ideas is a series of hypothetical events that might happen in the future, and our brains can assemble these cause-and-effect idea-chains for our benefit.

Accordingly we can think in terms of past and present and future and cause-and-effect. In essence our brains can perform a quasi time-travel operation in that we can imagine things that happened before, in the past, and compare them with what is happening now in the present. Further, we can imagine something in the past or future as if it is happening in the present, and make comparisons. We can imagine a past action that happened at one time, and then stopped at a later time in the past. Further, we can imagine a past action that is continuing in the present as well as something that might happen in the future. With our conception of time as an ever-forward linear progression of equal increments, we can think of events having a measurable duration in time.

The mind-body problem

We think of things in the world such as rocks and trees and cars and skyscrapers and the pens in our pockets as physical manifestations. We can also think of the ideas of these things, that is, mental conceptions which reflect our sense of these real-world things. In our minds we have ideas which seem to have no physical form, as if they are intangible shapes floating like clouds inside our brains. But our bodies are physical, so a question arises: How can something shapeless and formless and flighty as an idea cause something physical to happen? How can an idea such as *let's lift our arm* cause our physical arm to lift?

This is not a real problem but rather a misconception. While we can think of an idea as if it was a shapeless floating cloud inside our minds, it is only one way of thinking about an idea. Every idea in our head corresponds to a physical presence in terms of an arrangement of neurochemical pathways in our brain. For example, before we actually move our arm, when we are preparing to move our arm, there are specific neurons in the brain ready to fire: action potentials are readied, electrical impulses are geared to go, and the brain is waiting for other neurons to tell it to fire. Scientists can see these neurons about to fire using a magnetic resonance imaging machine. Then, neurons are triggered, muscles tighten, and the arm lifts. Now, when we think of this process, we can think of what's about to happen as if there were formless ideas in our mind, but we can also understand this as a series of entirely physical events in our bodies.

Still, the notion that shapeless ideas in our heads are capable of causing physical movements is a powerful illusion. We think that these ideas, as such, do the moving and shaking, when in reality, it is the physical neural connections which do the moving and shaking. Perhaps the confusion arises because we are aware of the ideas in our heads as ideas, and we are not aware of the electric pulses of our neurons. We can not feel physical neurons inside our heads, that is, we can not sense neurons-as-neurons in our heads.

If ideas as formless mental clouds did somehow cause physical movement, then that might suggest that there was a one-to-one agreement between ideas in the mind and actions of the body, but this is not the case. For there are instances when people do things which are clearly not done with any prior mental awareness. The doctor taps a knee, which causes a leg to jerk forward without the patient having an idea of moving their leg beforehand. The physical leg moved without a corresponding idea. Instances such as when a person talks in their sleep or sleepwalks suggest that there is no direct relation between ideas and action.

Basics of thinking

Perhaps the first rule of thinking is that it takes time. While some types of thinking happen almost instantaneously, others take longer, particularly if what we are thinking about is complex or puzzling. Thinking can take seconds or minutes or hours or days or years.

Another rule is that much of our thinking involves generalizing. Consider that there are hundreds of types of trees, from tall shrubs to skyscraper-tall sequoias, from sycamores to maples. For most people, distinguishing the various types is difficult and unnecessary. Rather, it is easier to find what is common to all types, such as the trunk and branches and roots and leaves, and lump them together under the concept of tree. That's all we need.

We think with generalities. When necessary, we can think about specific species of trees, such as when tree doctors or poets or landscapers need specific terms such as conifers or weeping willows or giant sequoias. But usually all we need is the umbrella concept of *tree*. We often simplify things that vary continuously such as time because it is easier to work with rounded figures than exact amounts. For example, we make appointments for four o'clock without specifying the precise chronological time in minutes and seconds. Color varies continuously as well, but we generally think in terms of discrete colors such as white, red, orange, yellow, green, blue, purple, gray and black. So while the real world is complex with mind-boggling variation, in thinking we often simplify things.

We try to map reality by creating a condensed stripped-down description of our world. Like a road map, only pertinent details are needed such as key roads and bridges and junctions. When we try to understand the world, what we are doing is similar to mapmaking in that we try to figure out the important features while disregarding the unimportant details. We want our maps to be accurate yet simple, covering what we need to know, and not bogging us down in distracting trivia. Our ability to generalize is necessary since our brains, while powerful, are not capable of thinking about everything in detail. This capability is a strength because we can get at the heart of concepts, to work with the most important parts of an idea, while ignoring the irrelevant aspects. But it is also a limitation because sometimes the minimized aspects are important, and ignoring them may undermine or distort our understanding.

There is an aspect of perception which might be called *signal sharpening* that happens when our senses choose a few key signals as being the most important ones, amplify them, and then disregard its neighbors. For example, in vision, when a set of nerves detects a range of incoming photons, the neuron with the strongest signal forwards the information to the brain while nearby neurons are instructed to cease firing. So a particular signal gets sharpened and amplified. It's how we process sensations. We magnify a slight difference to turn a gradient into an either-or binary proposition in the same way that one star emerges from a clump of various particles.

Along with our ability to generalize, and to think in time, we have the ability to remember particular thoughts. Some memories last for years while others fade rather quickly. Through practice and repetition, we can reignite our memory of difficult ideas, to keep them from fading, such as mathematical formulas or long lists. Some people can remember the thousands of digits in the number pi or memorize the entire texts of books. We tend to forget unimportant things such as what we ate for lunch yesterday or the title of yesterday's movie. It is easier to remember the plot points of a story, since they follow in a sequence, with each resolved plot point pointing to the next one, in a string, so that the successful recall of one point leads to remembering the next one in the sequence, and so on. In the story *The Wizard of Oz,* Dorothy's house gets twirled skyward by a tornado, and it lands on the Wicked Witch of the East, killing her. That cause-and-effect event triggers approval by the Munchkins, who tell Dorothy to seek the Wizard, and so forth. Each cause-and-effect event suggests the next one. So it is relatively easy to remember the entire sequence in summary form, and to retell the story to somebody else. We find it easier to remember poems that rhyme, because the similar-sounding words prompt us to remember the next line. The brief poem *the solution to pollution is dilution* is an easy way for doctors to remember to flush a wound with saline to remove debris and bacteria.

We are skilled at finding an underlying pattern that unifies a bunch of seemingly unrelated things. We see bananas and apples and oranges and pomegranates and we can identify the underlying pattern that they are all fruits. We can look at a collection of objects and sense an underlying pattern, to identify what belongs and what does not belong.

We can apply reason to our thinking. We know, by the rules of logic, that if Socrates is a human and if all humans are mortals, then Socrates is mortal. We can think deductively, working down from a generalization to particular thoughts, and inductively, where we take particular ideas and then generalize. By thinking and learning, by experimenting and getting feedback from what we do, we gain experience. We can imagine things that don't exist such as a blue winged unicorn.

Edifices of knowledge

Luckily we don't have to know everything. While life is complex, we don't need to know how every part of every system works. We only need to know how to interact with that system. If we wish to travel by commercial airliner from San Francisco to Sydney, for example, we do not need to know how an airplane engine works or how to land a plane, but we do need to know how to buy a ticket, how large our luggage can be, whether a passport is needed, and so forth. It is simply the passenger's system fitting into the larger air transport system. A temptation is to try to learn everything, but we only need to know how to fit into the larger system in most cases.

We need to know how the world works: how plants grow, how to get food, how to handle the daily tasks of living, and so forth. We need to know how to keep ourselves healthy by eating properly, exercising, and caring for ourselves. It is good to know why watering the roots of a mango tree is better than watering its leaves. A zookeeper needs to know that elephants need dust on their backs to prevent sunburn. We can not know everything, but it helps to know important things, and it helps to have a sense of what information is available and how to get it, if needed, or who to ask about how to solve a particular problem. A mathematician does not need to remember every formula but they should know which books or websites they are in. It helps to know what information is known to avoid wasting time rethinking old puzzles. Sometimes it is helpful to learn something once, even though it may be forgotten later, since the knowledge of its existence can be useful later. Relearning will happen faster than if it had never been learned. Further, that one-time learning might provide an insight into how to learn something totally different later on.

As we go through life, we build our personal edifices of knowledge. These worldviews hopefully explain a lot and help us get through life. It helps if the ideas in our worldviews are internally consistent, so that there are no glaring inconsistencies or gaps or blatant contradictions. It's a smorgasbord of things that we think are true. As our worldview becomes more detailed, explaining more aspects of life to us, it can become harder to accommodate new ideas. If we come across an idea that does not fit easily into our edifice of knowledge, then we have a conundrum. If we try to assimilate it, then it might require us to rethink much of our system, which could be a lot of mental work. Many people avoid thinking about difficult things, so it is often easier to simply ignore or dismiss contradictory incoming information. There is a term in psychology called *cognitive dissonance* which describes our uneasiness of trying to hold contradictory thoughts in our minds at the same time, and how our minds are predisposed to end the conflict in any way possible.

In such a manner, we grow our storehouse of knowledge.

The process of thinking

What characterizes healthy thinking is being purposeful with some form of organization. It is the mind of a person who knows what they want in a general way. Their minds have a focus. Not all thinking is goal-directed, of course, since there are times when the brain needs to rest, such as when a change of pace is required.

We can think of the mind as if it has two sections with different functions.

The first section we might think of as the **carpenter-mind.** It is like a central workstation where most thinking happens. Tools along the walls of the workshop are like the mental capabilities that we think with, such as associating ideas, seeing patterns, making a comparison, thinking by analogy, and so forth. There are boards and nails and glue as well, which are like the ideas in working memory that the tools work on. We can work on a single project, or switch between projects, but at any given moment we are usually focused on one project at a time. When we think, we may hammer ideas together, disassemble a conclusion by unscrewing the ideas which hold them together, and so forth. Since the area of the workshop is limited, it helps if it is spacious and uncluttered.

If we are actively trying to think through a problem, or to understand something, or to plan a sequence of future events, or to do other higher-level thinking, then it is helpful if the mind is mostly focused on that particular task. In such situations, the mind should do one project at a time and focus completely on that one project. This is in accord with Buddhist teaching, that we should live fully in the moment, so that when we're eating, we eat, when reading, we read, when being with someone, we focus exclusively on that person.

But it is not possible to focus completely on only one task. While our carpenter-mind does most of the thinking about a particular problem, our mind needs a gatekeeper to handle things like interruptions and to manage how we think.

Accordingly, we might think of the second section as an overseer of the workshop, or the **manager-mind.** It might be alert for interruptions, schedule upcoming appointments, keep an active behind-the-scenes vigil to watch and react to external events as well as overseeing the carpenter-mind. If the carpenter-mind becomes engrossed in a problem, the manager-mind can be alert for the ring of a doorbell and decide how to deal with it. The manager-mind is like an air traffic controller, juggling flights, bringing order to a complex system, keeping ideas from bumping into each other, making sure that departing flights leave on time and that arriving flights don't crash from lack of fuel, while the carpenter-mind is flying the planes of thought. Its purpose is to help the carpenter-mind be productive.

The mind is not generally equipped to think about two unrelated projects at the same time. What is thought of as multitasking is essentially switching rapidly from single-task to single-task. A person who tries to focus on two separate things at the same time will have trouble concentrating fully on both.

The carpenter-mind and the manager-mind need to work together. The carpenter-mind should do the heavy-duty thinking while the manager sits off to the side, handling the phones and coordinating the overall thinking. It is the manager-mind that listens for the sound of our name being called, so that it can interrupt the carpenter-mind as it tries to solve a math problem. An actor might be totally focused on playing a role, even thinking what the character is supposed to be thinking, but when the director says *cut*, then the manager-mind directs the actor to return to being himself or herself. In another example, when Abraham Lincoln was a young lawyer arguing a case, he could be fully cognizant of the arguments he was making in the case, and focused on making specific points to a jury while interviewing a witness, which was like his carpenter-mind, and yet there was a second overseer-type mind as if he could look down on himself and see himself thinking, and sense how listeners were reacting to his arguments. Lincoln could have both perspectives at once, and this dual-minded approach helped him win legal battles.

Fluidity of thought

The mind should resemble the watery environment from which life emerged in the sense that it should be fluid and flexible, not fixed, permitting new combinations, and having enough energy to move ideas about in new patterns. But instead of chemicals being shuffled in a fluid energy-filled area like within a living cell, it is ideas being shuffled in new combinations. The shuffling should be fast enough for thinking to happen but not so fast that it prevents coherent thoughts from forming, that is, it should follow the Goldilocks principle of *not too slow, not too fast*. The mind should be able to link and unlink ideas as needed. A person should be able to change their mind about something, like a dance floor where couples can mix and mingle and touch in a light embrace, temporarily hugging, temporarily splitting apart. Part of the thinking of Daoism is that we should be open to seeing things in new ways and to be open to new possibilities as they happen, since change can bring unexpected surprises and opportunities.

The mind needs facts to work with. These are ideas which hopefully have a basis in reality. When a mind is trying to solve a problem, there should be enough relevant facts for a solution. If the mind is trying to calculate the length of a triangle's hypotenuse, then it helps to know the Pythagorean theorem as well as the lengths of the two shorter sides. If it is trying to estimate the cost of building a shed, it needs to know the cost of lumber and screws. It should be able to hold diverse views, even if the ideas conflict with each other. As Abigail Adams said, "a person's intelligence is directly reflected by the number of conflicting points of view they can entertain simultaneously on the same topic." The mind is open. It welcomes a variety of thoughts.

The mind should not be afraid to think certain thoughts. A carpenter who is afraid to use a power saw will have trouble building a cabinet. Similarly, a thinker who is afraid to consider thought X or thought Y might have trouble solving a problem.

The mind should not become obsessed with one particular thought if it is irrelevant to the solution. It is like getting stuck with the wrong dance partner for an entire evening.

There should be sufficient space inside the mind for thoughts to move about, like a roomy dance hall with enough space for many ideas. While it should not be cluttered with irrelevant or wrong or useless ideas, it should be able to store ideas and retrieve them when needed.

How a mind thinks is important. Ideally it should use reason and logic and common sense to ask itself questions, such as: Does this new arrangement of ideas make sense? Is it logical? Does it feel right? Is this consistent with what happened before? Do the ideas click together into a coherent pattern? When thinking a new thought, there should be an assessment of whether the new thought is useful. It helps if thinking is goal-directed and proceeds in an orderly fashion, so what needs to be thought about first, gets thought about first, and what needs to be thought about second, gets thought about second, and so on.

Since thinking takes time, there should be enough time to solve a particular problem. But thinking should not proceed indefinitely. Various outcomes are possible. The mind could come to a conclusion that may be wrong or right. It could figure that it still doesn't know but that further thinking won't help so it should stop. It might determine that it needs new facts to rethink the problem at a later time, hopefully with a better result. But it should not keep thinking and thinking in a seemingly endless repetitive loop.

Throughout a person's life, the process of internal mental deliberation should be never-ending but not merely recycling the same old thoughts. Rather, thinking should build on what was learned before. We should learn throughout our lives, trying to make sense of the world and how we fit in it, finding new pleasures and facts and perspectives. If each person tries to construct a map of the world, then it is good to keep adapting this map to accommodate new facts and perspectives.

What cripples a mind is stuckness. This is getting fixed to one way of thinking. A stuck mind blocks out new views and opinions and information, and it refuses to entertain counter-arguments or inconvenient facts. The best minds are open and questioning, fluid and dynamic, and remain open to new ways of thinking. They are like businesses with a sign that says open. They are not shuttered or closed for renovation. Ideally our minds should flexibly adapt to our present circumstances. For example, we should not be trying to drive a car when sleep is needed, or sleeping during a date with a prospective romantic partner.

There is a risk of negative feedback loops in the mind which can happen when a person has a self-critical thought, which dampens their mood, which in turn leads to other self-critical thoughts which are irrational and distorted from reality. A state of mental stuckness can happen to pretty much anybody at any time. While knowledgeable people tend to be open-minded, since that is how they acquired their knowledge in the first place, their accumulated knowledge can become a barrier to considering fresh ideas. They may be reluctant to rethink a well-thought-out system of thought, or to overturn a long established and trusted idea, since thinking takes time and energy. It is not easy to do. It is probably the case that most humans are loath to think about things if there is a reasonable excuse not to. People don't like being in a state of uncertainty since it causes tension and stress.

Executive function

The ability to manage one's own mind is described by psychologists as **executive function**. It is a state of mind in which it can pay attention to what is important and yet be able to shift its focus as needed. It can plan a sequence of future steps, set priorities and filter out distractions. It allows a person to manage time constructively. Impulses are controlled. A mind can follow through on actions leading to a self-chosen goal, so that a person thinks about what they should be thinking about, when pursuing that goal. If a person is inside a burning house, then they should not be trying to write a poem or practicing calligraphy but focusing on exiting.

A key human mental activity is thinking in the present about what to do in the future. The more that our plans reflect the real world, the more likely it will be that we will get what we want. Since reality is complex, it is practically impossible to predict with certainty how things might play out, but as our thinking becomes better, then the likelihood of success improves.

In terms of human evolution, the human mind is a relatively recent adaptation, and structures within it have evolved at different rates. Most animals have simple stimulus-and-response mechanisms to help them survive; for example, if a neuron in a moth detects light, it will move toward it. While the human mind is much more advanced, it has similar reflexive mental structures, which evolved first, embodied physically in an area of the brain called the amygdala. This structure permits rapid responses to external events. It helps humans cope with extreme situations in which fast action is required for survival, such as running to high ground when a tsunami floods the beach, or swimming quickly to the shore if there is a large fin darting above the waves. It takes control. It shuts down higher-order thinking. It makes the human run move quickly.

The prefrontal cortex evolved later. This brain structure sits on top of the amygdala. It permits complex thinking, which takes time but usually yields better results. What is important is the interplay of these various cranial structures, so that the amygdala helps a person survive a tsunami and the prefrontal cortex helps a person plan a job search strategy. What can be difficult for a human is knowing how to handle an ambiguous situation: should we respond instinctively or should we take the time to think through a logical response? It is almost as if these areas of the brain battle for control.

When a healthy mind comes upon new information, it is skeptical. We keep new ideas at arm's length, like a gatekeeper questioning the veracity before admitting it into our storehouse of knowledge. It asks itself questions such as: How reliable is the source of the claim? What is the quality of the evidence? Has anybody tried to disprove the claim? Does the source of the claim have an agenda and what is it? We should cultivate a skeptical frame of mind and not accept anything on faith.

What characterizes healthy thinking, then, is that it is purposeful and focused, with proper coordination between the carpenter-mind and the manager-mind. It can follow through on its thought processes without getting distracted or waylaid by irrelevant thoughts. Its thinking is fluid, linking and unlinking ideas, and that it has time to think, with enough facts to work with. It is not afraid to think certain thoughts. It is not obsessed with anything, not stuck, not blocked. It uses reason and logic and common sense to grow its storehouse of knowledge, with a skeptical cast of mind. During its internal deliberations, it comes to a point when it makes a decision, even if it knows that its information is imperfect or incomplete. It does not succumb to what the Bhagavad Gita describes as "analysis paralysis".

A healthy mind focuses on life, on enjoying life, on growing and learning and acquiring skills. It should not be focused on death and dying, on pain and suffering, or on what, if anything, comes after life. People who ruminate endlessly on morbid thoughts, or whose minds are fixated on fear, are not healthy in an intellectual way. It is almost like they are crippled mentally and can not perform fully in the theater of life. That is not to say that one should not consider pain and fear when making decisions, because these things are helpful in that they steer us away from negative outcomes.

The puzzle of fate and free will

To illustrate the puzzle of fate and free will, let's consider a hypothetical example. Suppose there is a young boy at the Tastee Creamy Dessert Shop. He wonders what type of soft-serve ice cream to get. At this moment in time, he's thinking about his upcoming choice. Will it be vanilla or chocolate? He does not yet know what he will choose. He sees the future as open and undetermined as a blue sky of unfettered possibility. He thinks to himself that anything is possible.

So the question is: Does the boy have the power to spontaneously make a decision, on the spur of the moment, a decision that is *only* determined by him, by him alone, such that his decision is not influenced by any external factors, and so that his decision, when he makes it, will surprise even himself? Does the boy have free will? Or has his choice been predetermined by the workings of fate?

Consider that the ideas presented so far may seem reasonable: that causes cause effects, that time moves forward from past to present to future, and that it is impossible for something to emerge from nothing. We see these realities daily with our own eyes. They are neither mysterious nor something we must accept on faith. We know that tipping the cup spills the coffee and that the spill did not happen by itself. We know that February follows January and not the other way around. We know that a rabbit did not magically pop into existence from non-existence inside a magician's hat.

These ideas, taken together, suggest a world in which everything that happens, happens as a result of something that happened earlier in time, and in which there are no uncaused events. Our universe can be conceived as a giant mechanical engine pushing things inevitably onward, in which fate controls everything that happens, like the idea from Hindu philosophy of karma.

And yet we have a powerful notion of having free will, as if somehow we can break free from these chains of cause-and-effect and do something spontaneously, something uncaused by the past, by thinking and willing something to happen that had not been in our minds a second earlier. We make choices. We are aware of making these choices. We think we *willed* these choices.

So there appears to be two contrasting viewpoints which both feel right but which seem to be logically inconsistent. The first is that we have total spontaneous control over our decision making by an act of willpower. The second is that fate rules.

So, which is it? Are we creatures with a blue-sky type destiny unfolding because of our uncaused choices? Or are we creatures of the past, fated to act based on what happened before?

This is the puzzle of fate and free will.

Suppose in our example that the boy chooses chocolate. At first glance, it seems like his choice was an act of his personal willpower. But if we look more closely, we see that the boy will not have been aware of past instances that steered him to choose chocolate. His parents prefer chocolate. An advertisement that he saw a few days ago showed a young girl enjoying a chocolate bar. A few weeks ago he came down with a sniffle after having eaten a vanilla ice cream cone, so he came to associate that flavor with being ill, even though the vanilla ice cream didn't cause the cold. A year ago his friend said that chocolate was the "super bestest" flavor. He might not know about a genetic predisposition that prompts his taste buds to prefer chocolate. He probably does not know that three of his four grandparents hated vanilla.

Most likely, he won't remember most of these predispositions or even begin to understand how they forced his choice.

All he knows is that he wants chocolate.

He thinks he chose chocolate because of an act of his personal willpower.

But that is an illusion.

In reality, as the boy understands more, as he is better able to remember his past, and as he understands his own biology more fully, he will begin to realize that:

His choice was totally determined by the past.

What happens is that, in daily life, we are conscious of our choices, with the future ahead of us, uncertain, and the past behind us, mostly obscured, so that we have a predisposition to see ourselves as causal actors unchained from the past. We have the illusion of untethered choice. We have a tendency to think of our minds like a rational kingdom within the natural kingdom of the world, with our minds exerting our personal will, free and undetermined from the past, but this is not the case. Our minds are a part of nature just like everything else is a part of nature, in that our minds follow the laws of nature, just as everything is determined by the law of cause-and-effect.

A brief thought experiment can illustrate this.

If we try to do something, in a few seconds from now, something that is totally uncaused by anything in the past, right out of the blue, so that we do not know now what we are going to do in a few seconds time, that is, we will totally surprise ourselves by our spontaneity, then we will find that that is impossible to do. Try it. Can you do it? It seems impossible.

Consider the task of trying to do something uncaused. Even that act will have been caused by something from the past, that is, the question in this book. So anything we might do to demonstrate our supposed free nature will have been in fact caused by the prior written question, by the simple act of reading the *try to do something* statement, and then responding to the suggestion. The question determined the response. How one might respond is determined by previous ideas of what constitutes a spontaneous act, but in no possible way could whatever we do be described as having been uncaused by the past.

Notice that the question in this book, also, was not an uncaused out-of-the-blue spontaneous act, for it, too, was determined by past events, by the thinking in previous books, by past experiences and conversations with people and so forth.

Suppose a person tries to do something uncaused. If they jump up and down, yell "I'm free", dance like a robot inspired by shamans in pink costumes, well, then perhaps that is their idea, an idea from their past experiences, about what being free means. But it is not really their idea after all, but an idea planted in their brain from before.

Simply, the past causes the present. There is no way around this. It is the inevitability of time and circumstance and the logical playing out of cause-and-effect. It is how things work. It is fate. This reality is true for all of us. Everything is spilled milk, a giant sequence of determined causation, that is true for all of us on this planet twirling around our sun.

If we accept that the law of cause-and-effect applies everywhere, all the time, to everything that happens, then we can see that all things that happen, had to happen, and could not have happened any other way. Philosophers describe this view as determinism that can be stated as follows: The past *determines* the present entirely, and the present *determines* the future entirely in unbroken chains of cause-and-effect. There are no accidental occurrences that emerge out of thin air, and no rabbits that are created spontaneously out of a magician's hat. Everything happens for a reason. Nothing happens without a prior cause. At the tiniest levels of subatomic particles such as electrons, there may be randomness in how they move, but nevertheless what they do and where they go still determines what happens. It is not the case that something could happen which does not have some kind of prior cause, whether what happens is predictable or not predictable.

In short, fate rules.

But grasping the reality of determinism is difficult for almost all humans.

Can we influence the workings of fate by thinking about it, by knowing the future, and in that way, escape fate's grasp?

There is a story about a man who went to a fortune teller who peered deeply into a crystal ball and said in a low firm voice, *tomorrow you will see Death.* So the frightened man jumped on his horse and rode at breakneck speed through the Sahara, day and night, to a distant city, only to see Death, standing there, surprised. The man, shocked, had a heart attack and died instantly. Death was shocked too: *how did that man get here so quickly?* The story suggests the inevitability of fate, its firm stranglehold grasp, so that even if we do everything possible to avoid our fate, we will succumb.

Free will properly understood

Now the next step is understanding how humans can have free will in this context of determinism. Throughout human history, most people have not understood how this works, and this lack of understanding has caused grievous misfortune to humankind.

Consider two perspectives.

The first perspective is what might be called the God's-eye view as if one could step outside of the universe and peer in as a detached spectator, and see all of the cause-and-effect relationships correctly throughout all time with perfect and total knowledge. We know every cause-and-effect relation governing the interplay of all physical things, from the tiniest quarks to the largest galaxies. We know every cause-and-effect relation governing every idea ever thought by any thinking being. We know everything with complete accuracy and certainty throughout the infinite span of time. That is the God's-eye view.

The second perspective is the human's-eye view from which we have limited imperfect guesses about a few cause-and-effect relations, which may or may not be correct. We have scant knowledge about what happened in the past, and our ability to predict the future is fraught with uncertainty. A human brain, despite having billions of neurons, cannot possibly comprehend the complexity of reality. This is our viewpoint, the human's-eye view, from which all humans see.

If we accept the principle of full cause-and-effect determinism, and if we accept that there are the two viewpoints of a God's-eye view and a human's-eye view, then a conception emerges of human free will. It is that from our own, limited human perspective, we can have a human-type free will which involves making choices based on our hopefully intelligent thinking and guessing about the future, while at the same time realizing that every thought we think and every choice we make is fully determined from the God's-eye perspective. We can make choices as if we have God-type free will, while knowing that we don't have God-type free will, and this is what human-type free will is all about. Since we can not predict the future with accuracy, we must make choices based on our thinking, even though we know that our thinking has been determined by the past, and that when the future happens, that it too will have been fated to have happened as it happened.

Accordingly, human-type free will is a subset of god-type free will. God-type free will ultimately rules. It causes everything, and it contains within it human-type free will. It is as if all living creatures are in a play directed by the all-powerful past. Everything we do and say and think is controlled by what happened before, but within that fixed script, we have a sense of being actors with a consciousness of our choices.

It is a mistake to use the reality of determinism as an excuse not to make choices. Suppose a human accepts that everything is determined and, as a result, decides to merely sit on their couch, forever, not doing anything, not making thinking-based choices, saying to themselves that *everything is fated* so why bother to do anything? We can describe this mistaken approach with the term *fatalism*. A fatalist is someone who thinks about the future like we think about the past.

But it is wrong to think that one is relieved of the duty of making choices simply because of determinism. We do not have a license to do nothing. Rather, we must make choices. If a human believes in determinism and, as a result, gives up striving because they think that the future is fated, perhaps deciding to exist on a couch for eternity, simply letting whatever will happen, happen, well, most likely there will be negative consequences for such a person. Soon they will get hungry and thirsty. Family and friends might think that they are crazy and commit them to a mental hospital. The mistake of the fatalist is presuming to have God-type knowledge but no human has or can ever have such knowledge. We only have imperfect limited human-type knowledge.

Accordingly, we must act as if we have free will, and make choices from our human's-eye view, while knowing that everything we do is determined. Determinism must not be confused with fatalism. We must think, choose and act simply because we do not know how things will play out in the future. An essential part of our existence is action, and it is activity that gives our lives meaning. Our process of choosing is our exercise of free will, which is really free will from our own human perspective. This is free will, properly understood.

What is peculiarly perplexing is that we can, from our human perspective, increase our ability to influence events in our favor. This may seem contradictory but it is not, so clarification is needed.

Consider that the ideas in our heads can be thought of as causing other ideas. For example, suppose there are two ideas: the idea of an umbrella and the idea of rain. One can think of these ideas as linked in a cause-and-effect idea chain, something along the lines of (1) if it rains (2) an umbrella may keep us dry. The idea-chain is that the idea of an umbrella *causes* the idea of staying dry.

The point is that we can, by using our human-type free will, link ideas together in cause-and-effect idea-chains in our minds that help us cope with life. We hope that these mental constructions will mirror the real world, that is, that the idea of an umbrella keeping us dry mirrors the reality that a real physical umbrella will really shield us during a real rainstorm.

These mental constructions are the essence of human free will. It is not God-type free will in the sense of uncaused spontaneous action but human-type free will in the sense of making choices from our human's-eye perspective. A human may see that it is raining, and by thinking in terms of cause-and-effect idea chains, may open an umbrella to stay dry. From our human perspective, this act of thinking is an exercise of human-type free will. If, however, one steps outside the universe, and examines what happened from the perspective of an imagined deity using the God's-eye view, it is apparent that the human's act of thinking was totally determined by things that happened in the past. From the God's-eye view, everything was fated, not only the human using the umbrella but the human thinking about using it beforehand.

If we re-examine the story about the man and the fortune teller and Death, we can assess the accuracy of the story. What is true is the relentless inevitability of fate. What is false is the man's faith in the fortune teller's prognostication. Humans, including fortune tellers, can not foretell the future with accuracy. By believing the fortune teller, the man was thinking that he had acquired God-type knowledge, and this supposed knowledge caused him to do things

AN INDIVIDUAL HUMAN

that led to his death. His mistake was presuming to have a God's-eye view of the workings of fate.

But as humans, we are not hopeless. We can make our lives better by exercising our human-type free will.

Further, we can expand our human-type free will by forming idea-chains which ...

- are wider and wider in terms of geographic space
- encompass longer and longer spans of time
- are more accurate
- better reflect reality
- are unpolluted by random nonsense
- are ordered logically

From our human-type perspective, we can grab a greater share of the determining by thinking better, by knowing more, by getting educated, by thinking logically, and by getting a better handle on reality. It is how we can improve our lives.

To illustrate, consider that the idea-chain that *if it is raining, an umbrella can keep a person dry* is a rather simple construction. It may happen that it is raining on a particularly windy day, and that the wind may flip the umbrella inside out. So a person might think along these lines: (1) It is raining (2) It is windy (3) Wind can flip the umbrella inside out (4) A raincoat with a hood can shield most of the body so (5) Wear a raincoat. By using these extended and more sophisticated idea-chains, that meet many of the criteria described previously, a person is better able to stay dry in this example of human-type free will.

There is an idea, expressed by the Roman emperor Marcus Aurelius, that we should "Love the hand that fate deals us, and then play it like our own." That is exactly right. We must accept our circumstances, and then make the best choices that we can, given our circumstances.

The idea that there is a God or gods outside the universe,

peering in, seeing everything throughout all time, is an exercise of human imagination to help us think about fate and free will. The idea that there is a God's-eye view from outside the universe contains a built-in contradiction: If there is a God, separate from the universe, then how can this outside-the-universe God see inside the universe? If God and the universe are separate, then how can there be any interaction? It does not make sense.

Such is a theory about how fate and free will operate, but what should guide our human-type choices? This brings us to the subject of ethics.

The Basic Principle of Ethics

There is a fundamental idea underlying our desire for living that can guide our choices.

The **Basic Principle of Ethics** is that good is what is good for you, in wider spaces and longer time frames, as best that can be determined.

The good part is fairly obvious: good things are what help humans, such as food and air and water and clothing and shelter and love and friendship and money and knowledge. They help humans flourish. We need these things to live and to enjoy life. When we desire something that we think will help us, we describe it as good, which is why foodstuffs at a grocery are called goods. What is considered to be good can vary from person to person according to their personal preferences and internal logic. For example, a miser may think that an abundance of money is good, an ambitious person may think that honor is good, a hermit may think that solitude is good, and an entertainer may think that applause is good.

There are several ideas related to the idea of good.

First, good is what is good for one's whole self and not just for a part. While an activity such as smoking may be good for the brain since nicotine stimulates neurons and aids possibly with thinking, it is bad for the lungs which become clogged with cancer-causing particles which impedes breathing; accordingly, smoking is not good for one's whole self. This principle of being good-for-the-whole extends to structures larger than a single individual, but to combinations of individuals, such as a marriage or a membership in a business enterprise. In each case, good should be what's good for the whole group, not just a part. For example, a marriage which is good for one partner but bad for another partner is not really a good marriage.

Second, the principle of the golden mean usually applies, since too little or too much of anything can be bad for a person. For example, while water is necessary for good health, drinking too little or drinking too much can be harmful. There is a happy area between too little and too much which depends on the person and the situation. There are times when choosing an extreme is better than choosing the middle road, such as in warfare, but usually the golden mean is the best choice. This is consistent with the classic sense of human agency of choosing the mean between the extremes. For example, courage is identified as a virtue which is a mean between the extremes of rashness, or too much courage, and cowardice, or too little courage. It means acting "at the right times, about the right things, toward the right people, for the right end, and in the right way," according to Aristotle.

Next, the *wider spaces and longer time frames* phrase is about what is good in wider and wider spaces and longer and longer spans of time. For example, suppose a person does not have a pen. It is good to have one since it enables writing, and it has a slight economic value as well. But suppose, without asking permission, the person grabs a pen from somebody else. Now, in the immediate space surrounding their body, they are better off since they have that pen. They have the capability of writing that they did not have a moment earlier. But if the space is expanded outwards, to include both persons, then one person is better off but the other person is worse off. The pen grabber might find that the penless victim is angry, which is not good for the pen grabber, since there is the possibility of retaliation. If the space is expanded further to include the wider community, then it is even worse for the pen grabber since there might be negative repercussions in terms of criticism and possibly dealing with authorities. The point is that a clearer picture emerges of what is good by widening the space.

The same reasoning applies not only to wider and wider spaces but to longer and longer spans of time. In the immediate moment upon possessing the pen, the pen grabber is better off, but as time is extended further and further into the future, it becomes clearer that they are not better off. They are more likely to experience retaliation or social sanction or punishment. So what initially appeared to be good is not good by seeing things from a longer span of time.

Last, the *as best that can be determined* part suggests that our ability to make good choices depends on thinking correctly. We think about the possible consequences of what we might do. We guess about the future. Our guesses may be confused or incomplete or incorrect. As best that we can, from our human's-eye view, we strive to see things from a god's-eye view. Being good requires thinking, and this thinking may be wrong or right, and it is always imperfect.

It should be noted that the thinking, itself, takes time, and that more complex thinking of the wider-longer sort takes a human longer to do. This may not be practical in some situations, such as when a human is under severe time pressure and has to decide what to do quickly. While higher-order thinking of a rational nature is usually better than knee-jerk instinctive responses, it is not intrinsically better because it is a higher-order of thinking, but it depends on the situation. Since ethical calculations take time, it follows that a human, who doesn't have time to think, will have trouble acting ethically.

Accordingly, ethical problems can be challenging. They can flummox all humans. While some matters are simpler than others, there is no such thing as an absolute or guaranteed right answer to any given ethical problem. All such problems can be subjected to further study since our human ability to guess about the future is limited and fraught with uncertainty, and grows more uncertain as we try to think in terms of wider spaces and longer spans of time.

Most religions have ethical guidelines that are good and helpful. Most espouse a version of the *Golden Rule* which says to treat others like you'd want yourself to be treated. The Jewish scholar Hillel said something similar, in that "what is hateful to you, do not do to your fellow." Along the same lines, Kant's *Categorical Imperative* says we should act how we want everybody else to act. In the Judeo-Christian tradition, the *Ten Commandments* include rules such as *don't steal* and *don't kill*. Rules like these prevent much strife. They're succinct. They're simple. They're easy to remember. They're easy to obey, and obeying them is almost always the right thing to do.

But the *Basic Principle of Ethics* is deeper and more comprehensive than any of these guidelines. It is like the spirit underlying them. It gets to the heart of what ethics is about. If a person follows the *Basic Principle* faithfully and completely, they will almost surely obey the other guidelines espoused by most religions. They won't kill. They won't steal. They'll treat everybody how they'd like to be treated. They'll realize that what's good for them, in wider spaces and in longer time frames, as best that they can determine, is to not kill, to not steal, to play fair and treat people kindly, because it is in their best long-term interests to do exactly that.

Further, there are a few circumstances in which the simpler ethical guidelines should not be followed and in which the *Basic Principle* should be followed. In such situations, the *Basic Principle* can point to the best course of action. For example, the *Ten Commandments* says *don't kill*. But how can one cope with a mass murderer brandishing a machine gun, who has been killing people indiscriminately, and in which the only way to stay alive is to kill the gunman? Clearly the *don't kill* rule would not apply in such a situation. Neither would the *Golden Rule* be helpful in such a situation. In these rare situations, however, the *Basic Principle* could lead to the right course of action. By expanding the space and time, a person, by using reason and by thinking clearly and logically, might conclude that unless they kill the gunman, that they will become victims shortly. The only rational conclusion about what is good for the person, in wider spaces and longer spans of time, as best that they can determine, is to kill the gunman. It is the right thing to do. The other ethical guidelines waffle about this. The *Basic Principle* points a clear path to the right choice.

An advantage of the *Basic Principle* is that it can apply to diverse situations and problems while there is a limiting aspect about the other guidelines. For example, there may be cases where lying is required. For example, if a thief asks a person where a wallet is, then according to a must-tell-the-truth categorical imperative, the person would have to reveal the wallet's location and, as a result, be complicit in a robbery. In contrast, the *Basic Principle* helps a person analyze the negative consequences of telling the truth and would suggest that a better course is to say nothing or to lie.

Generally, however, most other ethical rules apply in nonviolent situations, and they are almost always good for such purposes. There is a remarkable consensus among major religions and philosophical traditions about the proper ways to treat our neighbors. They say:

- Be kind to others
- Treat people nicely
- Be fair in our dealings
- Share
- Tell the truth

These rules are good ways for almost all people to behave almost all of the time. Since they are simple, they are easy to understand, and they usually help time-pressed humans make good choices. They require less thinking. It is often as simple as *do this* or *don't do that*. But the real world is complex, and there are exceptions, and sometimes thinking is required.

The *Basic Principle of Ethics* is logically consistent with a reason-based approach to reality, since it builds on our understanding of time, cause-and-effect, and fate and free will. It encourages people to merge an imagined future into our present decision-making. By thinking through a cause-and-effect idea-chain leading to an imagined future, we can bring an imagined future outcome into our present consciousness. Accordingly, we can compare a possible future outcome with our present situation, or compare two or more possible future outcomes, and hopefully make a good choice.

The principle encourages us to focus on the future when making decisions. Suppose a person wants a beautiful photograph. That is the goal. In the present moment, the person thinks about possible future actions to reach this goal. Drive to the mountains? Or walk to the beach? A person can ponder steps toward reaching each goal, such as expenses and routes and obstacles to overcome, and by thinking through likely future outcomes, make a choice. Is spending money for a car trip worth the added expense? If one can think clearly and distinctly by creating longer and longer cause-and-effect idea-chains, then a human can have, in the present moment, two contrasting choices. If these mental conceptions correspond to the real-world sequences of what might actually happen, then a person can choose wisely.

The principle embraces the realization that ethical decision making can be difficult. It is imperfect and fallible and prone to errors in human judgment. That's why it contains the phrase *as best that we can determine.* We can not always determine what's best. We don't have a god-like ability to see far into the future because we're humans. As we try to see farther and farther into the future, our guesses become more tenuous, and it is difficult to maintain accuracy since more variables come into play. If we're trying to figure out what to do tomorrow, then our guess will probably be accurate. But if we're trying to figure out what we should do in five years, then our guess will be more tentative. There are no guarantees that we will guess correctly. Being ethical requires being smart, being knowledgeable, thinking logically, and taking our time to think through what might happen, but we could be wrong.

Accordingly there is a trade-off between expanding the space and time, and accuracy. A wider-longer guess may be better but risks being wrong; a narrower-shorter guess may be more accurate but may be short-sighted. Humans strive for perfect God-type insights but are doomed to come up short with only human-type insights.

The principle suggests that a brain-challenged human, clueless and unconnected, uneducated, or suffering from mental impairments or otherwise being closed off to new ideas, will have trouble acting ethically. They will have trouble doing what is good for themselves as well as for others. If they do the right thing, then most likely it will have been by luck or by habit or by following what others do, assuming of course that what others have been doing is right and good. But when a new situation presents itself, and it is not clear how one should act, then such a person will probably not be able to figure out the right course.

Notice that the *Basic Principle of Ethics* is built around what is good for an individual human and not for an abstract entity such as a group or community or city or nation or ecosystem. Goodness is rooted in the individual, as the principle begins with *Good is what is good for you.* This is the basic starting point for thinking about ethics. There is a danger with any ethical system that is not based on the individual, since such a system could permit harm to a particular human if it only benefits the group.

The Principle of Accountability

Since we do not have God-type wisdom but only human-type wisdom of a limited nature, the best that we can hope for is imperfect human-type free will, which comes as stated previously from thinking correctly, logically, with thoughts that are unpolluted by random nonsense and linked together in increasingly longer idea-chains that hopefully reflect reality, and then making good choices. We try to think like a god but we can only think like a human. This is our limitation. Accordingly, regarding our actions, from our vantage point in the present and looking back at what we've done in the past, we are not accountable to God or gods or angels or devils or other supernatural beings.

However, what we do, where we go, what we say, how we act, what we buy or sell, and so forth can affect other humans, positively or negatively, and as an effect of our actions, other humans may be better off or worse off, and they can help us or hurt us in response.

The ***Principle of Accountability*** is that we are accountable to other humans.

We are accountable to other humans even though everything is determined by fate. People who believe in gods or God can not avoid repercussions from humans by blaming a deity for what they, as individual human actors, have done. Similarly, people who don't believe in gods or God can not avoid repercussions from humans by blaming the mechanistic workings of cause-and-effect. We are all accountable to other humans. That is how it is.

A hypothetical example might illustrate the point. Suppose a driver of a moving car gets a text message on their phone, distracting them from driving, and they read it without stopping and rear-end a police car. When the officer tickets the driver for a moving violation, the driver can not wiggle out from punishment by blaming fate. If the driver said to the officer that *it was fated that I got that text and fated that I read it, so therefore fate bumped your police car, not me, so give fate the ticket.* The officer might reply *yes the crash was fated but so is the ticket, because you are accountable for your actions because you have human-type free will.* So the driver would face the consequences, perhaps a ticket or losing their license to drive, rightfully so. The reality of determinism does not slip us off of the hook of responsibility when it comes to our dealings with others.

Types of learning

Learning is a mind-expanding process in which cranial connections are wired into new configurations, enabling the mind to think more complex thoughts with wider-longer idea-chains. At first learning is slow and difficult, especially for infants and toddlers, but as a person grows from a child to an adult, many types of learning become easier. The more we know, the easier it is to learn more complex things. Benjamin Franklin wrote that "Being ignorant is not so much a shame, as being unwilling to learn."

Often it is difficult to guess beforehand the value of something we might learn. In our youth, we rely on parents and teachers and friends to point us to hopefully useful subjects. There's a risk that what we study could later prove to be rather pointless. A student focusing on calculus for several years who later becomes a dancer might feel that her earlier effort was a waste of time. Nevertheless, it's good to know what is already known. The more we learn, the easier it gets to learn, as if learning is a muscle that strengthens as we exercise it.

There are two basic types of learning, with a few variants: trial-and-error learning, and learning by instruction.

Trial-and-error learning is when a human tries something new and does not know what will result. It is an experiment to see what might happen, and the result can be positive or negative or inconclusive. Most scientific research is trial-and-error by necessity since it is the only way to learn things that are not presently known. This form of learning is slow, usually expensive, and sometimes dangerous. For example, the French scientist Marie Curie experimented with radium, often without protection from radiation-absorbing materials, and it probably caused her premature death from cancer.

A benefit of trial-and-error learning is that the lesson really sticks in the mind. Even if nothing is learned, there is a small upside in that there is less chance of repeating the experiment again, if knowledge of the failed experiment is shared with others. A drawback is that there is no guarantee that something valuable will be learned. Experimenting could waste time and money or it could lead to a glorious new insight or tool. Sometimes it requires repeated tries before a solution is found. Thomas Edison tried shooting electricity through a thousand different filaments until he finally found one suitable for the electric light bulb.

Learning by instruction is a process of disseminating known information. It can happen in one-on-one communication, such as a mother instructing her child about how to tie a shoe, or a teacher addressing a lecture hall of several hundred students. It is much less expensive than trial-and-error learning in most cases. A pupil must trust that the teacher is right.

A more efficient variant is when there is an intermediary between teachers and students, such as a book or pamphlet or video. Then a student can learn at their own pace without the teacher having to be physically present, if they're motivated to learn. It is possible for a student to act as their own teacher, choosing what to study and in what order. There is a risk, however, of wasting time with such an approach. A good teacher can steer a student away from superficial or incorrect subjects. Many religions value study and learning. In the musical *Fiddler on the Roof*, the character Tevye sang that if he was a rich man, he'd spend seven hours a day studying the holy texts with rabbis. If one is at the forefront of knowledge, facing unknown questions, seeking understanding, then a self-guided program of investigation is the only way forward.

A way to remedy the weakness of learning by instruction is to practice what was learned. Benjamin Franklin wrote, "Tell me and I forget; teach me and I remember; involve me and I learn." Practice is especially important in developing a skill such as playing the piano. At first, it might be hard to play. The fingers don't know where to go and the notes are unfamiliar, but over time, with practice and focus and repetition, there is less mental work involved. The brain rewires the neural connections so that thinking becomes streamlined and efficient, so that instead of hesitant neurons stumbling, misfiring, there are a few linked-up neurons confidently firing in sequence. The fingers know their places, the sequence of notes comes without halting, and music flows like grass waving in a gentle wind.

Confucius has a slightly different breakdown of the types of learning. There is learning by reflection, which is the noblest. There is learning by imitation, which is the easiest. There is learning by experience, which is the bitterest, although it can be the most trusted way to acquire wisdom. Oscar Wilde said "Experience is the hardest kind of teacher; it gives you the test first and the lesson afterward."

The structure of knowledge

Knowledge builds on knowledge. Something new and unknown is explained in terms of what is old and known.

Suppose there is something unknown that we are trying to define. Let's call this unknown thing the **name.** The name is something we are trying to define but we don't yet know what it is. So the first step is to describe the category of known things that this unknown thing belongs to. This is the **category.** In other words, the thing that we are trying to define, that is, the name, is similar to other things in the category, and this category contains things that we know about. Now the next step is to show how the unknown named thing is different from the other known things in the known category.

Let's illustrate with an example. Suppose that somebody did not know what a cell phone was, that is, a cell phone is the thing that we are trying to define. It could be explained as follows: that a cell phone (that's the name of the unknown thing) is a telephone (that's the category, that is, the cell phone belongs to the category of telephones, and we know what telephones are in a general sense). Now we come to the **point of difference.** How is a cell phone different from the other types of telephones? A cell phone differs from all the other types of telephones because it can work without a cord. That's the point of difference. Most telephones have cords. A cell phone doesn't have a cord.

So we can restate our example as follows:

A cell phone (name) is a telephone (category) that works without a cord (point of difference).

AN INDIVIDUAL HUMAN

A framework such as this one makes it easy to build concepts upon each other. For example, if somebody knows what a cell phone is, but not what a smartphone is, then a definition might be that a smartphone (name) is a cell phone (category) that has a computer built in (point of difference). Human knowledge can grow incrementally from simple ideas to complex theories. Our knowledge can build from basic things like a telephone, to a cell phone, to a smartphone, and keep expanding from there, in all types of subjects and in all fields of knowledge.

Learning happens better when new ideas are added to an organized system of thought. An isolated idea unrelated to other previously understood ideas is hard for the mind to process, so when a new idea comes along which can be linked to other known ideas, it is easier to understand and learn. For example, an isolated nonsensical idea such as *cucumbers dance in Manhattan* is hard to process, but if the idea is linked to other ideas, such as an *October parade to celebrate fruits and vegetables*, then it begins to make sense; one might imagine people dressed in cucumber outfits to promote healthy eating, possibly. The act of learning is plugging new ideas into our known systems of ideas.

Since reality is complex, a way for humans to understand the complexity is with models. Typically models are smaller and simpler than what they represent. A model plane made of plastic and glue is much smaller than a real-world airplane, yet it preserves the proportions of the larger plane while being small enough to hold in a hand. Similarly, a subway map is a model of a geographic space which helps riders navigate the system. In another sense, a model can represent an ideal, such as a model employee who embodies the productivity that a company values. A simulation is a model-in-motion of a system which offers a scaled-down representation of how real world variables interact with each other. A computer flight simulator, for example, can teach flying safely, with no risk of crashing.

An important part of learning is play. At birth, our cranial nerves are there physically but they are unorganized. During our childhood, our intellectual growth is amplified by all kinds of play, which is a fun and mostly safe way to try new things, to experiment, to learn skills such as running and jumping and fighting and dodging and climbing and swimming and singing. When we are adults, if we are confronted by an unexpected situation or difficulty, our brains have had prior practice through play, so we can respond quickly. Our responses have been rehearsed through earlier play. We often don't realize that we're learning when we're playing, because play is fun. Dance and music teach us to coordinate our body movements.

The game of peek-a-boo helps babies learn facial recognition and surprise. The games of hide and seek, tag, capture the flag, dodgeball, cops and robbers, leapfrog, jumping jacks, freeze tag, blind man's buff, pat-a-cake, sharks and minnows, musical chairs, tug of war, and many others help us develop basic skills. Ball games like basketball and football help us develop physical coordination. Games like Concentration help us develop our memories. Simon Says teaches the ability to follow instructions. Chess can teach strategy. Play continues throughout life, as young lovers explore each other by flirting, which is a safe way to try out possible sexual partners while not committing to only one person. Video games help us adapt to the world of computers and digital technology. We can try on new identities to expand our sense of self. When we're playing, we're immersed in a simplified fictional world where the only thing that matters is playing the game itself.

Systems of life

Generally, our perceptual and mental equipment is designed for dealing with what is roughly the same size as us, such as chairs and cars and hats and houses and trees and cats and other humans. A single human can deal with another single human, for example, but it is more difficult to deal with something substantially larger, such as a crowd, or something substantially smaller, such as an amoeba.

Accordingly, the ***Principle of Similar Scale*** is that we are best able to cope with things that are roughly the same size as ourselves.

We are made of systems that are smaller than us, such as cells and organs.

We are a system.

We make up larger systems, such as families, firms and nations.

It is important to understand how our particular bodily system works and how smaller subsystems and larger suprasystems interact and how they affect us. We need to know how to manage our smaller subsystems and how to fit in with our larger suprasystems. If a doctor says that our internal subsystem needs a specific vitamin, then we go to the external suprasystem of the pharmacy to buy those vitamins.

A few observations will be made.

First, systems at different levels of complexity share the properties of life. They desire to keep existing. They have a border with an *inside* and an *outside* and a boundary separating them from other systems. They foster movement of resources between their external and internal environments. They gather inputs from outside, use them, and excrete outputs. They try to keep their parts moving in a coordinated and orderly way. They need to take in as much energy as they use. They reproduce. They adapt to changing circumstances.

Second, at different levels, components have different properties but similar functions. Consider energy: in cells, it is adenosine triphosphate; in organs, it is glucose; in our bodies, it is food; in our families, it is money; in our firms, it is profits; and in our nations, it is natural resources. In each case, the function of the energy is to keep things moving. Or consider borders: in cells, it is the cell membrane; in organs, it is the surrounding fibrous tissue; in humans, it is the skin; in families, it is the exterior walls of the house or apartment; in a firm, it is the exterior walls of the factory; in a nation, it is the territorial border. In each case, borders have the same function: to keep the bad stuff out and the good stuff in.

Third, balance is important. If the heart weakens while the lungs strengthen, health can deteriorate. Cancer is an example of an out-of-control subsystem disrupting the overall balance. In a nation, if a government shunts resources toward wasteful projects while its infrastructure crumbles, transportation can atrophy.

Fourth, coordination is important. The brain and heart and lungs need to coordinate their activity, so if there is danger, the brain signals the heart and lungs to work faster, and to resume their normal pace after danger passes.

Fifth, as a corollary of the *Principle of Similar Scale,* systems exert the most influence on other systems at the same level. Accordingly, cells influence other cells, humans influence other humans, and nations influence other nations. A human has the most influence at their own level: they can wake up, eat breakfast, get dressed, go to work and so forth. Their influence diminishes as the degrees of separation between the levels becomes wider. For example, a human has some influence on the subsystem of their lungs, such as by controlling their rate of breathing, but they have no influence on cells within the lungs; for example, we can not instruct a lung cell which proteins to make. A human has less influence on larger systems such as their families and their firms, since other members have their own agendas, and they can affect or modify what choices we might make. A human's influence is practically nonexistent in the even larger suprasystem of the nation.

Nevertheless, our membership in these larger systems is important; what happens to them, happens to us. If the government fails to prevent crime, we may become victims. As Marcus Aurelius wrote, "that which is not good for the bee-hive cannot be good for the bees." A related idea is that systems on one level can not do the thinking for systems on another level. An individual human cell does not have the brainpower to tell a person where to get coffee, for example. Similarly, a national government is not geared to making specific decisions about what groceries a specific person should buy or what prices a retailer must charge for cosmetics, for example. There have been failed experiments when governments tried to micromanage the day-to-day decisions of citizens, with disastrous results.

Sixth, systems need to maintain their particular patterns of order, and what happens at different levels can affect those patterns. For example, within the brain, there is a subsystem regulating pleasure in which chemicals such as dopamine are released when the body acts to benefit its overall health. When we see a beautiful sunset, for example, pleasing chemicals are released, in effect rewarding us for what we did to see the sunset. In this way our brain learns how to get similar experiences in the future. But it is possible to interfere with this system of internal rewards by taking psychoactive drugs such as cocaine or heroin. These drugs can repurpose the brain to not work toward enjoying sunsets but rather to taking more of the drugs. This is bad for long-term health. Drug addiction can cause all sorts of systemic failures. It is a violation of the *Basic Principle of Ethics* in which a person elevates the short-term pleasure of the drug over the longer-term danger of the addiction.

Seventh, life flows in both directions among the various levels. It flows from the top down. For example, a nation gathers resources, enabling businesses to create widgets, generating profits for salaries, so employees buy groceries, enabling them to eat dinner, which becomes glucose in the bloodstream, which cells break down into adenosine triphosphate to power what they do. Cells, energized, power up the organs, powering up the human to work in the business, make more widgets, which helps the national economy. We depend on these flows happening smoothly and regularly. Disruptions can affect us.

Last, patterns governing the relations between lower-order systems and higher-order systems can be instructive. For example, transportation planners can model traffic flows by studying the human circulatory system.

Goldilocks transformations

Our lives are punctuated by moments in which we go from one state to another state. These transformations can be slight, gradual, abrupt or radical. What follows is a general rule.

The best transformations are gradual when only a few things change while the rest stays the same.

These are Goldilocks transitions: not too little, not too much, but just the right amount of change. It is how life evolved. It is how we think and grow, slowly and steadily, adding a new skill or learning a new lesson gradually, not trying to master playing the piano in a week, not trying to cram for the end-of-the-semester test in one caffeinated night. When we climb from the first floor to the second floor, we do not hop up in one springy move, but rather climb one step at a time. Each step is something we can handle; there is effort involved but not so much that it might overwhelm us. If we change jobs, our new job should have pretty much the same tasks we mastered from our old job with only a few gradual shifts in responsibility. It is easy for us to adapt to gradual changes in the weather; a slow transition from a sunny day to a rainstorm is an easy adjustment, while an abrupt transition brought on by a tornado is more dangerous. If humans lived in a world with constant tornadoes, then most likely we would find ways to adapt to this new environment.

Gradual transitions are how we learn. For instance, when we learn something new, most of what is learned is actually something that we already know, that we've understood and locked on to, while there are a few unfamiliar elements. The brain is keen to appreciate the unfamiliar, and it rewards itself with dopamine when it senses something unexpected. But if what comes rushing at us is radical in every way, with nothing understandable, we are bewildered and learn nothing. For example, when Galileo asked clergymen to look through a telescope to examine the pock marks on the moon, they could not make sense of what they saw, since the new information was so radically different from their point of view. Some suspected that the images were illusions or tricks.

If transitions are too slight, nothing much happens. If the height of each stair is only a few inches, then the transition is not challenging enough, so climbing one floor might take fifty steps rather than fourteen, which could be unnecessarily tiring. Like stair steps, there are twelve notes in the western musical tradition which proceed from one octave to the next, with human ears attuned to being able to distinguish each note as it climbs up the musical staircase. Our ears hear that a C# is higher than a C note, for example, but the human ear might have trouble distinguishing a frequency midway between those notes.

A pleasant melody has a repeating phrase, with perhaps only one or a few notes changing while most stay the same. If a succeeding phrase is totally different from the first, it may sound jarring and discordant. Changes in guitar chords within a song tend to be in the same key, with most of the notes staying the same, but only a few notes changing when the chords change.

Abrupt 180-degree turns are risky. A worker who changes everything in one fell swoop, such as their job and house and city and friends, all at once, risks something going awry. Radical shifts can be funny when they are delivered in non-serious or non-threatening situations. It is the essence of humor to juxtapose opposites, to lead listeners down a soft path and then whack them with a jarring punch. When a listener realizes that it is not serious, tension is released in laughter. In fiction, characters go through abrupt changes because the shifts are compelling to watch, but even then the changes can not be so drastic that the story no longer makes sense.

In our lives, radical shifts can hurt us. We grow by lots of gradual changes. We do not spring from child to fully grown adult in one wild weekend. Growing takes time, and as we live to old age, our transitions again should be gradual, to offset the lessening of physical capability with greater knowledge.

A gradual way to learn is to travel. During the Renaissance, young people traveled throughout Europe on the so-called grand tour, staying in foreign cities, studying and learning and making new friends. By visiting an older civilization, one can get a sense of one's own culture.

Human agency

If one accepts the *Basic Principle of Ethics* and the idea of human-type free will, then a picture of human agency emerges.

Human agency is the consistent and regular application of one's human-type free will to strive toward distant goals by the systematic linking of longer and longer cause-and-effect idea chains.

It is usually easy to identify people with human agency. They get things done. They accomplish projects that take months and years to finish. They stay focused on a distant goal. When obstacles block their path, they are flexible enough to overcome the obstacles and keep progressing toward their goal. They may change their goal; they may decide, halfway through, that their goal is unworthy or unrealizable or that another goal takes precedence. Persons with human agency, according to psychotherapist Amy Morin, don't fear taking calculated risks, and they don't shy away from change.

The most successful humans have human agency. They usually bring about positive transformations, assuming that they act in accord with the *Basic Principle of Ethics*. Perhaps the most dangerous humans have a high degree of human agency but lack any commitment to morality, such as serial killers, evil dictators and mass murderers. Their thought processes are confused and their goals are short-sighted and bad. They think, incorrectly, that their goals are good, but they can't think through what is best for themselves and for others in the long term, and they embark on their sinister course.

Why we die

Now we come to perhaps the ultimate and final transition, from living beings to dead ones. There are no examples of a living creature staying alive indefinitely. All creatures die. That is the sad truth. There are creatures such as extremophiles who can harden themselves into a form that can withstand extreme cold, and exist in a state of suspended animation, such as bacteria that can lie dormant for long periods before they are awakened by water or heat or some other condition, but if they ever awaken, then they too will die eventually.

It is a horrific paradox that living creatures, whose main essence is a powerful desire to keep living, are doomed to die. Our act of juggling various subsystems eventually fails. The heart stops beating. Brain cells die. The change from living to dying is the ultimate abrupt change that almost all humans fear and try to avoid. Death is not good for us. It violates the essence of the *Basic Principle of Ethics*. What we can do is to try to lead full and healthy lives, devoid of illusion and nonsense, and part of living well is understanding why there must be death.

One word explains death: bumping. Life requires movement of oxygen molecules and blood cells and muscles and neurotransmitters, and movement can cause bumping, and bumping can cause damage. If quarks never bumped into other quarks or if molecules kept to themselves or if blood cells never rammed into other blood cells, then we might not have this problem, but we do. It is part of the reality of our existence.

Most bumping is harmless, but sometimes it causes damage. As time passes, living things struggle to keep their internal parts repaired, which is difficult, since the structures doing the repairs can get damaged as well. A cell must take in energy and expel waste but this movement may damage its membrane. The cell must get the repair right, quickly, while keeping good things in and bad things out. If the structures making the repair are damaged, the repair might go wrong.

It becomes increasingly difficult for every living being to maintain its vital energy flows while keeping its structure repaired. This difficulty afflicts beings at every level of complexity, from cells, to organ systems, to humans, to families, to businesses, and to nations.

The essential built-in problem is that we need a fixed structure such as a backbone or cell wall or skin or cartilage to manage the energy flows, but that fixedness is also our downfall. The environment changes. The structure that worked well initially has trouble with new developments. Things bump. Damage results.

Consider the lifespan of a car. When it was built, it had the latest features: shock absorbers, mufflers to lessen the engine noise, and power brakes. Its signal lights and windshield wipers conformed to government requirements. As time passed, however, gunk built up in the engine, oil needed to be changed, debris clogged the filters and the tires needed more air. Early repairs were quick and easy such as adding air to the tires and changing the oil. But over the years, serious and lasting damage began to build up. The steel chassis endured the stresses of bending and turning on the roads. Paint began to wear off in places, allowing rust. The external environment changed. Government required engines to use unleaded gasoline. Cars had to have air bags for safety. Some modifications were difficult. Car manufacturers stopped making certain replacement parts, so it became increasingly hard to find them. Repairs became more substantial, such as a defective drive train or a malfunctioning steering column. Sooner or later a repair will come along which costs more to fix than simply buying a new car. The energy needed to swap out the drivetrain becomes so laborious and expensive that it doesn't make sense to even try to replace it. It is easier to junk the old car and buy a new one.

Essentially that's what nature does. Nature comes up against this problem of trying to keep a living being repaired and functioning and adapted to changing conditions, but the problem over time becomes too difficult for nature to solve. Nature decides to do what a car owner decides to do: to get a new body. Nature finds it is easier to make new and better-adapted humans rather than to struggle to keep the existing humans repaired.

Still, it is possible for humans to get smarter at making temporary fixes to extend our lives. Through technological advances, humans are discovering how to keep our bodies healthy and functioning. For example, if our heart fails, doctors can replace it with a mechanical heart. Scientists are making better medicines to fight infections and better tools for identifying microbes and cancer cells. It is possible to extend the average human lifespan by such methods.

But even then human life can not be extended indefinitely. Any such effort will run into intractable realities. Suppose, for the sake of argument, that humans figure out how to manipulate nature to make ourselves practically immortal, enabled by advancements in medicine, gene therapy, cell and organ replacement and such. Suppose, further, that scientists learn how to get energy from a relatively sustainable source such as directly from sunlight, and learn how to recycle all of the materials needed for life including proteins and other carbon-based compounds. These practically-immortal humans would confront a much bigger problem. Change would upset them. Any change, such as a warmer or colder climate, different animals or plants to contend with, or deadlier strains of bacteria, would threaten their systems. A planet populated with practically-immortal humans would not welcome babies. But since the species as a whole would be fixed with given genes, it would be vulnerable to external changes such as other species which might evolve to feed on such humans. The American philosopher Will Durant said "That the death of a part is the life of the whole", so while death is horrible for individual humans, it's good for the species since it permits gradual adaptation to changing circumstances.

A world in which humans lived forever would be a static world, one in which new developments, even the idea of news itself, would upset the established order. It would be a boring world. Nobody would really want to live there. Making humans immortal would make living unbearable. But of course the idea of humans achieving near-immortality is a fiction and practically impossible to achieve, given the realities of movement and friction and damage to our bodies internally and externally.

We can look at death as if it's the price of life. We can imagine the trade-off between immortality and change by comparing a relatively-immortal thing such as a statue with a mortal creature such as a living human. Which will exist or live longer? Arguably the statue will exist longer, since it is hard, impervious to sleet and snow, and immune from diseases. However, the statue can not think, or love, or feel snowflakes on its 'skin', or change its mind. The price that a human pays for good things about living, such as feeling and loving and growing and learning, is the eventual result of death. If we could turn ourselves into statues, which we can not do, but if we could, it would be a lonely and cold and rigid and boring and mindless existence on a pedestal. We could not even glance at the pigeons pooping on our shoulders.

Such is the tradeoff between immortality and change. It is why the living creatures with the longest life spans, such as giant sequoia trees which can live several thousand years, exist in rather boring and staid and predictable environments which never experience wild swings in temperature. A general rule is that smaller living beings tend to live shorter lives, although some bacteria can keep alive during adverse environmental conditions by hardening themselves into a protective shell, that is, by turning themselves into a rigid statue of sorts, waiting patiently for the environment to once again become more favorable.

Accordingly, death is rooted in birth. It is a horrible trade-off. To enjoy the miracle of birth and to do what we must do to keep living, the sacrifice for this wonderfulness is death.

Religion

Essence of religion
The prospect of death spooks almost all humans, and it can prompt us to make illogical and frankly weird choices. It inspired the Egyptian Pharaoh Khufu to build a giant pyramid at Giza as his personal tomb. It inspired Chinese Emperor Qin Shi Huang to

command sculptors to make eight thousand terracotta warriors to supposedly protect him in an afterlife. It spurred King Louis IX to embark on the ill-fated Seventh Crusade to supposedly win favor with God by conquering Jerusalem. These projects were a colossal waste of resources and often led to substantial loss of life without contributing to human betterment. The religious impulse to waste resources by illogical pursuits is not only in kings, but in all of us. We should try to understand why it is there, and for us to understand both the positive and negative effects of religious thinking.

If we consider our origins from evolution by random processes for four billion years, and our physical composition including our powerful yet limited brains, then it seems inevitable that belief in religion should have flourished. The motivation is that our powerful desire to keep living is undercut by the savage reality of our dying. We are squeezed into this nasty vise: We want to keep living, but we can't.

So our brains come to our defense. Since we can imagine what might happen in the future, we can imagine an afterlife. The illusion is immensely comforting. Human imagination goes further, conjuring supernatural beings who are somehow able to hide themselves from human view, parent-like with human-type emotions, judgmental, wanting to be worshiped and loved, and who created the afterlife and serve as its nightclub bouncer, choosing who goes in and who doesn't.

When our ancestors experienced earthquakes and diseases and thunderstorms, they figured that something had to cause these events. It is part of the strong human tendency to think in terms of cause-and-effect. The earth shook; humans got sluggish with fever; lightning flashed and thunder boomed. These things did not happen on their own, uncaused. But what caused them? Since our ancestors did not understand plate tectonics or virology or electricity, they imagined supernatural causes. To win the goodwill of these imagined gods, they sacrificed animals and built statues and prayed and chanted and danced in the hope that the god or gods would perhaps help them or at least not hurt them. When the idea of one all-powerful deity came along, our ancestors were hard-pressed to explain the bad things that happened, so this idea sometimes degenerated into a two-god explanation: a good one called *God* and a bad one called the *devil*. When good things happened like abundant harvests, it was because of the good one, and when heart attacks and famines and plagues and droughts happened, it was because of the bad one, or else it was the good one turning angry because humans did not worship it enough.

So, humans, desiring cause-and-effect explanations, with constant hunger for life and suffering from the nagging fear of death, living in ignorance with lively imaginations, found comfort in supernatural explanations. Most societies gravitated around one system of fantastical thought. Competing systems were problematic since they suggested that one's own system may be wrong. When attempts at logic and persuasion failed to convert people, violence often resulted. Given the wide variety of religious belief systems around the world, one would have thought that over time, if one system had been the right one, properly reflecting reality, protecting people and helping people lead better lives, conferring immortality on its believers, protecting them from invasion, connecting with the real and authentic god, that it would have emerged by now, by evolutionary pressures. But this has not happened. What has happened is that a variety of religious systems have emerged in an evolutionary unfolding, as various systems of fantastical thought compete to hold a place in the collective human imagination.

While there are many religions around the world, there are properties common to many. They tend to promulgate an all-inclusive system of belief with explanations for all of the big questions, often with ideas about the supernatural, an afterlife, and the soul as an unseen supernatural aspect of a human. Each tends to foster a religious mindset through which believers perceive and interpret the world. Believers can have an intensely personal and private feeling of connectedness to a spirit world. Many religions foster the idea that everything has a purpose, even humans. There is often an idea that people have a measure of God-type free will, so that their choices can be subject to a subsequent review by a supernatural authority. Each religion tends to set standards for behavior.

Almost all religions encourage belief in creative fantasies, many of which are absurd. Most defy common sense and the laws of nature. Most assert that some beings called gods do not die, even when science and experience and common sense suggest that immortality is impossible. Religions hold fantastical ideas such as that a deity created the world in seven days, that the first woman was crafted from the rib of the first man, that dancing on the parched plains can prompt rainfall, that people are reincarnated into various animals after they die and that they need to live a good life to come back as a human, that the sun is a deity riding a chariot through the sky, that one can foretell the future by looking at constellations of stars, that one can experience a spiritual connection by taking hallucinogenic drugs, that we are regularly visited by aliens but that authorities hide such encounters, and so forth.

These systems fall apart under simple questioning. If the prophet is still alive, where is he now? If Adam and Eve were the first man and woman, did their children commit incest with each other since they were unable to find other partners? If one tribe is the so-called chosen people, then why has such misery befallen them again and again? If God is all powerful, why is there a devil? How does one explain evil? If people used to be animals but were reborn as humans, why don't they remember their earlier existence? Why are most prophets men?

These fantastical explanations rarely get exposed to rational-critical analysis. An argument with a religious believer usually comes to a halt after a few such questions, with the believer asserting that their beliefs must be accepted on faith. So questions stop. The inquiry ends. This undercuts a chief leg of the *Basic Principle of Ethics* in that the *as best that can be determined* part gets blocked.

Since a fantastical system of religious belief is illogical and often defies common sense, it needs to find ways to persist in the human imagination. It is a system of sorts which evolves like every living being, changing over time, constantly working to keep itself believed by humans. It helps if the system has some measure of internal consistency, so that there is a logic to how it explains things of a metaphysical nature. It needs to discourage people who ask questions. Children need to be taught. Believers who bump into inconsistencies might need clarification.

So, in many societies, a priestly class emerged to manage discrepancies within the fantastical system and to enforce conformity. They were often self-chosen people, usually men, who would school new recruits into the intellectual mechanics of their particular system, and teach them how to justify its logic and how to keep believers from veering from the faith. Membership was often predicated on some form of personal sacrifice, such as giving up sex or alcohol or particular foods. If people asked why one god was all-powerful and yet there was a bad god, for example, then priests could try to explain such discrepancies. They could motivate people with rewards and punishments, both earthly and supernatural, and those with political power could punish non-believers with fines or ostracism or jail or death. They could promise a pleasant afterlife to believers and threaten a nasty afterlife to non-believers.

Manipulation was often needed to reinforce belief. Some human behaviors are driven by strong desires, often involving sex or food, so to manipulate people, the fantastical system could identify certain behaviors as sinful. When people did these supposedly sinful behaviors, they could be made to feel guilty after having done them. Most religions try to restrict sex in some ways, with an extreme example being the Shakers, an American sect which demanded celibacy; they forbade men and women to be alone together, so that they couldn't even pass each other on the stairs, or shake hands, or blink their eyes, or have women sit cross legged; unsurprisingly, without sex, Shaker numbers dwindled over time. Priests could persuade people that they committed their supposedly offensive behaviors through their own god-type free will, defying the wishes of the unseen deities and displeasing the gods. Priests could offer spiritual relief, perhaps saying specific words, giving a blessing, or performing a rite, for the apparent purpose of interceding with the god or gods on behalf of the offending human to restore the deity's love. In such a manner, priests could use guilt to keep ignorant people faithful as well as solidify their role in the community.

Rituals were another way of reinforcing belief, such as repeating particular sequences of words, offering somewhat edible parts of animals as food for the unseen gods, praying, genuflecting or bowing or showing other signs of submission, wearing particular types of clothing or avoiding specific foods, building and maintaining structures devoted to house an unseen god or goddess, and so forth. Weddings, funerals, baptisms and so forth often required the services of a priest who could be paid for conducting the ritual. Since priests do not generate wealth by farming or trading, they must get sustenance from believers. When there is a self-selected group, attracted to a fantastical system of belief, a clubby insularity can form that often works against self-examination and reform.

Since the forces underlying religion are permanently etched into the human condition, it seems that belief in religion will be around as long as people are around. Superstitions, ideas of the supernatural and of afterlives and gods and goddesses and all other types of the fantastical are a natural way of coping with the weirdness of the human experience. It does not make sense to try to get rid of these belief systems, or to punish believers, or to try to highlight their absurdity with reason and logic. Our bitter human predicament of wanting to stay alive but being unable to do so is so vexing that all kinds of mental gyrations will happen despite our best efforts to promote rational thinking.

Accordingly, a general attitude of toleration should guide us. Let people believe as they wish. It is extremely difficult and unwise to try to force people to think one way or another. The atheist philosopher Will Durant advised against trying to foist atheism on believers, since religion helps them to be happy and to cope with life. He wrote "To be in haste to destroy the faith of such people is surely the mark of a shallow and ungenerous mind."

The way to counter irrationality is not to try to impose rationality but rather to try to understand why we think what we think and have a healthy respect for human limitations. There can be no certainty about what's what. There are only guesses. People only really get to find out if there is an afterlife after we die, and if selected dead people ever made such a discovery, they can't return to life to tell us. The supernatural may exist and it is impossible to prove that it does not exist. There could be gods who pop up tomorrow in living color.

An exception to a general attitude of tolerance is when people are confronted by intolerant people who seek to impose their beliefs through intimidation and violence. In such circumstances, people are forced to become intolerant of intolerant people. It is a weakness of sorts—that people who are tolerant and uncertain of their own beliefs, lacking the stubborn sureness of a fantastical belief system, must somehow become sure and stubborn when dealing with sure and stubborn people. Uncertainty and questioning are short-term weaknesses but long-term strengths, since a skeptical attitude can lead to greater understanding.

So if we consider religion to be an organized system of fantastical thought living in the human imagination, we can think of religions as living creatures, evolving in their own right, trying to stay in the minds of their human believers. They adapt and learn from each other, borrow ideas and stories and try to fit them into the culture of their believers. Like all things, religion in a general sense is neither right nor wrong, but people need to understand why religion does what it does to avoid the bad parts and to enjoy the good parts. Religion is like humanity's childhood, our beginnings, and it should not be dismissed out of hand as foolish but rather explored and understood so that its good lessons can be extracted and its misconceptions avoided. If we remove fantastical thinking from religion, then what remains is usually helpful advice on how we might live our lives. Indeed there is a fairly remarkable consensus among religious and philosophical traditions about such issues.

Benefits of religion
The benefits of religion include the following…

- **Ethical wisdom.** Most religions have guidelines regarding good behavior and these rules are usually good and helpful. They are almost always the right thing to do. Rules such as *Don't steal, Don't commit adultery,* and *Don't murder* are sensible and simple and easy-to-learn. Religions can help inculcate good habits such as tolerance, forgiveness, respect for parents and elders, cooperation, sharing, neighborly affection and marital harmony. A key virtue based on the Vedic tradition, and found in Jainism and Buddhism and Sikhism and Hinduism and elsewhere, is the goodness of nonviolence, or ahimsa, which is not only the avoidance of hurtful thoughts and actions, but a prescription for peace. In the Atharvaveda, some poems extol the virtues of peace; one goes "Give us agreement with our own, and with strangers give us unity, in this place join us in sympathy and love, may we agree in mind, agree in purpose, around us rise no din of frequent slaughter."
- **Comfort.** The ideas of an afterlife, a powerful unseen god as a protector and benefactor, and so forth are immensely comforting to time-pressed humans squeezed in a crucible between life and death, trying to cope with the death of loved ones and bodily decay. Beautiful storytelling and poetry and rituals can amplify the comfort factor, which helps to lessen anxiety.
- **Imagination.** The act of contemplating what's not visibly present spurs humans to exercise their imaginations.

- **Literacy.** Religions often indirectly encourage reading and writing of their sacred scrolls and books.
- **Change of pace.** The practice of religion usually involves a turning away from work and study and raising families, and toward otherworldly concerns. Praying can help humans break out of repetitive negative mental habits. Attending a weekly service offers a break from the day-to-day pursuits of wealth and business, and a chance to do something less demanding and less physically stressful.
- **Socialization.** Religion often brings people together to meet, mingle, share, make friends and meet future spouses. In Confucian philosophy, there is an emphasis on harmony within the family, encouraging children to respect their parents, and for parents to love their children.
- **Helps warriors fight.** The idea of a powerful god on one's side can help warriors allay their fears, and struggle fiercely against a tough foe. Belief in an afterlife can smother fear, and supposed rewards in heaven can motivate a hesitant soldier.
- **Benefits of a priestly class.** These are usually smart people who are exempt from the struggle to earn a living. In their free time, they can develop skills that would normally not get developed, such as writing and singing and storytelling. They offer society a reservoir of talent that it would not normally have access to. Monks in the Middle Ages preserved many ancient texts by re-copying them, preserving valuable information for humankind. Priests organize efforts to support widows and orphans and the poor. They can intercede on behalf of parishioners who are in trouble with political authorities.
- **Conformity.** Religion can foster social cohesion, prompting people to think in a like-minded fashion. Social harmony is particularly vital for societies under stress.
- **Decision-making.** By spurring people to think about things

unrelated to their daily concerns, religion can help people indirectly to discover their unconscious desires. If people are confused and stuck in their thinking, for example, then seemingly unrelated mental activities, such as examining the stars for patterns or reading tarot cards or praying to a statue, can distract a worrier from worrying, and get them to focus on what they are really feeling and wanting. This understanding can help their decision-making.
- **Mental discipline.** Activities such as prayer can help a human clarify to themselves what they want, and this clarification can help them actually get what they want. Chanting, breathing exercises, meditation, contemplation of paradoxes such as trying to hear *the sound of one hand clapping,* saying a repeated word rhythmically, and other such methods can pull a mind out of the whirlpool of endless rumination. According to Confucius, meditation can help us find peace within ourselves, and to help us stay focused on whatever goals we've chosen.
- **Discouraging vice.** Most religions discourage smoking and gambling and alcoholism and drug addiction. Many sponsor activities to help people recover from addiction.
- **Pilgrimages.** Religions encourage travel which can help personal growth.
- **Altruism** in the sense of generosity, or what Will Durant called *selfish altruism*. Most religions encourage people to share their excesses, to give to the less fortunate, and so forth. These acts are generally consistent with the *Basic Principle of Ethics* because they bring indirect benefits to the giver in the future, such as living in a society with fewer destitute people. A single act of generosity is like throwing a pebble in a pond, bringing ripples of kindness and good feeling in ever-widening circles. If we can temper our desires by only wanting what we really need, then it is easy to give away our surpluses. Siddhartha advised us to take care

of ourselves first, and after we have enough, then we can give to others. Islamic thought emphasizes the importance of keeping neighbors out of poverty through sharing.
- **Culture.** Many religions encourage painting and music and sculpture and dance and literature, enriching humanity in a general way.

Drawbacks of religion

The drawbacks of religion include the following...

- **Distortion of reality.** Since most religious systems are built on fantasy conceptions, there is a disconnect from reality. This can be tolerable if the religious ideas stay in the minds of believers, providing comfort, and do not harm a person in their day-to-day striving or in their dealings with others. But humans need a solid grasp of reality since it is how we survive and thrive. Bad ideas can cause injury and pain, not only to the believers themselves but to those they interact with. For example, the religion of Christian Science asserts that sickness is not real but an illusion caused by the devil, and that the proper way to fight disease is with prayer and not with medicine. This distorted thinking can result in needless deaths. In another example, in the Middle Ages, a religious leader called on Christians to retake the Holy Land from the Muslim infidels, spurring more than a million soldiers to march to their deaths.
- **Anti-science.** Richard Dawkins said "Religion is corrosive to science; it teaches people to be satisfied with trivial, superficial non-explanations, and blinds them to the wonderful, real explanations that we have within our grasp; it teaches them to respect authority, revelation and faith, instead of always insisting on evidence."
- **Discouraging thinking.** Religious systems want to keep their believers believing. So they try to squelch mental

activity which might threaten their hold on their subjects' minds. This can lead to a society-wide type of mental stuckness in which people get glued to one type of thinking, and cease growing intellectually. Religion can amplify a natural human tendency to avoid exploratory thinking.
- **Altruism** in the sense of one-way giving. If altruism is a one-way transfer of something valuable to somebody else without any expected future compensation, then it violates the *Basic Principle of Ethics*. It is not good for the giver. The giver does not get any future benefit. A person who gives money to an alcoholic, for example, is engaging in a one-way transfer, so that the giver becomes poorer while the recipient is no better off. Society is not wealthier as a result. Altruism can be good if giving results in the general improvement of society, since that indirectly benefits the giver. The problem is that many religions don't distinguish between the good type of altruism, which is generosity with an indirect future benefit to the giver, from the bad type of altruism, which is a one-way transfer of wealth.
- **Self-sacrifice.** An extreme form of altruism is martyrdom. Some religions honor their martyrs and see their act of sacrificing their own lives as the ultimate good. It is an extreme manifestation of the idea that we have to give up something precious to please a fickle yet powerful deity. Examples include Abraham about to burn his son Isaac as an offering although he later changes his mind, Jesus giving up his life so that others can find eternal life, and Aztec kings hurling their daughters to their deaths to please a deity.
- **Free will.** Many religions promulgate the incorrect understanding that people have God-type uncaused out-of-the-blue free will, when people only have human-type free will. This flawed understanding is a serious impediment to emotional management as will be shown later. According to many religions, people are supposed to have this god-type

free will so that they can choose or not choose to love the deity, to follow the deity's rules, and so forth. If they choose the course prescribed by religion, they are considered to be good, and if they don't, they're bad. When people do bad things, they feel guilty, and religious authorities can manipulate feelings of guilt to further control their believers. Further, the bad-deed-doers can be punished by religious authorities or by the supposed deity, perhaps by denying entry to the good afterlife.

- **Waste of resources.** Time and money spent on religious rituals, funding a priestly class, building elaborate structures for worship, traveling on pilgrimages and so forth could have funded education and science to benefit humanity.
- **Discouraging pleasure.** Many religions apply a wet rag on the flame of human pleasure. Some discourage sexual intercourse when it is a healthy and enjoyable activity. Some prohibit sex unless it is done by a traditional man-woman married couple for purposes of procreation. Sex is a strong human drive and most people, regardless of prohibitions, are going to engage in sexual activity, so preventing it can inflict psychological stress. Many religions push restrictions on eating or dietary habits, or discourage artistic expression by prohibiting the creation of images. Many religions urge people to stifle the self or engage in various acts of self-denial.
- **Anti-women.** Most religions are male-oriented and emphasize subordinate roles for women that focus on child-rearing and the family. Most prophets are men. God is usually described in masculine terms.
- **Focus on the afterlife and not on this life.** Many religions suggest that people should not pursue their self-chosen lifetime goals but rather devote their lives to serving a deity or serving some religious purpose to secure a supernatural reward. This can lead to people wasting their earthly lives.

They don't pursue what they want to pursue, but rather pursue what a religion or priests or society in general thinks that they should pursue. The focus on an afterlife can skew a person's priorities. A person who makes choices based on what happens after their death may undercut choices that would help them in their current life. The philosopher Epicurus criticized fear-based religions for postponing joy, adding that "Life is ruined by putting things off", so that believers die "without truly living."

- **Violence.** Most religions do not condone violence, but most have a vested interest in perpetuating a system of fantastical thought. So non-believers, or believers who question their faith, are threats to the system. An entire community has a vested interest in believing as a way to secure admittance into an afterlife, and doubts and questions and denials risk upsetting their plan. Logic and persuasion are often ineffective, so fervent religiously-minded people resort to the only tactic left: to harm the unfaithful. In the Middle Ages, non-believers were declared to be heretics and murdered, and priests declared elderly women to be witches and had them burned to death.
- **Genocide.** It can be particularly dangerous when there are two different faiths in the same physical space. Even though both faiths may profess things like love and tolerance and goodness and kindness, each faith is a stark and visible reminder that their own thinking may be wrong. Will Rome be pagan or Christian? Will France be Protestant or Catholic? Will India be Muslim or Hindu? Such madness has led to horrific civil wars.
- **War.** Belief in religion can result in extra-dangerous warriors who are not afraid of death. Belief erases doubt and imparts a false sense of confidence that an unseen god has one's back and will protect the warrior in battle and bring death to the enemy and victory to the believers. It replaces

a complex ethical calculation from the *Basic Principle of Ethics* with a mindless command to kill the infidels. In extreme forms, warriors might be motivated by a weird fantastical calculus, such that if they commit a suicide bombing, they will not only have subsequent immortality, but be rewarded by having dozens of virgin brides in this supposed heaven. So, warriors are rewarded for committing murder on Earth, to enjoy glory and sex in heaven.

The ways that religion insinuates itself into the human imagination are complex. Since religious thinking varies widely, this simplified construct of benefits and drawbacks will not be applicable in many cases, but what is important is to get a general sense of the positive and negative aspects of religion. With such a perspective, an atheist may begin to enjoy the good aspects of religious thinking while avoiding the pitfalls.

Atheism

Atheists are humans who don't believe in the supernatural, in gods or God, in miracles, in the soul or an afterlife. Atheists are a diverse bunch, not unified around any type of orthodoxy or formal belief system, but rather they represent a scattering of all kinds of belief systems sometimes described as humanism. Agnostics who maintain that God or gods *could* exist, but they're not sure, could possibly be included under the umbrella of atheism. A person who identifies the entire universe and all of its rules as 'God', but who doesn't believe in an afterlife and who doesn't see God as a separate being that answers prayers, then such a worldview is consistent with the idea of atheism. Theists, who believe in a particular religion, could also technically be called 'atheists', since they don't believe in most gods such as the gods of ancient Greece or Baal or Santa Claus, but rather only believe in one particular God, such as Yahweh or Jesus. Richard Dawkins observed "We are all atheists about most of the gods that humanity has ever believed in, some of us just go one god further."

If we think of atheism as a type of religion, competing with real religions for followers, it seems on first inspection to offer nothing of value. There's no afterlife. There's no powerful unseen deity for assistance. What is at the end of the road? Just nothingness, oblivion, and an infinite span of unconsciousness.

What atheism offers, however, is a better grasp of reality that can help people live better when they are alive. We can make better choices to help us grow and think and learn and to be genuinely good people. We can become more tolerant and open-minded with a focus on expanding human agency and enjoying life and working toward human betterment.

Being a human is a really tough task since a person is confronted with a bewildering forest thick with choices and without a clear path forward. What should we do? How should we manage our time? What habits should we develop? What should we learn? How can we balance different areas of life? Which friends should we choose? How can our lives be lived to the fullest? If life is a smorgasbord of choices, what is the best possible mix? A belief system based on atheism can help us navigate through the weirdness of life.

Perhaps it is a fair assessment that most humans do not have an optimal mix. Some are stuck in dead-end jobs. Some have unproductive interactions with others. There are highly intelligent people who don't know how to work with others, or how to manage a project, or even how to have friends. And nobody gets it right forever, because even the most successful and best adapted among us eventually succumb to bodily decline and death. Perhaps most people have a period in our lives when we have our act together and when we are relatively happier. It varies from person to person. Some have happiness in short bursts, while others have long stretches of happiness, while others lead miserable lives. Life is not fair.

Why we won't meet aliens

Belief in aliens is essentially another form of religious belief. The thinking goes that creatures from other planets visit the Earth yet they hide themselves from authorities and journalists. There is a strong consensus in the scientific community that such visits are unlikely, although ideas about aliens are common in fiction books and movies.

In the vast universe, there are trillions of stars and planets orbiting around them, so it is highly likely that there is life out there which sprang into existence spontaneously like on Earth. But it is highly unlikely that we will ever encounter intelligent aliens because they are extremely far away. Between us and them, there is only a dark and freezing nothingness devoid of energy, with no air, no refueling stations, no food, no warmth.

The difficulties that beset aliens trying to visit us are the same ones that beset Earthlings trying to visit them. Suppose humans wanted to find intelligent alien life. Our first task would be to identify where these aliens possibly were. In which direction should we go? The universe expands outward in all directions. With vast distances, even information traveling at light speed can take years to reach us. The closest star is Proxima Centauri which is 4.25 light years away. That means it takes the fastest thing that we know—light—more than *four years* to go from our sun to the closest star. The universal speed limit is the speed of light, which is incredibly fast at 186,000 miles per second or 671 million miles per hour. So if our spacecraft could travel at the speed of light, it would take more than four years to reach this star.

But humans can not travel at the speed of light. We can't even travel at a fraction of the speed of light. So any possible journey would take hundreds of years. The original astronauts would not live long enough, so it would be their offspring, and their offspring's offspring, and so on, for generation after generation, to complete the voyage. There would have to be enough humans so each new generation could find acceptable partners. These unfortunate space travelers would have to spend their entire lives aboard a metallic structure, never having walked on a beach or swum in a river or felt the gentle pelting from a rainstorm.

A built-in constraint with space travel is that the faster we go, the riskier it gets. As we accelerate, we risk bumping into things, and even a tiny speck of dust at such speeds could burst apart the spacecraft. Its captain would have trouble seeing this dust, and the only way it could detect it is by using light waves, which have a built-in speed limitation, as explained earlier. So we'd have to travel relatively slowly and carefully.

Our spacecraft would have to contain enough life-sustaining materials to keep enough humans alive for generations, including plants to recycle carbon dioxide back into breathable air. It would have to spin to create an artificial gravity. So, the bigger the spacecraft, the more energy it would require to sustain life and to spin and to propel itself forward, and the more likely that a collision with even something tiny like space dust would be fatal. If a spacecraft reached the nearest star, Proxima Centauri, it would probably not find life-supporting planets nearby with conditions similar to Earth. So our unfortunate hypothetical space travelers would have to clamber back into their spaceship to renew their hunt.

It took humans about four billion years to evolve from single-celled creatures. But humans have only been around for 250,000 years, that is, only a tiny sliver of the time. If alien life evolved at a similar rate, we'd have to hope that their evolutionary timeline matched ours, but that is unlikely to happen. If humans ever did encounter aliens, most likely they'd be boring single-celled creatures hardly worth talking to. Could we live on an alien planet? It might have a different gravity, unfamiliar chemicals, or lack air suitable for breathing.

Such are the difficulties for humans trying to visit possible alien planets.

The same insurmountable difficulties would beset aliens trying to visit us.

That's why we don't have any alien visitors.

A more likely scenario is that humans, over time, with better technology and patience, will figure out ways to colonize Mars and maybe a moon of Jupiter or Saturn. This task will still be extremely difficult and fraught with uncertainties. It would take hundreds of years or longer.

These predictions, of course, are based on a current assessment of human technology, and new information could render them incorrect. It is logically impossible to rule out the existence of intelligent aliens on Earth in the same way that it is logically impossible to rule out the existence of gods or God. We can't prove with certainty that something doesn't exist because we can't travel everywhere in the universe to possibly verify such a claim.

Nevertheless, for all practical purposes, based on the current understanding of humanity, it is almost certainly the case that *we are alone in our solar system.*

A human with other humans

As stated previously, we are parts of larger suprasystems such as families and businesses and nations, and how we mesh with them has a huge impact on our well-being. The rules of life outlined previously apply to these larger structures. Accordingly, guidelines such as the *Basic Principle of Ethics*, the *Principle of Accountability*, the *Principle of Similar Scale* and others can act as templates to help us understand how these larger systems work and how we can interact with them.

Socrates said "Know thyself." An idea from Confucian philosophy is similar in that we should understand ourselves first before we try to understand others. A character in the TV show *Fleabag* said "We're all we've got." That's right. We are social beings. We evolved to live with other humans in communities. We need others and others need us. A force bringing us together and pushing us apart is our emotions.

Emotions

The power of emotions

All of us are subject to emotions. It is not possible for any human to be fully free from their powerful influence. Even the wisest, most rational-thinking human can be swayed by them. A person, grieving over the death of a loved one, can simply not wish away the sadness by an act of willpower. A person who has lost their temper during a traffic dispute will have much difficulty regaining control. Emotions can distort our perceptions; for example, if we have something, lose it, then get it back, then we are more likely to love it even more than if it had never been lost, even though this is somewhat irrational. If we are in love with somebody, we are often blind to their faults.

Emotions spring primarily from our interactions with others, although of course our physical state influences our emotional state as well, so after a good night's sleep, we are less likely to be grumpy and irritable. Emotions can entangle us, twist our interpersonal relations into knots, and either help us or hinder us in our pursuits. So the task is to avoid their harmful effects while enjoying their good ones.

It is generally insufficient to try to sidestep their influence by trying to think rationally. We cannot rid ourselves of emotional thinking but we can strive for better emotional management which is easy in theory but hard in practice.

It is helpful, then, to try to describe the emotions.

It is easier to say what an emotion is not, rather than what it is, but in this roundabout fashion, perhaps what is meant can become clearer. Emotions happen when human agency breaks down. If we think in terms of the carpenter-mind and the manager-mind metaphor, then one can think of an emotion taking hold as if both carpenter and manager minds fuse together, stuck slightly, so that our mind has less ability to regulate itself. Our thinking gets polluted with random nonsense or distorted by outside events, or the idea-chains themselves are illogical or irrelevant. Our minds become like a computer program that is stuck in a temporary infinite loop. It loses some flexibility. It is no longer helping us adapt to external events.

Consider that it is difficult in our day-to-day scrambling to figure out what we want and how to get it, and it is hard to understand our complex and ever-changing world. Our intellectual capacity is relatively powerful compared to other living creatures but it is ultimately limited and microscopic when viewed in the context of the universe. So we resort to simplifications and generalizations and guesswork. We make choices based on imperfect and incomplete information, and in this vacuum, emotions can interfere with our striving.

Emotions are not inherently bad. Rather, the determination of good or bad is made in the context of whether a particular emotion helps or hurts us. It could happen that emotions distort a person's thinking but the overall result of the distortion is positive. For example, a person, angered by something irrelevant, may channel that anger into a productive activity such as gardening, and become a better gardener as a result. On the contrary, it could happen that a bad result happens to a rational-thinking person who has better emotional control; for example, such a person in a dating situation may appear cold and calculating, and fail to form a desired love connection.

Still, overall, if a person is less affected by emotions, and uses clear reason-based rational thinking to make decisions, forming wider-longer idea-chains, then their chances for getting what they want are better.

A way to illustrate the effect of emotions is to contrast someone with human agency with someone beset by emotions.

A person with human agency may have a goal Z, and they have plotted a series of steps in their mind to reach their self-chosen goal. They think that idea A will cause idea B, that B will in turn cause C, and so on to reach Z. Their ideas are orderly and logical and reflect what might really happen, that is, idea A will cause real-world event A, and so forth. While everything that happens is determined from the god-type perspective, from their own human-type perspective, they are exercising their own human-type free will by linking up the A to Z idea-chains in their mind. It's their doing. They're in control. There are no outside influences on their thinking *between* idea A and idea Z. They set a course. When they do A to Z, they are active. It is likely that they will achieve their goal.

In contrast, a person befuddled by emotions may have the

same plotted path from A to Z in their mind, but random external events happen which distract them from their goal. A phone rings and an ex-lover needs consolation, or a needy neighbor drops by unexpectedly. The person becomes wrapped up with these other people and their problems rather than focusing on achieving goal Z. It is not so much that these interruptions happen, but that the person responds emotionally to these distractions and, as a result, their A to Z idea-train derails. They no longer do the full determining since random variables are doing some of the determining. The person is not fully in charge. When they stumble en route from A to Z, they are not active but passive. It is less likely that they will achieve their goal.

Emotions tug on our heartstrings and distract us from our goals. They can be quite powerful. Yet they are not necessarily bad; in the example, it may happen that the person enjoys interacting with the ex-lover or neighbor rather than striving to reach goal Z.

Dual perspectives

This brings us to the subject of emotional management.

Previously an argument was made that there are two perspectives: the *God's-eye view* which sees everything as determined, and the *human's-eye view* in which we act as if we have free will by making choices. The determinist perspective emphasizes the inevitable nature of everything that happens. The causal perspective emphasizes human agency. With the determinist perspective, we see ourselves as if we are a reed in the wind, being blown about by powerful forces, and things that we do are not worthy of blame or ridicule or praise since we are not ultimately responsible for our actions. In contrast, with the causal perspective, we see ourselves as if we are a vital force of human agency making our own choices and planning our own lives, taking charge of our actions, and we are accountable for what we do.

We can see things from either perspective. For example, suppose we spill milk on a sofa. We could view the spill as not being our fault since it had been fated to have happened and could not have happened any other way, which is the determinist perspective. Or we could view ourselves as a causal agent, actively choosing to have spilled the milk, like it was our fault, which is the causal perspective.

If we accept that there are two perspectives, then a general strategy for managing our emotions is to cultivate the skill of being able to shift perspectives depending on the situation. For example, a jilted lover can choose to see the rejection as having been inevitable, and bounce back into dating others quickly with a shrug of the shoulders, by seeing it from the determinist perspective. A lover accepted by another can choose to see it as a result of their own human-type free will in actively winning the affection of their beloved, and enjoy a sense of accomplishment, by seeing it from the causal perspective. What is key is being able to shift perspectives depending on the situation. One can be mindful of both perspectives—the determinist and the causal—and be ready to apply either when the situation permits.

This dual perspective aids emotional management. As humans we are predisposed to think and act emotionally, and in many situations, it is good that we think and act emotionally. In our lives, sometimes we should choose to enjoy the good emotions, such as those that help us to be happy, such as love, while sloughing off the emotions that cause problems, such as hate.

A prime benefit of having the correct understanding of free will is greater freedom from life-denying emotions such as guilt or shame. Things may have happened in the past that we are not proud of, but we need not feel guilt or shame if we shift our perspective to the determinist one. It happened. It was inevitable. It was not our fault. We can forgive ourselves. We can choose the determinist perspective to see how it was fated that our hand knocked over the milk, spilling it on the sofa. Further, we are unlikely to blame others when they spill milk. It is easier to free ourselves from these imprisoning emotions simply by seeing things from the external everything-is-fated viewpoint.

Further, when we act responsibly, make good choices, and do things that we are proud of, we can reaffirm our sense of self-worth by seeing things from the causal perspective. We can take credit for our accomplishments and our good deeds. We did them. We caused these good things to happen from our own human-type free will. If we become overly infatuated with our accomplishments, so that our self-esteem becomes infested with pride, then we should choose the everything-is-fated external view and remind ourselves that we are the lucky beneficiaries of positive developments in our past, to keep our pride in check.

Suppose a man seeks the love of a woman. He might consider possible actions to win her heart: buying roses and shiny shoes and concert tickets, doing a jiggle-dance when handing her the flowers, singing her a song on the guitar, complimenting her appearance, and so forth. Let's call the man Jerry and the woman Janice. Jerry must evaluate possible future actions, guessing about their possible effectiveness. He is trying to construct chains of cause-and-effect ideas in his head which hopefully mirrors reality, ideas which are logical, which don't include extraneous or irrelevant ideas or which are otherwise cluttered with nonsense. He knows that everything up to this present moment has been determined by the past, including the ideas in his head, and that everything that is about to happen will be determined as well by what happened before, and yet he doesn't know what will happen, so he must actively make choices as if the future is not so determined.

Will these choices work? Will they help Jerry win Janice's affection? To the extent that the cause-and-effect ideas in Jerry's mind (1) reflect reality (2) are logical (3) are sequenced in the right order (4) are relevant (5) cover wider and wider geographic space and cover longer and longer time frames, and (6) are not polluted with random nonsense, then Jerry is thinking actively. To the extent that they don't, Jerry is thinking passively.

So Jerry goes on his date with Janice. He may or may not win her love. If he wins her love, he can see himself as the causal agent and enjoy the emotion of falling in love. He can brag to himself that he did it, that he caused her to love him, and that he is the master of his fate and the captain of his soul, to quote from the poem *Invictus*. Or, if he does not win her love, he can see himself as a creature of fate and not get too sad about this state of affairs since he knows that everything was determined and that he never really had a chance. He can shrug his shoulders, forget about Janice, make a mental note to himself that doing a jiggle-dance when handing flowers to a woman is ill-advised, and have a healthy ability to pursue the next woman he encounters. Whatever happens, he has managed his emotions for his personal betterment. He is likely to be happier than if his mind is stuck in either the determinist or the causal mode.

It should be noted that thinking actively and getting the idea-chains right is no guarantee of romantic success, since the universe is fraught with unexpected variables. It could happen that doing everything right does not lead to the goal, and that having polluted random idea-chains does lead to the goal. It could happen, for example, that Janice's choice of lover could itself be predicated on her own faulty idea-chains, and that's that.

Classifying the emotions

It is helpful to try to classify the various emotions. The following arrangement is based on the philosophy of Spinoza but other arrangements are possible, and all such classifications are somewhat arbitrary. While particular emotions are hard to define, they spring from basic aspects of our nature:

- our sense of time as the past and present and future
- our desires: wanting things such as food, water, love, shelter, approval
- things in the world, such as a lamp or a bar of chocolate
- people in the world: individuals, family members, groups of people, the public in general

- how we think about our desires, things, people
- our memories of what happened in the past
- our imagination of what might happen in the future
- the law of association

Most emotions can be described in terms of these factors. For example, our perceptions of things and people can imprint in our brains an idea of what they're about. A person can remember a thing, and by conjuring such a thought in one's mind, may be affected emotionally by the memory of the thing. It can be an idea of a thing from the past, or a thing that might happen in the future, and still, by imagining such a thing, the person can be as affected as if the thing was visibly present.

There are three basic categories:

- Emotions based on pleasure such as love
- Emotions based on pain such as hate
- Desire in the sense of a general appetite

Emotions and desire are bound together so it is not easy to differentiate one category from the other. The general sense is that desire motivates our behavior, while how we react to our desires causes our emotions.

The first two categories, pleasure and pain, can be thought of as transitions between states of vitality. Pleasure-based emotions are transitions from a lesser to a greater state of vitality, so we feel better during the transition. Pain-based emotions are transitions from a greater to a lesser state of vitality, so we feel worse during the transition. Obviously, pleasure feels good and pain feels bad. In the immediate moment, pleasure is almost always good and pain is almost always bad, but during longer spans of time and over wider expanses of space, what happens is subject to the *Basic Principle of Ethics* and the good-versus-bad estimation depends on how things play out. For example, a person rejected by a lover might feel pain, but as time passes, the rejection might lead to finding a better lover.

Both pleasure-based emotions and pain-based emotions are passive transitions in that they happen to a person who is being shaken about like a dandelion in a windstorm. As a general guideline, it is usually better to have active transitions in which a person, through their own human agency, improves their vitality to get what they want.

Generally when the mind thinks about its own activity, it feels pleasure. When it thinks about itself clearly and distinctly, conceiving of itself accurately and in sharp focus, devoid of illusions, its pleasure is greater. The mind does not like to think about bad events from the past, or painful transitions, and it does not like to contemplate its own powerlessness and vacillation.

Emotions are subject to the law of association. If a person feels two different emotions at the same time, then when they feel one emotion, they may feel the second emotion as well, even if there isn't a reasonable explanation for them to feel the second emotion. For example, if a man falls in love with a woman, and he happens to be wearing a certain hat that he likes on the day that they first met, then he might feel the emotion of love for the woman just by wearing that hat. If the man sees a similar hat, then he might feel a greater love for the similar hat simply because of the association. If a rival wears a similar hat, he may feel conflicting emotions. A person feeling two contrary emotions at the same time may be in a state of vacillation.

What follows is a rough categorization of the emotions which are, by nature, varied and complex and often don't fall neatly into a category. Rarely are they easy to delineate. What follows is a conceptual outline of the primary emotions, but in actuality, people experience a mix of various emotions and states, sometimes with conflicting pains and pleasures, often mixed with desires. The emotional experience of each person is unique. Accordingly, it is impossible to list every emotion, or even to define them precisely.

Pleasure-based emotions
Selected pleasure-related emotions will be examined first.

Love is pleasure coupled with the idea of an object as the cause of that pleasure. For example, suppose Jerry loves chocolate. It is a physical thing, and Jerry has the idea that this thing, if eaten, will bring him pleasure. He sees chocolate as being the cause of his pleasure, so he loves chocolate. It should be noted that chocolate does not necessarily cause pleasure, since other people may abhor its taste. Rather, Jerry has come to associate eating chocolate with feelings of pleasure. He has a cause-and-effect idea-chain in his mind that *chocolate causes pleasure.*

Except in the case of self-love, the object of the love is usually something external to a person, such as another person, a thing, a political movement, a job, an idea, a state of being, a philosophy, a hairstyle or a song. It means a person wants to be close to what is loved, and if close, to keep that closeness. Generally, love is something that a human is conscious of, and directs their attention to maintaining its affection.

Different types of love range from extreme forms of liking, to romantic love, to love of one's parents or children, to the reciprocal affection between friends, or even to abstract concepts such as the love of God or gods, or loving the habit of walking in the woods, or loving a type of cinema. When infatuation consists of obsessive romantic thoughts that are not focused on a real person but rather with a fantasized conception of them, then the love might be described as limerence. There is love of ideas, love of a cause, and of course self-love. There is love between a woman and a man which is bound up with sexual love and physical pleasure. For example, suppose Janice loves Jerry. Jerry is the object of her love. She believes Jerry will bring her pleasure in the future. When a person is first attracted to an object, it might be described not as full-on love but more like an inclination or predisposition.

Love can grow and change over time. The feeling of love might be powerful when people meet for the first time, and the unfulfilled attraction might even amplify these powerful feelings. If they marry, as time goes by, these feelings of love can change into more of a contemplative type of feeling. A person, about to eat chocolate, loves it, but while eating it, and perhaps afterwards, does not love it as much because of the feeling of satiation. Love is about wanting something, and once a person has the wanted thing, the love may be more or less.

We can extend our understanding of any emotion by thinking in terms of time, objects such as things and people, the *Principle of Association*, and so forth. For example, if we feel that an object of our love is harmed or destroyed, we will feel pain, or if it survives or is out of danger, we will feel pleasure. These feelings happen by association, that is, we associate ourselves with our loved object. If a person feels that their loved object feels pleasure, then they will feel pleasure as well. If a person thinks that a third thing affects their loved object pleasurably, such as a book or a movie, then they will feel a love towards this third thing too. For example, a man may not like a movie, but if he believes that his lover likes the movie, then he will begin to like the movie.

Most people want others to love what they love and to hate what they hate. So, if a person loves a particular song or flower arrangement, then they will want others to love the same song or flower arrangement. When one person is in love with another person, they want that person to return their love. If we have no particular feeling toward a person, but that person appears to be deeply in love with us, then our first reaction toward this person might be complacency, which might grow into love or it might atrophy into indifference. If a person feels loved by a second person, but the first person believes that they have done nothing to cause such a love to happen, then they might grow to love the second person in return.

If we love a person but think too highly of them on account of our love, then this emotion may be described as **partiality**.

If a person sees that a second person has done something helpful to a third person, then we might feel the emotion of **approval** which is love toward one who has helped another.

If a person feels pleasure at the good luck of another, or feels pain at the bad luck of another, then they may feel the emotion of **sympathy**. It is when the feelings of one person are aligned with the feelings of another.

If a person feels pleasure at their own efficacy and power of action and reputation, then that emotion is called **self-esteem**. But self-esteem can be taken too far. If one thinks too highly of oneself, then it is **pride**, which is a misguided pleasure that can become problematic. It is as if self-love bloomed into a stinky flower that thinks it has the fragrance of springtime roses. A proud person often boasts frequently, talks incessantly of their own virtues and the faults of others. They may think they are pleasing to everybody when in reality their presence is an annoyance. As Benjamin Franklin said, "He that falls in love with himself will have no rivals." It is a human tendency to notice faults in others that one fears seeing in oneself, and this is especially true of the proud person.

It is difficult to draw a sharp distinction between self-esteem and pride, since it is a matter of degree and context. It is up to a human to try to figure out which is which, whether an accomplishment or character trait is rightful self-esteem or excessive self-esteem, that is, pride. A way to distinguish them can come from responsible friends who tell the person the truth, but will a proud person listen to what they say? It is in the nature of a proud person to disregard the views of others, and so it is often difficult to get through to such a person, and to tell a proud person that they are, indeed, proud, and to have them listen. It seems as if the persons who most irritate proud people are other proud people. It's like when two proud people are together, their personalities resonate with mutual annoyance. Still, it is hard for us to tell a proud person that they're proud, without manifesting pride ourselves. Accordingly, a proud person may stay proud for years, and not realize the effect that they're having on everybody else. It's as if they're so accustomed to their own smell that they don't realize how it annoys other people.

Almost all religious and philosophical traditions warn correctly against pride. It is often cast, rightly, as a sin, and as a dangerous and noxious mindset. It is generally true that pride, overall, harms the proud person, since it cuts them off from other people with a false sense of undeserved elevation. It prompts jealousy and conflict, and it can work against community spirit. In Greek mythology, there is the tragic story of Niobe, a mother of fourteen children who bragged that she had more children than a goddess, but after hearing that proud insult, the gods slew the fourteen children in front of her.

Another example illustrates the danger of pride. In 1726, Voltaire was a rising young literary star in Parisian society. But he traded insults with an aristocrat about an issue as trifling as their names. Voltaire was *proud* of his fame and the Chevalier de Rohan was *proud* of his aristocratic family name. The dispute escalated. Voltaire was pummeled by Rohan's thugs, imprisoned in the Bastille, and exiled to Britain. So an amazing thinker got tripped up by his own pride.

If we do something that we believe others approve of and praise, then the emotion is called **honor**. If we see that others desire something or someone, and then we desire the same thing as a result of this observation, then that is called **emulation**. For example, a child may want candy simply because they see other children wanting candy, even if the child is not hungry.

Devotion is love towards someone or something that we admire. Admiration tends to lessen as we imagine more situations involving the object of our devotion, so that as we get to know a person or a thing better over time, our earlier devotion erodes into a general feeling of affection. While the public may admire a movie star or politician or scientist, people closer to the actual person, who have more interactions with them and who see them in more contexts, may have less devotion yet greater affection.

If we conceive the presence of a negative quality in a thing or a person that we hate, then we may experience the pleasurable emotion of **derision**. If we feel pleased with ourselves in a form of self-contemplation, we may feel the pleasurable emotion of **smugness** or **self-complacency**, which is a watered down form of pride.

Hope is pleasure, coupled with the idea of something happening in the past or future, which is uncertain at the present time. Accordingly, hope is intermingled with the emotion of fear. If the uncertainty is removed, and doubt has vanished, then hope turns to **confidence**, which is pleasure coupled with the idea of something happening in the past or future, which was at one time uncertain, but which is no longer doubted at the present moment. Confidence is what a human believes to be true, but may or may not be true in reality. If we had hoped for some good outcome, but doubted that it would come to pass, and then it comes to pass, we feel joy.

Pain-based emotions

Hate is pain coupled with the idea of a thing or a person as the cause of that pain. Typically when we hate a person, we have the false idea of that person as a free-willed actor in the God-type sense who deliberately chose to cause us to feel pain. According to this incorrect interpretation, the offender could have chosen an alternate course of action, but they did not, and instead they chose to hurt us, so we hate them as a result. But that's wrong. The hated person never had a choice. What happened, happened, and it could not have happened otherwise. So hate is built on bad thinking. Hate can build inside us unless we feel that the hated thing or person suffers a setback or is destroyed, in which case we will feel pleasure. While hate can be a helpful emotion in a few circumstances when it helps us overcome an adversary, in most cases it is unhelpful because it clouds our judgment.

If we think of some thing or person as being accidentally a cause of our pain, then we feel the emotion of **aversion**, which can lead to **prejudice**. The linguistic roots of the word prejudice are *before* and *judging*, that is, judging happens before knowing. Prejudice is a snap judgment usually leading to a bad evaluation.

For example, if one person has been affected painfully by a second person, and that second person belongs to a different race, then the first person might transfer the negative feelings to the entire race of people. Prejudice is a mental mistake springing from the human tendency to associate ideas in our minds. It is an illogical linking of ideas, since a person's race or class or nation or sex or religion is not responsible for the initial aversion. Unfortunately, real thinking takes time, so correct evaluations are often replaced with simplistic prejudice, which is a form of stupidity.

If a person feels that they are hated by another person, but that this hatred is undeserved, then the hated person will be motivated to respond by hating the hater. As a general rule, hatred is increased by being reciprocated. According to the Buddhist tradition, "hatred begets more hatred." It can be a mutually reinforcing spiral of animosity that can erupt into violence.

One way to flummox hatred is to return it with love. This causes confusion in the mind of the hater, who may wonder why the hate is not being returned. The confusion offers a chance that the hatred might be flipped into a love which is greater than if the earlier animosity had not occurred. Not responding to hatred with more hatred is one way to de-escalate violence. Many religions, properly, advise against hatred. For example, in the Christian tradition, Jesus advised people to "love their enemies" and counseled "to one who strikes you on the cheek, offer the other cheek also." Of course no one should try to hate something simply so that the hatred, if converted into love, will become a greater love. In the same way, no one should want to be sick, so that after returning to health, they might feel even healthier.

Fear happens when we think of something in the past or the present or the future in which we think that a bad outcome may happen, but we are not sure. Emerson said that fear "always springs from ignorance." Accordingly, fear is pain, coupled with the idea of something harmful in the past or future with which we are not certain. Seneca wrote that "the mind that is anxious about future events is miserable" and that we should focus instead on the present moment. Fear is a serious disability, according to the Bhagavad Gita. Fear can build upon itself, with the initial fear leading to more fear, until the mind is transfixed with doubts and becomes befuddled and confused. If time passes and something bad happens, then fear can turn into **despair**, or if something bad does not happen, then fear can turn into **relief**.

If we had hoped for something good to happen, but it did not happen, then we feel the emotion of **disappointment**. This is pain coupled with the idea of something happening which was the opposite of what we had hoped.

If something bad happens to a person that we think of as being similar to us, then we might feel the emotions of **pity** or **sympathy**. We do not hate somebody that we pity, but we can try to free the pitied person from their misery.

If we hate a person, and think too meanly of them as a result of our hatred, then we feel the emotion of **scorn** or **disdain**.

If we hate a person, and the hated person has good fortune or comes to possess something that we think is valuable, then we may feel the emotion of **envy**, which is pain induced by another's good fortune. People are naturally envious of one another, rejoicing in the shortcomings of others, and wincing at the virtues of others. In a love triangle, if a person feels that a loved object is closer in friendship or affection to a rival, then the person may hate the rival and feel the emotion of **jealousy**. Envy usually describes a situation when we want something that we don't yet have, while jealousy is more of a fear of losing something that we already have, such as a lover fearing that their beloved will leave them for another.

Generally people do not envy the virtues of those people that we feel are below us in a social hierarchy. For example, we do not admire a homeless person for their ability to find edible food in dumpsters, although such a skill might help the person stay alive. In contrast, another homeless person may indeed admire such an ability, since both of them are roughly equal in status and it is clear to both of them how that skill can be beneficial.

If another person has a skill which is particular only to that person and not to humans in general, we probably will not envy such a person. We may wonder how they do it, or how they acquired this skill, but most likely it will not inspire our envy. We will not usually envy an autistic savant who has the ability to perform complex multiplications in a split second, without a calculator, since that skill is peculiar to that person, and not something that most humans value or are expected to have. In contrast, if a skill is thought to be one which most people should have, but which a person lacks or is deficient in when compared with others, then they may feel pain as a result. For example, if a person stutters while everybody else speaks without stuttering, then the stutterer will try to minimize or distort the shortcoming, or embellish their other skills to compensate.

If we think that there is something delightful that only one person can have, then everybody will try as best they can to see that nobody else gets possession of the delightful thing.

Parents, when trying to motivate their children to succeed in school, or behave properly in society, often use the spur of honor or envy to achieve such results.

A person, who contemplates the weakness of their body or mind or social position, might feel the painful emotion of **humility**. A person who keeps their head low, who constantly talks of their own faults as well as the virtues of others, who blushes and wears unkempt clothing, can be described as a humble person. But human nature discourages us from feeling too meanly of ourselves, or focusing on our own inadequacies. So it is usually the case that a humble person is, in reality, secretly ambitious and envious. One can think of humility as a reverse form of pride. Humility and self-esteem and pride can be described along a single axis, from left to right, with humility being a negative pride, pride being a positive pride, and self-esteem being a middle ground between the two extremes. A shy person places too much importance on the opinions of others, and this can impede their social interactions. The American actor Lucille Ball found that her career blossomed when she ceased worrying about what others might think, and she overcame her earlier shyness.

If we believe, incorrectly according to the reality of determinism, that we have performed some action freely, by the free and uncaused-by-the-past decision of our mind, and we believe that our action was bad or harmful, then we may feel the painful emotion of **guilt**. According to Maimonides, repentance begins with personal recognition of our wrongdoing, renouncing the error, confessing it to the person we've wronged, followed by reconciliation and making amends, as part of a six-step strategy to assuage our guilt. But it would be better to simply not feel guilt in the first place.

If one thinks too meanly of oneself, one experiences the painful emotion of **self-abasement**.

Shame is pain, accompanied by the idea of some action that we have done in the past that we believe that others feel is bad or evil or otherwise worthy of blame. It is associated with the idea that others believe that the reprehensible action had been done voluntarily. **Modesty** is fear or dread of possible future shame, by restraining oneself ahead of time from doing the supposedly base actions.

If a person is afraid of doing something that their peers do not fear, then the emotion is **cowardice** which is an outgrowth of the emotion of fear.

If a person wants to avoid evil but is bewildered by the amazement of the evil that they fear, then the emotion can be described as **consternation**, which is another outgrowth of the emotion of fear. Consternation is like a double fear which stymies a human, making them unable to act, by the fear of one thing, and the amazement about that thing too. The two types of fear leave the person baffled and unable to think about how to get out of their predicament.

Desires

All humans have an underlying hunger for life that is baked deeply into the marrow of our beings. We desire life. We desire to keep living. We desire to have things that keep us living such as food and water and shelter. We desire to make copies of ourselves by mating.

Our desires are powerful. They push us to do all sorts of things to improve our ability to survive and thrive and mate. Creatures which didn't have such powerful urges, or which had less powerful urges, did not survive and did not reproduce. They vanished. They got eaten. They starved to death in cold caves. They didn't have enough sex. But here we are, thanks to our ancestors, who figured out how to make fire and hunt mastodons and who had lots of successful sex over a course of several hundred thousand years of trial-and-error evolution. When what we do helps us survive and thrive and reproduce, we are rewarded internally by feeling good; when we fall short or stumble, we are punished internally by feeling bad.

A couple of points should be made.

First, we should realize that we didn't *choose* our desires, but rather they were *chosen for us* by random factors and happenstance based on our evolutionary beginnings. It's as if evolution chose our desires for us, and frankly it has done an excellent job of pushing our species to the top of the food chain to make us into Earth's most amazing creature.

Second, these desires are what our genetic code wants and what our species wants. They're not necessarily what we want. Satisfying these innate urges will not necessarily make us happy or lead us toward meaningful lives. Natural selection only wants us to survive, to grow rich and powerful, to mate, and to pass along our genes to the next generation.

Third, we should try to understand our desires. There are two basic types.

Some desires are what we might call *quenchable* or what the Stoics call *natural desires* or what Epicureans call *necessary desires*. After we fulfill them, we're satisfied. We don't want any more. For example, if we're thirsty, we drink water, and after drinking water, we don't want any more water. Our thirst is quenched. Breathing is a similar type of desire; if unsatisfied, we will feel pain quickly, so it's necessary, but we can't overdo it by consuming twice as much air.

Other desires are *insatiable*. After fulfillment, we want more. For example, a happily married woman with a great husband and a satisfactory sex life may desire another lover. A successful entrepreneur wants to start another enterprise. A movie star wants to become internationally famous. What happens is that these satisfied desires are replaced with new desires, so that we are forever living in a state of dissatisfaction. It's like we're on a treadmill with no end in sight. Stoics describe these as *unnatural desires* and Epicureans describe them as *unnecessary desires*. We don't need them to be happy. We all experience these desires to varying extents, like the line from the popular song that goes *everybody has a hungry heart*. We're happy until our neighbor buys a flashier sports car, and then we're dissatisfied and want an even better car. We feel social pressure to outdo our neighbors and friends. As H. L. Mencken said, "A man's satisfaction with his salary depends solely on whether he's making more than his wife's sister's husband."

This suggests, in turn, that simply trying to satisfy our so-called treadmill desires will not necessarily lead us to contentment and happiness. Simply enjoying what we've got and being content doesn't spur the human race to improve, so that being satisfied with the status quo is a form of collectively sitting on our loins.

Our ability to master our desires is rather limited. It is probably the case that we are best able to control those desires which have the least impact on our lives. Denying our desires doesn't feel good. Our intellects and our rational thinking brains don't really help us much. It's as if our intellectual minds act like a wingman to our desires. So we give in to our desires, most of the time. We seem to be constantly in a state of restless achievement.

The Stoic philosopher Epictetus suggested that we should not try to desire things that are beyond our control, such as our social reputation; he advised that "Freedom is not procured by a full enjoyment of what is desired, but by controlling the desire."

Since we have little power to determine what other people think about us, we should not be bothered if they insult us or praise us. The Stoics cautioned against depending on others for approval because it gives them a measure of control over how we see ourselves. Epictetus advised against depending on the admiration of others, saying "There is no strength in it." Benjamin Franklin said "Happiness depends more on the inward disposition of mind than on outward circumstances."

If complete mastery is impossible, what we can strive for is a general understanding of these strong internal impulses, and manage them as best we can. Meditation can help us become better acquainted with our desires. We should pursue what we desire but realize that such pursuits can become excessive, and moderate them when possible. We should strive for a feeling of overall contentment and inner peace. According to Buddhist teaching, we should "Practice the middle way", to live between poverty and luxury, to seek a balanced way of life. The Stoic philosopher Seneca offered a similar sentiment, saying that we should have enough money so we don't descend into poverty, but not so much that we'd have a deep sorrow after losing it, and that wealth is fine provided we don't cling to it. Buddhist teaching emphasizes that desiring to control certain desires is itself a form of desire, and one aspect of becoming more enlightened is dealing with this paradox.

Consider the story of Alexander the Great. He was a king's son, highly educated by a wise philosopher, Aristotle, and he had an incredible intellect. He was indefatigable. With his amazing charisma, he led a small but disciplined Macedonian hoplite army to conquer the largest empire in the world at the time, and then *he desired more*. He drove his army deep into Asia past the Hindu Kush mountains into modern day Turkmenistan and Uzbekistan. On the banks of the monsoon-swollen Hyphasis River, his loyal soldiers were tired and sick with dysentery, beset with mosquitoes and rats and poisonous snakes. He begged them to battle the next opponent. But the men would not budge. They wanted to go home. He threw a temper tantrum, he sulked, to no avail. Finally, he gave in. Defeated, unable to keep satisfying his seemingly eternal lust for fame and glory, he retreated to Babylon, and died a few years later.

So there we have it: the most powerful human at the time, constantly hungering for more. He didn't know how to moderate his desires. His desires controlled him.

Desires grip us in different ways. They vary from person to person. Unlike the alternatives of pleasure and pain, desires are not necessarily opposed to each other, and they can co-exist in many ways. They can lead us in sometimes contrary directions. It is possible to desire things that hurt us, such as alcohol or tobacco.

What follows are descriptions of selected general desires, with the caveat that it is not easy to classify desires as different from pleasure-based and pain-based emotions. Since there is considerable overlap, the terms themselves are hard to describe precisely, and vary as language varies.

Regret is the desire to have something, the idea of which is kept alive by the mind's memory of it, but at the same time the mind is constrained by remembering other things which remind us that we don't have the desired thing. We imagine the desired thing in the present even though it is something that happened in the past, or might have happened in the future, such as getting an award or being loved by a lover. But then we are aware at the same time that we don't have that award or love, so we are filled with a painful longing of what might have been. So we feel regret.

If another person has helped us in some manner, done us a favor, complimented us, or given us something of value, and if we seek to return the favor, then we experience the desire of **thankfulness** or **gratitude**, which springs from love. If the benefit is received without gratitude, then the giver may feel pain.

If we seek to help somebody that we pity, then we experience **benevolence**, which is our desire to confer a benefit on an unfortunate person. Benevolence is desire arising from compassion. If we seek to injure a person that we pity or love, and if we think that our intended victim can not prevent the injury or retaliate, then the desire is called **cruelty**. If we desire to injure somebody that we hate, then we experience **anger**. If hate is a simmering longer-lasting predisposition of aversion, then anger is the explosive boiling over of negative emotion, as if the carpenter-mind and manager-minds have melted into a ball of trouble, so a person feeling anger can be dangerously out of control. They become like a speeding car with no brakes. Anger subverts our mind's ability to calmly deliberate in a reasoned and reflective manner about what is the best course of future action. We've stopped thinking. Marcus Aurelius wrote that the things that make us angry are not as bad as the anger itself. When Dwight Eisenhower found himself angry at somebody, he would write their name on a piece of paper, and then, after a while, drop it in a wastebasket.

If there is another person with whom there is mutual hatred, accompanied by the idea that the other person injured us, then the desire to repay injury with injury is **revenge**. Over time, revenge often boomerangs to hurt the avenger as much as the target of the revenge. According to Marcus Aurelius, "The best revenge is not to be like your enemy."

If we are faced with an option of two evils, one greater and one lesser, with the condition that facing the greater evil and triumphing against it will produce a better outcome, then the desire of choosing the lesser evil is **timidity**. But if we choose a course of action that other people fear to do, then our desire can be described as **daring**.

Deference is when a person desires to act in such a way as to show respect to another person, as a way of pleasing them or refraining from displeasing them.

High-mindedness is the desire to help other people and unite them in friendship. **Nobility** is the desire to live ethically. There are offshoots of these desires which are characterized by reasonableness and common sense, such as temperance, sobriety, presence of mind in the face of danger, and so forth.

Desires can become excessive, such that the thing being desired is good but having too much of it can be harmful. **Lust** is an excessive desire to have sex. The immoderate desire of power is **ambition** which can cause sensible persons to stretch themselves into contorted shapes, such as when the Roman general Caesar toyed with the idea of becoming a king, which led to his assassination. **Luxury** is the desire of living richly, with gourmet foods and exotic wines and mansions with manicured gardens. Desiring too much alcohol is **intemperance**. Desiring too much wealth is **avarice** or **greed**. There is a story about a dog with a steak in its mouth, that saw its own reflection in a pond, and then tried to bite to get the apparent second steak, only to lose its real steak in the pond. According to Schopenhauer, if we become greedy for what we don't have, we should think how bad we would feel if we lost what we *do* have, with the lesson being that we should appreciate what we've got.

Emotional management

There are four general strategies to manage emotions.

A first general way to lessen the impact of emotions is to see that things happen by necessity. When we understand that whatever happens, had to happen, and could not have happened any other way, then it is difficult for us to get too attached to any outcome, whether such an outcome is helpful or harmful for us. We can shrug our shoulders and get on with life. It is consistent with Stoic philosophy which advises that we should "find a way to love everything that happens", and to essentially try to love fate. What happened, happened, so we might as well love the result, and appreciate the fact that we're still alive.

To the extent that we can understand that other people are similarly driven by the inevitable reality of cause-and-effect, then it is hard for us to become too emotionally involved with them. For example, if a baby cries, we don't blame the baby for crying, because we don't see the baby as a free-willed actor who chose, on its own, and by the free state of its mind, to cry, as if it had been deliberately trying to send displeasing sounds to our ears out of some sense of spite. Rather, the baby cries out of necessity. It is what babies do. We don't hate the baby.

A key to emotional management is to see that all humans are driven by necessity, not just babies. If we have the false idea that a person is a free willed independent actor who can choose what to think and what to do, and if such a person injures us, then we may hate that person simply because of the perceived choice. We may think, incorrectly, that the other person could have chosen to have been kind to us, but instead chose deliberately to harm us, so we hate them as a result. But hating hurts the hater. When we succumb to hate, it can distort our perceptions and cause us, in turn, to do things in the future that may bring injury to ourselves as well as to the hated person. Hate is an illogical and stupid waste of time and energy in most situations.

When people think incorrectly that others are agents with God-type free will, they are more likely to be bothersome to each other, and there are more ways for them to become entwined in needless emotional tangles which bring pain and confusion.

When people think correctly that humans are driven by necessity, then they are much more likely to be tolerant of each other and to treat people with kindness and respect. With such a mindset, it is natural to have a general policy toward others of forgiveness. In our dealings with people, there will be transgressions, misunderstandings, slights and unintended insults, and if we realize that all of these things had to happen, then it is easier to forgive people and to cultivate a spirit of goodwill and tolerance. Forgiveness greatly lessens the risk of retaliation. It dries up ill will and fosters harmony among people. Most religions correctly teach the wisdom of forgiveness.

A second general way of coping with emotions is to learn to identify when one is under their spell. When experiencing an emotion, one can realize intellectually what is happening, so one can say to oneself internally that *I am in love* or *I am angry* or whatever one is feeling as an act of self-awareness. It is a step toward quarantining an emotion to prevent it from doing further damage. While the emotion continues to exert its influence, the act of identifying the emotion as an emotion can activate and strengthen an internal mental watchdog to oversee it. While the carpenter-mind experiences the full intensity of the emotion, the manager-mind can try to control it. If an emotion is like a forest fire, activating the manager-mind is an attempt to cordon off the area of combustion to set up firewalls. Identifying emotions in others is necessary to develop the skill of empathy. It can be helpful to let others know when one is in the thrall of an emotion, so that they can be more understanding.

A third general way is to avoid getting too attached to anything, whether it is a physical object or a person or an opinion. In life, things change. Books can be lost or stolen, houses can burn down, lovers can leave us, cars can rust, political parties can atrophy, and if we get too attached to the way things were, we suffer emotionally. Bertrand Russell counseled against getting angry about somebody else's opinion. He noted that there are seldom arguments over factual subjects such as arithmetic, and plenty of arguments about opinions. People don't get into heated disputes about whether two plus two equals five. If an opinion contrary to our own makes us angry, then we may be inwardly worried that our own opinion is weak.

Many religions counsel wisely about avoiding unnecessary attachments. Buddhism counsels against what it terms "clinging, grasping attachment", which it describes with the term up d na, because it leads to unnecessary suffering. Stoics believe that we don't own our possessions but rather that we get to use them for a while. Epictetus wrote that "a man should so live that his happiness shall depend as little as possible on external things." There was an art collector whose life revolved around collecting paintings, but when his gallery burned down, he was so distressed that he committed suicide.

A fourth general way of coping with emotions is simply to know more. If emotions happen when our thinking is clouded or illogical or polluted by extraneous thinking, then knowing more, and having a firmer grasp of reality, is naturally helpful. Good information can protect us. For example, suppose a person knows that it is not wise to make a major life change when under emotional stress; then, if a family member dies, then they are less likely to change jobs or move to a different city while grieving. Their prior knowledge can help them avoid a bad choice.

There is an irrational component to all emotions. For example, while eating chocolate may indeed bring pleasurable sensations, to love chocolate is somewhat irrational. One doesn't woo a bar of chocolate by writing poems to it or buying it flowers. Understanding emotions from a clinical perspective can help us be less susceptible to their influence.

But knowing more, in and of itself, is not a guarantee of competent emotional management. Our rational sides are often overpowered by our desires and our emotions. A smoker may know the risks of smoking but be unable to quit the habit; a dieter may know intellectually that the triple layer chocolate cake will not keep the waistline in check. Just knowing the right thing to do, in itself, is often not enough. As Sigmund Freud observed, the id often overpowers the ego, meaning that our desires often triumph over our intellectual attempts to moderate them.

A risk is that, when we think of something, we get attached to what we thought, because we think that it was *our* idea. We lose some impartiality. When we get too close to something, even to our own thinking, it can impede our judgment. There are experts who became so attached to their expertise that they were unwilling to question what they knew. For example, the English demographer Thomas Malthus became so attached to his theory about how population growth would always outrun the food supply, that he failed to consider how human ingenuity could increase crop yields, and so far time has proved him wrong.

It is generally unhelpful to try to use reason and logic to try to will away a stubborn emotion. Rather, a better method is to counter it with a more helpful emotion. Humans are emotional creatures. Our impulse to think emotionally is often stronger than our ability to think rationally, perhaps because in human development, our emotional nature evolved before our ability to reason. The philosopher William B. Irvine compared emotions to a headstrong five-year old child who whines and begs and "won't take no for an answer", but unlike a parent dealing with such a child, we can't send our emotions to their bedrooms or give them a "time out." He wrote that the "intellect's best strategy for dealing with emotions is to use emotions to fight emotions."

The ultimate helpful counter-emotion is the love of knowledge and fate and the beauty of life itself, according to Spinoza. Loving these good things can help dampen the harmful emotions, and make them less volatile.

Exercises which enable better mind control can help too. Many religious practices help in this regard, such as meditation, yoga, chanting and breathing exercises. Prayer can help a person clarify in their own mind what they want. The Stoic philosopher Seneca's advice about controlling anger was simply to count to ten before reacting to a provocation, to allow the mind the time necessary to consider a better response.

There are times when our minds engage in a so-called chatterbox state, with thoughts in no particular order, seemingly popping out of nowhere, random and nervous, with no clear benefit, and this is natural and often unavoidable. The underlying cause can be the emotion of anxiety which is a type of fear. The problem comes if the chatterbox mental state interferes with our enjoyment of life. Paradoxes can help a person trick their own mind into ceasing the endless chatter. As a person tries harder and harder to think about a logically incompatible paradox, such as to *hear the sound of one hand clapping*, the mind eventually gives up trying to understand the nonsensical instruction, and relaxes. In the Buddhist tradition, there is a practice of focusing meditation on paradoxes as a way to liberate the mind. In the Tantric tradition, there is a similar emphasis on mental liberation but instead of trying to be still, it is exercising physically to the point of exhaustion as a way to achieve enlightenment.

If the chatterbox state is caused by something that we fear, then therapy can help a person overcome the phobia. The therapeutic technique of systematic desensitization conditions the mind to associate a feared object with a neutral object. Since it is difficult to hold two incompatible ideas in the mind simultaneously, the repeated associations may lessen the fear.

It helps to cultivate a spirit of intellectual detachment. It can extend to our thinking about our current state of fortune, whether we are flush with cash or penniless and begging. There is a story about a ruler whose kingdom was sometimes ravaged by pestilence, other times blessed with fruitful harvests, and he asked a sage for advice who, after pondering for a while, said *this too shall pass*. So good fortune will not last, but neither will bad fortune, and there is wisdom in not getting too attached to either state.

Attachment to specific things and people can be problematic. If something we own breaks, and that upsets us, then we experience needless fuss. If a friend or lover or family member dies, then we will be sad but we shouldn't be too sad because our focus should be on life itself. As best that we can, we should try to rejoice that the person had been alive, and realize that death is simply a return to the natural state of not being alive. A spurned lover should not keep dwelling on how great their lover had been, since such recurring thoughts can be practically addicting, preventing them from finding another lover.

A way to think about happiness is that it is a frame of mind which happens when remembering a positive transition from a lesser state to a greater state. During the past transition, a person learned something new or acquired a new skill or made a new friend or won a promotion or enjoyed a sumptuous dinner. In the present moment, they remember the past transition which feels almost as good as when they were actually undergoing the positive transition itself. They replay the step-by-step process of what happened to enjoy the memory. It is good in that it is a pleasant feeling. It is like a mental reward for the previous efforts undertaken to achieve the positive transition. But it can be unhelpful if the focus on the past transition distracts a human from achieving further positive transitions. That person might be happy but it is not what is best for them in the wider-longer sense. So a person should not necessarily strive for happiness-in-itself but should strive instead for positive transitions, keeping in mind that the happy feelings that result from remembering these past transitions are a by-product of the striving, which can be enjoyed from time to time, in moderation.

Ethics with others

The *Basic Principle of Ethics* extends to interactions with other people. They are a part of the mix. They factor into our thinking about what is good for us. If we want to dine at a restaurant, will it be better if another joins us? Sometimes we may want things from others, or want others to perform services for us, or want them to treat us in a certain way. When other people are involved, there is a greater level of complexity, with more possibilities and variables and ways for events to play out. We try to guess how others might react to what we might do. This usually requires more thinking and it brings greater chances of error.

What amplifies the complexity is that when there are two people, the second person makes their own calculations about what is best for them. There are two minds performing assessments. Even if there is a common area of interest, they may not agree. When there is agreement, social harmony is possible, or if there is disagreement, there may be discord. There may be one thing that two people want, and only one person can have it, so who will get it? What is the right thing to do?

A HUMAN WITH OTHER HUMANS

There is a strong motivation for humans to behave ethically, to do good, to be responsible and fair, because behaving ethically is good, in and of itself, for both ourselves and for others as time passes. We benefit and others benefit when people behave ethically. The motivation for good behavior should not be to win a reward or to please a deity or to spare us from punishment in an imagined afterlife. Rather, it is in our own best interest now and in the future to act ethically toward others, and it is in their own best interest now and in the future to act ethically toward us. In situations when persons are not acting ethically, it is usually the case that one or both persons have made suboptimal longer-time wider-space determinations. They are not looking far enough into the future, or they are making incorrect guesses about the possible future sequences of causes and effects. Such determinations are often difficult to get right, and as a result, acting ethically is problematic for humans.

The Golden Rule is an excellent starting point. We should treat others how we want them to treat us, and not treat them as if they were our tools, or use them for our personal benefit without reciprocating. We should respect their good goals and help them achieve their good ends.

It helps to cultivate empathy. We try to feel as another feels. We try to guess what they're thinking and feeling by imagining ourselves as if we were them, replaying our memories of what experiences they have had, and then imagining how we would have felt if those experiences had happened to us. We listen intently and read facial signals such as smiles and frowns and body posture, and try to glimpse inside their minds.

It helps our interpersonal relations if we cultivate a habit of generosity. Most gifts benefit the giver in some way. A donor might get a positive feeling or a tax deduction or a smile or somebody saying thank you. A multimillionaire gets prestige by donating millions to have their name emblazoned on a university building. Sometimes the benefit to the giver is substantial but not obvious at first, such as a corporation that subsidizes a train line that helps employees get to work, and which could help the firm attract the best workers in the future. In other cases the gift might be great but have only marginal utility to the giver. For example, near the end of his life, the industrialist-turned-philanthropist Andrew Carnegie donated his vast wealth to libraries and other humanitarian projects, which helped society considerably. If giving is widespread in society, then even though people give much, they get much. So habitual giving can lead to a better society for everybody in an indirect way.

According to Confucius, as we go through life, the practice of compassion and generosity starts by giving to oneself, and then it moves outward, to giving to one's family and friends, to one's community and nation, and then to humanity in general.

Humans need humans. We need each other. We need others to help us get food and shelter and medicine and clothing and information. We need them to teach us and to love us. At almost every stage of our lives, the care and affection of other humans is vital to our welfare.

Humans in larger systems

When two humans interact, such as friends or lovers, parents or siblings, an employee and an employer, or even two strangers on a train, they form a system. It is a level of complexity higher than that of a single human. Each human is the subsystem, and how the two humans interact with each other forms a suprasystem. There are inputs and outputs, such as in a conversation—one person talks, the other listens, and then they swap roles with the listener talking and the talker listening. In an employee-employer relationship, the employee works and the employer pays.

The suprasystem of a relationship has many of the characteristics of a living thing. It has a lifespan with a beginning, a middle and an end. It has an inside and an outside in the sense of how both persons understand the boundaries of the relationship. Sometimes the relationship is based on what not to do. For example, two strangers on a train are expected not to bother each other, particularly if one is trying to nap or read. The system needs to take in more energy than it expends for it to continue, that is, each person needs to benefit sufficiently in some way for the system to continue.

Since a great variety of suprasystems of humans are possible, a few basic ones will be covered, such as friends and lovers and employer-employee relations. But a few general points about all interactions are worth making.

Human interactions have a thinking as well as a physical component. Inside each mind there is an idea of the other person, such as who they are and what they are about. It is summary information, distilled from past encounters and conversations into a simplified clump of generalizations about the other person and about the relationship itself, its patterns of giving and getting, and so forth.

Since the human mind can not remember every word another person ever said, it tries to distill the vast panoply of shared experiences into a few actionable nuggets: that a particular friend loves stories about Uncle Ernie's sad attempts at fishing, hates pistachio ice cream, works part-time as a dog walker and has two dogs. So if we are trying to understand another person, or if another person is trying to understand us, the notion of dog-lover is easier to work with mentally than trying to remember the many details. Like most forms of human-held knowledge, it is simplistic, with helpful generalizations replacing the complexity of countless impressions. The encapsulated knowledge is like a newspaper with only headlines. We distill numerous sense-impressions into a condensed picture to try to describe the underlying framework of a person. All humans have limited mental processing power, and only so much room in our memories to devote to any subject, including another person.

Once an idea gets fixed in another person's mind, it is often hard to dislodge or change. Accordingly, it is important to make a good first impression. It helps to try to put favorable ideas about ourselves in the minds of others. We are in the reputation management business. If people like us, it is easier to get them to employ us, marry us, lend us money, and care for us if we are sick. Conversely, if most other people hate us, it is a sorry state of affairs, since we are cut off from what they can offer us. Information that other humans have about us can be distorted by their own biases.

Obviously we can not see inside another person's mind to discover what they think about us. All we can do is guess. If we ask them, they may or may not tell us, so we assemble clues. In addition to empathy, there are standard cultural signals such as smiling and crying and laughing, and there are culture-specific signals such as customs about eye contact.

Character

The idea of character is that there is something about a person that is consistent over time and yet unique. It is as if our identity is organized around a few central principles that guide what we do. While there are countless facets to our personality, we try to identify a few consistent themes and highlight them. To the extent that a good character is consistent over time, it is easier to understand. Stoics counsel that a person should be their same steady self, in times of plenty and in times of poverty, so external circumstances do not elicit a change of personality. A good person is more likely to see the wider-longer benefits of maintaining this consistency of character since it benefits themselves and others over time.

The uniqueness of character happens when the guiding theme is atypical, fresh, different and memorable, possibly creative in the sense of having an unusual combination of traits. If a person's character is similar to those of many others, it is predictable but risks being boring. The uniqueness factor can help a character-image stick in the minds of others. It can be a blending of disparate character themes, such as a dog-lover who believes that canines can predict the future by what they bark about. Conflict can assist character formation; according to Abigail Adams, "It is not in the still calm of life, or the repose of a pacific station, that great characters are formed."

A person that follows the *Basic Principle of Ethics* has a good character. They do what is best for themselves, in wider spaces and longer time frames, as best that they can determine, and their determinations will naturally suggest to them that they act not only for their own personal betterment, but for the betterment of others as well. So good people are polite, kind and generous. A way to assess character is how a person treats their inferiors: kindness toward equals or superiors may be out of a fear of retribution, so kindness toward inferiors may indicate a good character. Marcus Aurelius advised that we should "be tolerant with others, be strict with ourselves". There is a similar guideline in Sufism.

According to Confucius, we learn the basics of good character from our families and from schools. Such beginnings become the foundation for acquiring other virtues. We learn to respect our elders, to care for them when they're sick, and to heed their good advice, assuming, of course, that we have been born into good families.

People with good characters almost always tell the truth. Most religions insist on honesty. A lesson from the Hindu Vedas is to "speak the truth and don't speak untruth." In courtrooms, witnesses are asked to "tell the truth, the whole truth, and nothing but the truth." Humans need accurate information from other humans about what is happening since it helps us make smart choices. Truth-telling is consistent with the *Basic Principle* in that it is in the long term best interests of the truth-tellers themselves.

A person may get a momentary advantage or avoid unpleasantness by uttering a distortion, but lying is harmful in wider spaces and longer time frames, not only to other people but to the liars themselves. Lying cuts us off from other people since it teaches them not to trust us. Even one lie, if exposed as a lie, can undermine a reputation for integrity that had been built up for years. If the lie is not exposed, but is deployed against another person, the lie weakens people who might have been helpful to the liar in the future. In the story *The Boy Who Cried Wolf*, the boy taught the villagers to ignore him by repeatedly claiming falsely that there was a wolf, so when the real wolf emerged, villagers didn't believe him, and he was eaten.

Of course there are exceptional situations when lying is required. In the *Parable of the Burning House*, from the Buddhist tradition, children were playing in a burning house but refused their father's order to leave; so the father lied, saying their best toys were outside, so they ran outside and stayed alive. In this situation, lying was acceptable since it was the only way to avoid a loss of life. The father understood the wider-longer benefit of what to do.

A person with a good character is honest with themselves. They understand who they are and what they want. They know their strengths and their weaknesses and they have a spot-on internal assessment of their true self. They are devoid of illusions. They follow the Socratic maxim to "know thyself." The writer Fyodor Dostoyevsky said "Above all, don't lie to yourself; the man who lies to himself and listens to his own lie comes to a point that he cannot distinguish the truth within him, or around him, and so loses all respect for himself and for others."

There are other exceptions when untruths are permissible. One situation is when the truth about a trifling matter might hurt a person's feelings. If so, then it is usually better to simply say nothing than to lie. An aging wife who asks "how do I look today" should not be told that her wrinkles are widening into shadow-casting trenches. A second situation is when a person is under the threat of violence, and lying is the only way to stay alive.

But generally what helps us mesh with other people is having a reputation for integrity by consistent truth-telling. If a person tells a falsehood under the mistaken impression that the falsehood is true, then the falsehood should be corrected at the first opportunity. A saying attributed to Confucius is that "When you have erred, be not afraid to correct yourself."

A related idea is keeping promises, which is essentially telling the truth about a forthcoming choice, so that what is said now will probably happen in the future. Over time there is a huge benefit for consistent promise-keepers since others learn to trust them. Their words become powerful. They have weight. They mean something. If they say something will happen, something will probably happen. In contrast, promise-breakers may become flaky in the eyes of others, so people learn to stop listening to their gibberish.

Our good character is influenced by what we think about. Marcus Aurelius wrote "The soul becomes dyed with the color of its thoughts." A good character will choose good things to think about.

The Binding Principle

It may seem contradictory that bonds between people, which seem restrictive at first view, can bring greater freedom.

The **Binding Principle** is that bonds between humans can help us do things that we couldn't do by ourselves.

The whole idea of binding has been around since the *Big Bang*. It is one more example of how larger structures such as friendships can be understood as more complex manifestations of life's basic rules. Binding is how quarks and atoms and molecules cling together. Two hydrogen atoms and one oxygen atom bond to form a water molecule. Each atom exists as an atom, but when they bind together, something new is formed. Both hydrogen and oxygen in their gaseous states are flammable, so combining them into something that puts out fire confounds expectations. If a water molecule splits back into two hydrogen atoms and one oxygen atom, the atoms return to their original states. The act of binding and unbinding doesn't change the atoms. They exist as they existed before.

Like atoms and molecules, bonds enable new capabilities for humans. Individual humans behave in one way, but by binding together, they have new powers and capabilities that seem to emerge like magic out of nowhere.

A key is that an individual must be free to make and break the bonds. The new bonds should be stable enough to let the new arrangement do what it is supposed to do, and yet not be so fixed that no other arrangements are possible. Bonds between humans should be like the chemical bonds between carbon atoms and other atoms like hydrogen and oxygen and nitrogen. They should be stable enough to do things, but not be welded together permanently.

Bonds between people can be temporary or they can last for decades. The benefit is sometimes to one but usually to both individuals, and often to the larger entity, depending on the context.

There are many types of bonds:

- When two people bond for mutual companionship, it is friendship.
- When one person buys something from another, it is a buyer-seller relationship.
- When two adults bond to create a family, it is a marriage.
- When a person works for a firm, it is an employee-employer relationship.
- When a person belongs to a political body, it is citizenship.

Bonds vary greatly by culture and context and by the particular individuals in them. They vary in duration, purpose, size, maintenance requirements, and signaling. Sometimes there are penalties for breaking a bond; for example, in a buyer-seller relationship, there may be instances when returning a purchased item in exchange for a refund can have conditions. In another example, a married couple, divorcing, may incur penalties such as alimony payments. Some bonds are practically permanent. A prisoner on death row, for example, can not break the bond of imprisonment. Like most biological processes, bonds take time to form and time to break.

The combined entity created by the bond can often do things that separate individuals can not. For example, two friends can play a game of tennis, while each person, alone, can not do this.

Parents in a love relationship can have genetically-related children, which is something that a solitary individual can not do. Persons in a buyer-seller relation have a wide range of goods and services available.

What is generally best for people with human-type free will is to be able to choose helpful bonds, and to be able to break them as needed. This is freedom and it is good. Of course, not all bonds can be chosen; for example, we can not choose our parents, but in a few cases, if we find ourselves stuck with abusive parents, we may have a chance to escape.

The strength of the bond can be important. It might be to a person's benefit that another person is bound tightly to them. In the same way that a chemical compound might require energy for the individual elements to bind together or break apart, it takes energy for most human bonds to form or split apart; how much energy, and for how long, can vary considerably. A customer might change their mind after making a purchase and un-doing this bond requires little energy to dissolve; they simply return the item for a full refund. In contrast, some divorces can be protracted and expensive affairs.

What is important is having sufficient information before deciding to form a bond. This requires a degree of transparency. For example, before buying a house, a buyer might need to know the condition of the house, whether there are liens against it, the financial terms of the mortgage, what penalties there may be for getting out of the contract, and so forth. The deal should be clear. There should not be fraud involved. It is not good for a person to get stuck in a bad house or a bad marriage or become enmeshed in a fraudulent business arrangement.

Correct information before a bond is made can help a person see the wider-space longer-term benefits of a possible bond, and make an informed choice. Such bonds usually involve a short term sacrifice to enable a long term benefit. For example, a couple deciding to get married may have to sacrifice the chance of having sexual relations with others, but they secure the longer term benefit of having a committed partner to share the task of parenting.

Most bonds involve some type of maintenance, as well as signaling to each other as well as to others that the bond exists and that others should respect it. A printed receipt might signal a buyer-seller transaction. A wedding ring might signal a marriage. Two people spending time together might signal a friendship.

Many bonds have an on-again off-again rhythmic fluctuation. There is an alternating pattern of time together and time apart. Friends meet, friends part, and the pattern repeats. A husband and wife who spend every minute together may tire of each other. It is as if the bond needs to recharge during the periodic separation. The bond is more like an elliptical orbit than a circular orbit, with the bodies sometimes coming closer together, sometimes farther apart, as time passes.

Focus will now shift toward a few types of bonds.

Friends and enemies

In China two disabled classmates became best friends. Jia Wenqi lost both arms after touching a power line, and Jia Haixia lost his eyes in a quarry accident. But the men bonded, helping each other plant more than ten thousand trees as part of an environmental rehabilitation project. The blind man would ride on the back of his sighted armless friend to cross a river, and the two would cooperate to plant the saplings. Their cooperation shows how friendship can be mutually beneficial, allowing two people, together, to do things that neither could do by themselves.

Friendship is a bond between humans characterized by mutual affection, esteem, intimacy, goodwill and trust. It has a lifespan like a living being in that it can begin and grow and end. It has a "mind" of its own in the form of a shared understanding in the minds of the friends. Because it is based on the emotion of affection, it is not characterized by total rationality, so the relationship is usually not one of cold clinical calculation but rather one of warmth and shared interests. Interpersonal relationships have a pattern of give-and-take, of compromise, of taking turns. According to Aristotle, friendship is goodwill among virtuous people, such that friends want what's good for each other.

Friendships work better when the people involved have virtue and integrity, with each person having a measure of human agency. Each person has a wider-longer sense of what is good for themselves and for their friend and for their relationship as a whole. They treat each other with tenderness. They have good characters. They tell the truth. They keep their promises. Since criminals are prone to break faith with others when tempted by money or fame or lust, it is hard for them to maintain friendships, since they can not see the wider-longer benefit of staying true to their friends.

There is more to friendship than having a good character. It requires a personality which values friendship. It requires space in one's mind to hold the friendship, to record information about the other person, as if there was an internal mental module which represents another person's mind in summary form. It allows one friend to guess what the other friend may be thinking and feeling, as if a person could query the module as if to ask, *if I did this, how will my friend react?* It enables intelligent sensitivity.

The art of being a friend is a skill that can be learned over time. People can get better at this skill by working at it and by devoting time and energy to maintaining it. Friends stay in touch. They listen to each other. They enjoy activities together. They understand that friendship should not be one-sided with only one person giving, so they take turns giving and getting, with each trying to keep a focus on what's best for both of them over time. Ideally reciprocity strengthens both persons. Each knows that a sacrifice today may bring dividends tomorrow. Friends communicate clearly. If one friend feels sad, the other feels sad, so among good friends, there is a resonance of feeling. They signal to each other that they are friendly, such as smiling and listening. They are open to tempered criticism and feedback, and they are willing to change their thinking and behavior as their friendship grows. They can be frank with each other, even when it is unpleasant or unflattering, without becoming defensive.

Friendship is characterized by openness and transparency. Friends usually don't keep secrets from each other, particularly when the secrets could adversely affect the other person or the friendship itself. Some friendships have spoken or unspoken boundaries of what their relationship is about.

While friendships can form at any stage of life, it is probably easier for young people to become friends. Their lack of entrenched habits renders them more open and flexible to the possibilities of social interactions. According to Christopher Hitchens, "A melancholy lesson of advancing years is the realization that you can't make old friends." Harvard researcher Robert Waldinger suggested that when old friends fall away, it is vital to replace them with new friends.

It is easier for friendships to form between people with similar levels of status or wealth or power. When there is inequality, conversation can become difficult or one-sided. A commoner addressing a king was risky, since one wrong word or gesture could result in death. It is why it is difficult for friendships to form between civilians and police officers.

Friendships form easily when there are activities such as work or school which regularly bring people together. They can also form when people find themselves in intense competitive situations in which cooperation and trust are essential for success, such as soldiers in combat or teammates in athletic trials. They see the value of cooperation directly and personally. Sometimes sports rivals become friends, since they develop a respect for each other's competence while playing. This is how the friendship developed between the savage Enkidu and the cruel king Gilgamesh in the fictional Babylonian story. They fought but became friends. Enkidu learned to be civilized while Gilgamesh learned to temper his cruelty.

The types of friends that we choose can influence how we

develop, with the general idea being that we tend to become like our friends. If we choose friends who are ambitious, we'll become ambitious. If we choose friends who like to party, we'll grow to love partying. As Tennessee Williams observed, "Life is partly what we make it, and partly what it is made by the friends we choose."

It helps to cultivate a network of friends who have human agency. They know how the world works. They have resources. They are not stuck mentally in crippling patterns. They have correct ideas about us and they are predisposed to help us achieve our goals.

Since the human brain is finite, there are limits on how many friends a person can have. According to Confucius, it is better to have a few good friends rather than many casual friends. Buddhist teaching is similar, in that when choosing friends, we should choose quality over quantity. Epicureans believe that we can't be friends with everybody. A study by anthropologist Robin Dunbar concluded that the human brain can only handle about 150 interpersonal relationships.

There are many benefits of friendship. Good friends help us cultivate virtue with good habits. Friends can help each other navigate the wider world of business and art and government and academia. They can make introductions that lead to more friendships. They can provide valuable assistance when we're beset by bad luck. They can introduce us to a future spouse. A longitudinal study by Harvard University of 724 men found that good relationships are vital for our health, that loneliness kills, and that the quality of our close relationships is what matters, and that they matter much more than wealth or fame in determining how long we will live.

Friends can share a cause. In the nineteenth century, activists Susan B. Anthony and Elizabeth Cady Stanton shared a passion for empowering women politically. They became lifelong friends. Their skills complemented each other. Anthony excelled at organizing while Stanton excelled at writing. Anthony gave speeches and circulated petitions, while Stanton provided ideas and strategy and content. Anthony sometimes supervised Stanton's children. Together they published a sixteen-page weekly that advanced women's suffrage.

Friendships can form when people rally around a common challenge, like Anthony and Stanton did with women's suffrage. They bring a complementary skill or make up for a deficiency. They help prevent isolation and offer companionship. They look out for each other's interests. They can offer a place to stay, a loan, good advice, or an invitation to a party. They can dissuade each other from doing something illegal or immoral or reckless. They can offer a glimpse at how other people see them, and offer precious feedback into how they appear to the community in general. Ralph Waldo Emerson said that friends were like "mirrors to draw out and explain to us ourselves." There are health benefits too. Some studies suggest that friendships can lower one's blood pressure, reduce stress, and offer emotional support in trying times, imparting a sense of belonging. Friends can distract us when we're sad or upset.

According to Aristotle, there are several types of friendships. Some are based on utility, such as business partners floating a company, and some are based on pleasure, such as two young people enjoying their time together. But these friendships depend on their usefulness and pleasure; should these things change, the friendships may atrophy and wither. The best friendships, says Aristotle, are not determined by external factors such as usefulness or pleasure but rather by internal factors. These friends value each other for who they are. They respect each other's values. Emerson said that this type of friendship is "fit for serene days, and graceful gifts, and country rambles, but also for rough roads and hard fare, shipwreck, poverty, and persecution." A true friend stands steadfastly by you during trying circumstances. These friendships tend to be long lasting, often for life, although true long-lasting friendships are not common. Maintaining a friendship over time and distance is challenging, since people change, needs change, and circumstances change. The writer Somerset Maugham wrote that "It's no good trying to keep up old friendships; it's painful for both sides; the fact is, one grows out of people, and the only thing is to face it."

Good friends help each other become better persons. Together, they help each other enjoy life and find greater happiness and personal fulfillment.

Friendship involves risk. It is possible that both friends are good people but that the manner of their relationship is not helpful to one or both of them, perhaps because of an unclear understanding or miscommunication or because of some other issues. It is possible for a friendship to become toxic, if one or both people abuse the relationship for a self-serving purpose. So what may appear to be a friendship is really more of an abusive relationship that may involve gossip, unkind treatment, manipulation, one-way transfers of gifts, put downs and verbal abuse, insincere apologies, the breaking off of future plans without an adequate explanation, poisoning of other relationships, or other unwelcome surprises. It is possible for a bad friend to hurt a good friend by abusing confidential information to inflict emotional damage. A way to tell if a friendship is toxic is to assess how one feels after such interactions. If one feels diminished, less happy, and confused after such encounters, it may be a sign to break off the "friendship."

Unfortunately, it is the nature of the human experience that some people will become enemies. This happens naturally because we are emotional creatures with limited understanding, pressed by time while struggling to survive and thrive, desiring to live but doomed to die. Even if all humans were enlightened, clearheaded creatures in control of our emotions, there would be less fighting, but fighting would still happen because there are limitations on resources and on our ability to predict the future. There will be misunderstandings, breaches of etiquette, disagreements and discord. Since the human body is a complex system, it is vulnerable to many types of interference, and humans know how to hurt other humans. The Sting lyric repeats, *how fragile we are, how fragile we are.*

Enemies are the opposite of friends. If people were atomic particles, friends would be particles that attract each other, and enemies would be particles that repel each other. They push away. They don't want to be near each other. Each would like it if the other particle was far away or did not exist. If relationships are like music, interactions between friends are harmonious while those between enemies are jarring and discordant.

Enemies are not merely competitors who play in good faith by the rules, but people who try to injure their opponents, to separate them from their friends, their family, their property and sometimes their lives. As true friendships are rare, it is rare for two people to be true enemies. Almost all interpersonal relations marked by animosity are caused by misunderstanding and mistakes in judgment, not thinking through what's best, misinterpreting signals, and so forth. Most people, most of the time, try to do the right thing, but this is difficult, given our general human condition. We can learn from adversaries and rivals; as Benjamin Franklin wrote, "Love your enemies, for they tell you your faults."

Friction between people is usually resolved by some form of distance. People move away from each other, avoid each other, don't speak to each other, and that usually solves the problem. It becomes problematic when other factors push discordant people together, such as when two people work in the same company or live in close proximity, or if they are both members of the same group of friends.

As a general rule, free persons have few, if any, enemies. To the extent that persons have human-type free will, are open-minded and not pressed by external circumstances such as hunger or war or by internal circumstances such as disease, then they are likely to have healthy relations with most people. Since they have the correct understanding of fate and free will, they are more likely to make the intellectually correct call of forgiveness when transgressions inevitably happen. Seeing other people as driven by the past, they are less likely to see them as independent actors who chose deliberately to give offense, and so they are less likely to hate them or become otherwise entangled in unproductive emotions.

Conversely, persons who are stuck mentally, uneducated, closed-minded, rigid and unthinking, pressed by time or by circumstance or by disease, who believe incorrectly that they and others have God-type free will, then such persons are more likely to have enemies. Their relations are often characterized by mistrust and bitterness. They are difficult people, stubborn and feisty, hard to reason with, cocksure and petulant. Most societies encourage harmony between people and punish difficult people, perhaps with ostracism and shunning and sarcasm, and in extreme cases with legal punishments such as fines and jail.

It can be difficult to determine whether another person is an enemy or merely a difficult person, or whether someone is undergoing a temporary hardship. Enemies try to conceal their thoughts and intentions from each other so they may be hard to read. As friends share transparency, enemies share obscurity; as friends share love backed by trust, enemies share hate backed by fear. Since fear may cripple thinking, it thwarts opportunities to resolve the conflict with reason.

There are ways for a rational person to cope with an enemy. We can try to see that the enemy is not the person themselves but rather the confused ideas in their head. The enemy is a victim of their own bad thinking. How can we get inside their head to change their mind? We could try to shine our flashlight inside their mind to expose our enemy's flawed understanding to themselves. The enemy lacks a correct understanding of who we are and what we want, perhaps believing incorrectly that we are God-type free-willed actors who have deliberately chosen to hurt them or who are planning to do so. This is not the case. We need to tell them that. If possible, we can try to get them to see that everybody is driven by prior causes, and that neither we nor they are worthy of blame. We try to communicate our good intentions. A way to do this is to try to love the enemy and to try to treat them with kindness instead of violence provided that it does not expose us to further danger. Obviously this strategy is fraught with risks and it may not work.

Human reproduction

Evolutionary realities

Humans have emerged at this particular time in the history of life on the Earth with our bodies in the peculiar forms that they are in. Perhaps if the Earth had been constructed differently, or if the interplay of events and forces had happened differently, our bodies would be different. If Earth's gravity were more like the moon's, perhaps we might be more adept at jumping and tumbling. But we are who we are through the inevitable workings of fate.

We are born either as males or as females. We don't get to choose which sex we're born with. Our biological beginning as either a male or a female has profound ramifications on what it means to be a human, how we approach life, the character of our relationships, what capabilities we have, what expectations our societies have about us and how we are supposed to behave.

Our bodies are hard-wired for sexual reproduction. Our senses are usually predisposed to finding adults of the opposite sex to be attractive. We have instinctual urges to make babies and to protect them until they can fend for themselves. Humans have such an intense appetite for sex that we will figure out how to reproduce without formal instruction. Nerves are extra-sensitive to touch and pressure and heat and vibration, such as those in the genitals and around the anus, lips, breasts, earlobes, inner thighs, neck and hands. Touching can lead to further stimulation in cycles of positive reinforcement, culminating in intense spasms of pleasure. Sexual intercourse sometimes results in ejaculated sperm swimming automatically in search of an unfertilized egg. We can even imagine having sex without another person present while physically stimulating the genitalia. This happens according to the *Principle of Association*. We can associate images and touching to fool our body into thinking that there is another person present, and have sex all by ourselves.

Different roles

Each sex has a different role in reproduction. Women produce eggs and men produce sperm, and their union creates a new human. Whether a fertilized egg becomes a female or a male is determined by random biological processes, so roughly half of babies are female and half are male. The roles in gestation are unequally distributed. A woman carries the fetus inside her body for nine months while males have no required physical role during this time.

Accordingly, the bodies of men and women are different. Women have wider hips to enable a baby to pass through them, with larger breasts and pear-shaped bodies with a narrower upper forehead and rounder features. Men have wider shoulders and forehead and are taller. Men are stronger physically while women live longer. A man can usually force a woman to have sex, but not vice versa. Men tend to have a stronger sexual drive than women. For fertilization, orgasms are mandatory for men but optional for women.

When men are aroused, it can be obvious visually, although clothing provides a restraint and a visual barrier. When women are aroused, it is much less obvious. The penis extends outward when erect, while an engorged clitoris extends internally and is generally not visible. Men are more likely to choose female partners on the basis of their physical appearance, while for women, a man's appearance is only one of many considerations.

Since not every act of sexual intercourse results in fertilization, and since there is a nine month delay between fertilization and birth, a man may not know whether a child was created with his genetic code. In contrast, all women know that their children are theirs genetically since they emerge from their bodies in a dramatic way. The profound contrast between uncertain paternity and certain maternity has implications for dating and mating.

Accordingly, from the perspective of the individual, there is not much fairness in human reproduction. It is not fair that people do not get to choose their body type as either female or male. It is not fair that it is easier for men to force women to have sex and not the other way around. It is not fair that the experience of physical pleasure during sex is often unequal. Since men must climax to reproduce, and since women can reproduce without climaxing, female bodies did not evolve to maximize sexual pleasure.

Human reproduction leans toward the pair-bond model in that heterosexual couples mate in an exclusive arrangement and generally stay together for life. But these bonds are not as stable as those of other species such as penguins. People can change partners. Institutions such as marriage try to protect the pair-bond arrangement. The moral codes of most societies and religions emphasize lifelong fidelity to one's partner. Since sex is a private act that takes little time, and since a couple is sometimes apart, there is the possibility of cheating.

Nevertheless, the pair-bond model is beneficial for the formation of stable families and the raising of children. Babies and young children can not survive on their own, so it is better to have two parents to share the parental workload and child-rearing expenses. Children need food, clothing, living space, protection, medical care and education to become viable adults. Accordingly, most societies discourage cheating and switching partners, and they encourage couples to form stable long-lasting pair-bonds.

In modern times, technical advances have given humans greater control over our biology. These developments are changing the relations between the sexes, reducing inequalities, amplifying choices and empowering people. It used to be difficult for women to enjoy sex without risking pregnancy, but the advent of birth control has changed this dynamic, freeing women to enjoy sex without such concerns. Vibrators can help equalize the inequality of pleasure. Advances in weaponry such as handguns reduce the inequality of physical force. Surgery can alter the genitalia to enable sex change operations.

A general biological constant is evolution. Each human is like a living biological experiment in which nature throws out different genetic combinations to see what happens. With the exception of identical twins, each human is a unique mix of genetic material from two humans. This brings great variability to our physical characteristics: hair, facial structure, height, skin color, immunological defenses, brain size, and so forth. This variation is beneficial for the species because it enables it to adapt to changing conditions. But as individuals it may help or hinder our individual chances for reproduction. Nature does not care whether we as individuals reproduce or not. So here we are. We're on our own. We spring forth into life with physical characteristics not of our choosing. Some of us are born strong and smart and beautiful and others less so. We must work with what we've been given.

Beauty in objects

It is an odd aspect of our natures that we are attracted to things that we perceive as pleasing to the eyes and ears, such as a shapely vase or a colorful sunset or an enchanting human face or a beguiling painting. Beauty stimulates our minds to contemplate and to keep contemplating the object before us. Roger Scruton wrote that some artworks "take our breath away" such as Botticelli's *Birth of Venus* which "fills us with an untroubled and consoling delight." The two senses of seeing and hearing are primarily how we appreciate beauty; we don't think of something having a beautiful smell, for instance.

Beauty teases our powers of intellectual association, reminding us of other pleasant sights and sounds. We associate a curvy bottle of wine with a relaxed dinner. We associate a lovely garden with the soft welcoming feeling of nature. Wordsworth's description of daffodils swaying in the breeze reminds us of dancing with humans. Beautiful things remind us of other beautiful things.

Our appreciation of beautiful objects and landscapes and artwork is often characterized by what philosophers call *disinterested desire*. We simply enjoy looking and listening without necessarily wanting something specific in return. The act itself is enjoyable. We don't become more beautiful by contemplating something beautiful. We can't *consume* beauty to become more beautiful in the same way that we can consume an apple to gain energy. Rather, we're interested in a passive nonchalant way.

Perceiving beauty is an enjoyable intellectual exercise. It stimulates our sensory apparatus. We contemplate the inner order of a bird's wing or the symmetry of a cathedral or the round harmony of detail in a rose. Our minds enjoy this task of discriminating what we like best out of the range of choices. We wonder why we find something appealing, such as artwork that uses the golden ratio to create a pleasing aesthetic of balance and harmony. In his poem *Hymn to Intellectual Beauty*, Shelley described how he became infatuated with the "spirit of beauty", which seemed to pop up unexpectedly, randomly, to tease him, like "moonlight on a midnight stream" or "clouds in starlight widely spread" or "memory of music fled", so that he dedicated his life to pursuing beauty. We sense how things fit in with other things, how details are assimilated, and whether there is an underlying pattern.

To appreciate beauty is to appreciate life. Frances Hutcheson said that beauty is "unity in variety" in the sense of how disparate parts fit together into a sensible whole. We enjoy finding a unified pattern from a slew of seemingly random sights and sounds.

Some assessments of beauty are based on fear. Edmund Burke said that some landscapes remind us of our tiny and insignificant selves against the forbidding expanse of nature. We describe such beauty as *sublime* when we contemplate a barren cliffside or a towering mountain range, and yet we respect how we can persevere despite the awesome power of nature.

We wonder why something is more beautiful than something else. We judge. We compare. Why is object X more beautiful than object Y? It seems like an object has beauty as one of its properties, but its beauty is unlike other properties such as an object's size or density or texture or color. We can't objectively measure an object's beauty like we can its weight. Our assessment of beauty is highly subjective as in the saying *beauty is in the eye of the beholder*. Still, it's a judgment that only we can make for ourselves. Another person can say that X is beautiful, and that may influence our judgment, but we can't corroborate their assessment until we study it for ourselves. Try as we might, we can not make a deductive argument about *why* something is beautiful.

We're prompted to share our beauty assessments with others. Another person can have a different view, and each person is right in their opinion. But we become like "suitors for agreement" as Kant said when we try to persuade others why we think something is beautiful, or why one object is prettier than another. We may not persuade them because there is no "right" answer, although we probably influence each other's views. That may explain why there are fairly consistent standards worldwide, among different cultures and peoples, about what types of objects we think are beautiful.

If it seems puzzling to be attracted to things that don't satisfy an immediate need, then our evolutionary origins may offer an explanation. Humans evolved to appreciate beauty. Our ancestors who found things beautiful went on to reproduce successfully, and those humans who didn't find things beautiful did not reproduce successfully. Beauty brings us together. We enjoy sunsets that resemble waves of colorful mashed potatoes. So do people we might mate with. An enchanting sunset brings people together, and when the sun sets, they focus on each other. They date. What is brought to their next date? Flowers. Where do they go? To a concert. Their children will similarly like sunsets and flowers and concerts and so their appreciation-of-beauty genes will be passed on to successive generations.

We appreciate humans who can create beautiful things. We're attracted to people who paint pictures of sunsets, sketch flowers, and play music, as these activities signify genetic health.

Plato distinguished between *indeterminate desires* and

determinate desires. If we're thirsty, any glass of water will do, so our thirst is an indeterminate desire. But when we think something is beautiful, it matters to us. We want the prettier vase, not just any vase, but only a particular one will satisfy us, that is, it is a determinate desire.

This suggests that our hunger for beauty, whether it's pretty flowers or handsome houses or manicured gardens or stylish sports cars or attractive lovers, spurs us to keep wanting more. It's a powerful underlying motivation inside all of us. We want more money, a prestigious job, a prettier house. We want to win the love of that particularly beautiful woman or man that we can't take our eyes off of. These drives spur humanity to keep on our restless course of invention, requiring risk and hard work, and sometimes even war. These drives underpin our propensities to group ourselves into different social classes in a hierarchical order. We desire to belong to the "in crowd."

If every human was as beautiful as a supermodel, then few would be motivated to build a better mousetrap or invent a new computer game or earn a top salary. Such uniformity would be like a wet blanket on the flame of human ingenuity and drive. So contemplating beauty doesn't just stimulate our sensory powers and make us smarter, it spurs us to get out of our houses and build great businesses and sculpt fine statues and woo attractive partners.

Human beauty

Perhaps our comparisons of the relative beauty of physical objects helps us to better appreciate human beauty. We study dandelions and roses and daffodils. Perhaps when we select the prettiest flower, the exercise of judging floral beauty helps us select the prettiest human face.

As we shift our gaze from pretty objects to pretty humans, we find that we have an *interested interest.* We don't just enjoy looking at beautiful people in a nonchalant way. We want to mate with them. According to Judah Abrabanel, beauty is that which "delights the mind that recognizes it and moves it to love."

The perceptual sharpening effect happens when we're first attracted to another person. In a room full of possible partners, there might be one who is slightly more attractive than the others, or who we start noticing first. But as time passes, this one person appears to be even more attractive than our initial impression of them, as other possible partners seem to disappear in a relative way. The pattern is similar to that of star formation, in that our interest settles on one person in the same way that particle clouds gravitate toward one star and away from other stars. Perceptual sharpening helps us maintain long-lasting pair bonds, in that the lovers we've chosen seem to be more beautiful to us over time.

If we took a random sample of a thousand faces of people in their early twenties, photographed them, and ranked their beauty on a one-to-ten scale, the scores of the faces would be normally distributed, with most scores falling within the middle zone, with some less pretty and some more pretty. But if we took the prettiest faces and showed them repeatedly to the judges, then they'd seem to be even prettier than the initial viewing because of perceptual sharpening. A movie star will appear to be much more attractive than if they weren't famous. It is as if appearing in films elevates their attractiveness, transforming a pretty person into an extraordinary beauty. A painting such as the *Mona Lisa*, featured prominently in museums, seems to be more beautiful because of the accumulated attention from repeated exposures, even though, in an objective sense, it is only slightly more beautiful than other paintings of a similar nature.

Beauty is based on symmetry since it is an easy way to assess genetic health. In a symmetrical building such as the *Taj Mahal*, it is easy to see that it's built right by comparing the left and right sides. They match. In a symmetrical face, one side mirrors the other, and getting this symmetry right requires billions of genetic operations over years to happen correctly. Symmetry suggests not only genetic health but a disease-free upbringing devoid of accidents. It is easy for a viewer's brain to quickly tell whether the two sides match, particularly the eyes and eyebrows and nose, and less so for the ears since they are farther apart and sometimes partially hidden by hair. It is as if one side of the face asks the question, and the opposite side gives the answer, for all to see. Since the eyebrows are controlled by facial muscles and can move, an assessment of beauty based on the symmetry of the eyebrows is less important than the symmetry of the eyes.

While our physical features are mostly beyond our control, we can make ourselves more attractive with makeup, good grooming, clean clothes, bathing, exercising, using colognes and perfumes and so forth. Attitude helps too; a person who appears to be alert and smiling is usually perceived as more attractive than someone who appears to be sad or angry or sleepy. Assessing physical attractiveness is predominantly a visual matter, although a person's voice and natural body scents can also be a factor. We can surround ourselves with beautiful things to appear more beautiful by the *Principle of Association*.

As a general rule, men value beauty in women because it permits a split-second assessment of whether she is likely to bear genetically healthy children. Beauty correlates positively with intelligence, health, disease resistance, education, fitness, and so forth. Women, in contrast, are choosier as a general rule, and they value wealth, status, and power in men, including physical strength as well as beauty, and they are more likely to weigh their estimation of their mate's commitment to them and their offspring in their choices. Beauty correlates positively with fertility so that humans are most beautiful as teenagers and young adults.

Beauty is also based on average proportions. There are certain proportions within a face that are recognized around the world as being beautiful. In the female face, the distance between the pupils of the eyes should be about 46% of the distance between the inside edge of the ear to the other inside edge of the ear, when looking at a face from the front. The distance between the midpoint of the eyes to the midpoint of the mouth should be about 36% of the length from the bottom of the chin to the hairline. Women with these facial proportions tend to be considered as more beautiful than women whose facial proportions differ too much from these average proportions, and this is true across cultures. There are similar standards for male faces. Bodily proportions such as the size of the head compared to the chest are fairly constant as well.

Physical beauty correlates with average height, so that men and women who fall within an average range are more likely to be attractive. This is why the heights of attractive movie stars tend to fall within an average range. There are few tall or short film stars. If two actors compete for a role, such that one is extra tall while another is of average height, they will both appear to be the same height on a viewing screen. It's as if the camera removes the variable of height from the assessment, so that they are judged only by their physical beauty. In the competition, the average-height actor will have an advantage because their features are more likely to be proportional and balanced.

Features that stray too far from these norms or that are unusual or distorted can negatively affect attractiveness. Of course, as the human species evolves over time, these guidelines may change as well. However, during the past five thousand years, the standards for beauty have apparently not changed substantially, so that a beautiful human from ancient Babylonia would probably be considered to be beautiful today.

Biological realities

Biological differences entail differing strategies for mating. The forces of evolution and natural selection, operating over time by the continuing interplay of cause-and-effect, have brought about two distinct types of humans, men and women, who have radically different reproductive agendas. What follows are imperfect generalizations about the nature of these different agendas.

The male reproductive agenda is about quantity. Since men who have sex with more women are more likely to have copies of their DNA in successive generations of humans, men are biologically predisposed to have sex with as many women as they can. The male physical contribution to human reproduction takes only a few minutes, which is in sharp contrast to the female contribution which takes nine months. So it is possible for a highly attractive male to impregnate dozens of women and leave without doing anything more to raise the offspring.

In contrast, the female reproductive agenda is about quality. Women are biologically predisposed to be highly selective about partners since they have a substantial role in growing the baby inside their bodies. There is usually a bond formed during breastfeeding, so women are more likely to be closer to their child throughout its life. In contrast to men who have millions of sperm and who could possibly sire a child at the rate of one or more per day, a woman can only have one child every ten months. If women are fertile from age fifteen to age forty-two, then the upper limit of the number of children that a healthy woman could reasonably have is perhaps twenty seven at most, assuming one baby each year. A decreased sex drive relative to men helps women be choosier.

It is in the confluence of these opposing agendas that mating happens.

Given these biological predispositions, the most successful male reproducers in history have been powerful kings who had sex with dozens of women. They weren't particularly choosy about which women they mated with. In contrast, the most successful female reproducers in history have been beautiful women who were highly selective when choosing their mates and who usually chose the richest, strongest, and most powerful men.

If males and females have distinct reproductive agendas, then we can imagine that societies as well have reproductive agendas. They need to encourage procreation lest their numbers lessen over time. Some religious communities that discouraged sex found their numbers dwindling to the point of extinction; for example, the religious group called the Shakers mandated celibacy, prohibiting procreation, and as a result, there are few Shakers alive today. Most societies have institutions to protect the marital pair-bond, since families are better able to raise and control their children.

Further, in almost all cultures, sex is a private act. There are strong cultural and personal reasons why sex almost always happens behind a visual and auditory barrier since it discourages jealousy and allows the partners to concentrate on their mutual enjoyment. But privacy enables cheating since there are few telltale signs afterwards that intercourse happened.

Society amplifies the distinctions between the sexes with the concept of gender, partly to make it easier for people to correctly identify potential persons for mating, as well as to signal how to treat people. Dress codes and hairstyles emphasize the femininity of women and the masculinity of men, so that a person can correctly identify the sex of a stranger. How each sex is supposed to talk, think, behave and so forth is somewhat dictated by social norms, which vary substantially by society. Failing to follow these norms can lead to exclusion.

In all societies throughout human history about five to ten percent of people are attracted physically to persons of the same sex. It is how they are. Homosexuals did not choose their orientation. They suffer discrimination and abuse because of something that they did not choose and that they can not control. Since they are often treated as outcasts, they are forced to understand society better than heterosexuals as a matter of survival. It is easier for them to see through the myths that confuse every culture. They question how society works and bring a novel and fresh perspective to public life. Society benefits by having members who are not directly involved in the reproduction game, and who have free time to help elevate the general prosperity.

Many homosexuals become artists, writers, painters, sculptors, dancers, scholars, musicians, inventors, dancers, fashion designers, choreographers, entrepreneurs, entertainers, warriors and priests. For instance, the British mathematician Alan Turing, with his code-breaking skills, was a valuable asset to his nation's struggle in World War II; his brilliant machine deciphered the enemy's secret codes.

Most religions persecute homosexuality. This foolishness reveals a flawed understanding of fate and free will and human nature. Persecution damages not only the people who are persecuted but constrains the entire society in a general way since it inhibits talented people from contributing their particular skills. As humans become more enlightened and knowledgeable, they may realize how counterproductive it is to persecute people for what is not their fault, and hopefully people will become more tolerant.

Romantic relationships

A successful relationship benefits each partner. They both feel love, closeness, camaraderie and the warmth of good feeling. They help each other. The bond can bring the benefits of specialization from the division of labor. For example, household chores can be shared so that each one does what they're best at; one cooks, one cleans, each doing what they prefer. There can be restrictions; for example, a committed relationship usually rules out sexual liaisons with other people. Ideally, two people in love think about what is best for their relationship in the wider-space longer-time sense as well as what is best for each of them individually.

While there can be rational aspects of a relationship, its primary essence is love, which is an emotion. The phrase *falling in love* suggests a loss of control when it happens. We plunge into an abyss of feelings. Love is like a glue that connects us with other humans and makes life less lonely, and in this way it can be good. We can not human-type 'will' ourselves to fall in love in the same way that we can not human-type 'will' ourselves to fall out of love. It happens, or it doesn't happen. Love can bring happiness and heartbreak.

Will Durant wrote "Do not be so ungrateful about love ... to the attachment of friends and mates who have gone hand in hand through much hell, some purgatory, and a little heaven, and have been soldered into unity by being burned together in the flame of life. I know such mates or comrades quarrel regularly, and get upon each other's nerves; but there is ample recompense for that in the unconscious consciousness that someone is interested in you, depends upon you, exaggerates you, and is waiting to meet you at the station. Solitude is worse than war."

A prerequisite before falling in love is loving ourselves first. We must do this before we can love another. Emerson wrote that "We must be our own before we can be another's." Loving ourselves is something we learn hopefully as babies from our parents. Perhaps most people love themselves naturally but not always totally, perhaps by attaching conditions on self-love, but we should love ourselves fully and unconditionally. Dostoyevsky said that "Learning to love is hard and we pay dearly for it; it takes hard work and a long apprenticeship, for it is not just for a moment that we must learn to love, but forever."

Accordingly it is difficult to enjoy the positive aspects of love while avoiding the negative entanglements. Love is a risk in that it may or may not be returned. It is opening oneself up to possible rejection and making oneself vulnerable to another. One can build a castle around one's heart to block everybody out but then loneliness is certain.

Relationships should be based on openness, equality, fairness and mutual respect. It helps if lovers have their other emotions under control. A meek forgiving demeanor is good. As the saying goes, *Love is patient, love is kind, it does not envy, it does not boast, it is not proud, it does not dishonor others, it is not self-seeking, it is not easily angered, it keeps no record of wrongs.* Love is not clingy. It should not be a manipulative power-play. Lovers should not use each other as tools for self-gratification. There should not be threats or coercion. Real love humbles us and shakes us like an earthquake rattling the windows of skyscrapers. Love conquers us, reorganizes our priorities, flips our minds and attention away from our image in the mirror to our beloved.

A relatively recent phenomenon in modern life is the proliferation of images, in photographs, on billboards, in film and on the Internet. Images seem to be everywhere, and this is a huge change from just a hundred years ago. Since physical attraction is primarily visual, there is a risk that people become attracted to the images of other people and not to the real people themselves. Real love requires a real connection with another real person. A romantic obsession with the idea of another person or with the image of them is sometimes called *limerence*. This infatuation can be difficult to control. Limerence may be motivated by a desire to avoid intimacy and the risk of rejection. Seeing images of seemingly perfect people all the time can make it easy for us to develop unrealistic expectations for what our own real relationships should be like. This can lead to dissatisfaction with the real people that we might date, and make it difficult to form romantic connections.

Most societies have an arrangement in which two adults are joined in a pair-bond characterized by sexual exclusivity, often for the purpose of raising children. It is a way for the system of a love bond between two people to fit in with the larger system of the society. As an institution, a traditional man-woman marriage meets the various needs of men, women, children, and society.

For men, marriage solves the problem of uncertain biological paternity by making the sexual relation exclusive to the couple. The community draws a sexual cordon around a couple, in effect roping off two people from other partners. Violators of the pair-bond meet with community sanction; local leaders frown on others having sex with the couple, particularly with the wife. What this means is that a man can be fairly certain that his wife's children are his biological progeny. Cheating can happen occasionally but is risky: a man who sleeps with another man's wife risks being killed by the husband with impunity or else punished by the community. Since men know that the children are their own, they are motivated to invest in their upbringing.

For women, marriage solves the problem of the risk of unassisted

A HUMAN WITH OTHER HUMANS

child rearing. Children need food and clothing and protection, so having two parents instead of one is beneficial for women who wish to have children. Marriage says, in effect, that the wife will not be deserted during these vulnerable years. In most societies, men who break their commitment by divorce face penalties such as alimony.

For children, marriage enables a more secure way to grow with two adults, each with different skills, which provides greater stability. Children of two-parent families tend to be stronger, smarter, better educated, safer, better nourished and healthier.

For society, marriage solves the problem of how to manage new members. People are less likely to encounter poorly educated and possibly violent troublemakers wandering about.

There is a window of time in which couples can have children. It is only a few decades, beginning with puberty and lasting until a woman is in her forties to early fifties and somewhat longer for men. Reproductive ability decreases in middle age, so couples have a harder time conceiving as they get older, with a greater risk of birth defects. Physical attractiveness increases slightly during the late teens and early twenties, then decreases gradually. The effect of the limited time horizon is that people who wish to have families with children should not wait indefinitely to choose a partner, and that partners should pair up within the time constraint.

In the past few hundred years, there have been major changes in human relations, particularly in societies which value human rights. Various developments have brought about the empowerment of the individual, including a vast expansion of human knowledge as well as advances in tools and the ability to exploit resources. Machines replace human labor, freeing people from repetitive and monotonous drudgework. Productivity has increased exponentially. Throughout most of human history, women were regarded as subservient beings whose principal function was reproduction and child-rearing. Today, increasingly, women are treated as equals, with the right to vote and form businesses and hold political office. There are fewer restrictions on sex, choice of partner, and marriage. The possibility of divorce means that there is less risk of being stuck in a dysfunctional relationship, although it can be difficult for young children when parents separate. The institution of marriage is opening up to new arrangements, such as same-sex couples forming families and three parent families.

Another development is that it is increasingly up to individuals to create pair-bonds, instead of parents and matchmakers, and people do this by flirting and romance.

Flirting is romantic play, playful teasing with a fun cast of mind which allows people to gauge whether there is a mutual attraction. It is advertising one's availability and interest to a possible partner, with a focus on the possibility of romance. If a man is interested in a woman, for example, the flirting formula might be *I'm a man, you're a woman, ain't that great*?! It is as if a question mark and an exclamation point have merged into a new punctuation symbol like a raised eyebrow. It is a shared focus on the juicy unpredictableness of life.

Flirting is like being in a play of one's own making, scripted-on-the-spot in real time, with the ending unwritten, light-hearted and breezy with a dollop of roguish humor and mock rebelliousness. When talking, if something is important, it is treated lightly; if light, it is treated with thundering importance. Flirting is being adults but playing like kids while being somewhat ambiguous about one's intentions. Is it kidding or serious? Part of the fun is guessing which is which. Flirting fails when it's a narrow-minded means toward the goal of a future date or sexual intercourse. That is really more of a seduction or a power play which can be manipulative and dishonest if the true intentions are obscured. Flirting should be fun in itself, with a playful spirit that is present-oriented and not future-driven.

Flirting shuffles into the territory of romance when one is fairly clear that one is attracted to another person and wants to woo them. If flirting is dipping one's toe in the pool, then romance is full-immersion swimming.

The art of being romantic is not taught in schools and it often doesn't come naturally to most people. It's poetic infatuation, uncontrolled and passionate, something beyond our power that happens to us. Either person can initiate the romance; the writer Vera Nazarian wrote "Sometimes, reaching out and taking someone's hand is the beginning of a journey; at other times, it is allowing another to take yours." The feeling of falling in love can not be willed into existence by an intellectual focus, although one can work toward a state of openness and curiosity that can improve the chances of it happening. If love is a kind of blindness and irrationality, romance is a feeling of emotional helplessness, as if one is dependent on the love of another for their existence. For lovers, every shared moment is precious. There is a seductive element of fatalistic unavoidability in romance as if it is fated that love will happen, and that trying to fight the feeling simply makes it more powerful.

There is a conspiratorial element to romance as well. It is as if the lovers enter into a tryst of two against society, whispering, plotting, sharing their innermost thoughts in a secret language. The privacy spheres of two separate people merge into a larger private sphere.

Love is like a game with no rules. It means that lovers can experiment, violate conventions, and do whatever works for them both. Like everything, relationships are subject to the whims of fortune and circumstance, as well as pushes and pulls from other people, from children and parents and employers.

In successful relationships, the partners know how to communicate their needs and expectations. There is courtesy and good feeling. They learn how to resolve disputes thoughtfully. They enjoy sex. Magdalene J. Taylor said that sex reduces pain, relieves stress, improves sleep, lowers blood pressure and strengthens heart health. Couples know that sex is only one of many ways to express love, and that it is not an end in itself. A pattern emerges over time which is mostly routine but with room for surprises. It is as if a couple is continually choosing each other as a mate.

Expansion of knowledge

In the present time, our collective human knowledge is substantial, and our acquisition of new knowledge is proceeding at an exponentially rapid pace.

If we look at the wide expanse of history, and consider human development from when humans first emerged on the planet to the present, our progress has been extraordinary. According to some assessments, our species came into existence about 250,000 years ago. Humans knew hardly anything. There were no schools, no books, no teachers to tell us what happened before us. Humans didn't even know how to read.

Nevertheless, our prehistoric hunter-gatherer ancestors survived several ice ages. They learned how to control fire. They learned how to hunt and kill giant elephant-sized mammoths. In warmer climates, they figured how to time their migrations to locate bushes with edible berries. They learned how to use the stars to traverse the huge Pacific Ocean in open boats. They came to inhabit every continent except Antarctica.

Gradually, by collective learning, by communicating via symbolic languages, and by learning how to record and store information, human knowledge grew. The advent of writing on stone tablets and papyrus and later in books enabled the transmission of knowledge from generation to generation. About ten thousand years ago, humans learned how to cultivate crops like wheat and maize, and to domesticate herd animals like cows and sheep. They could stay in one location and not have to carry everything around all the time. About five thousand years ago, small cities emerged.

It was around this time that humans not only kept learning new things, but they began to ask about *how* to go about learning. In ancient Greece, Socrates emphasized the importance of asking questions. His pupil Plato developed theories about metaphysics and politics. Plato's pupil Aristotle pioneered the study of philosophy, science, rhetoric, mathematics, ethics, and logic.

But it wasn't until 1620, when Francis Bacon wrote *Novum*

Organon, that serious scientific investigation got underway. Bacon argued that nature's complexity was too difficult for humans to figure out just by guessing or by theorizing about how it works, or by trusting religious authorities or ancient scholars for answers. He advocated that humans study nature intensively, to observe its particulars and to measure phenomena with accurate instruments, and to pose hypotheses that could be validated or discarded by careful experimentation. Such investigations are based on an assumption that everything that happens has a cause-and-effect explanation of why it happened. We assume that there are reasons behind these processes. We may not understand what these reasons are but we assume that reasons do, in fact, exist.

At present, scientists do not understand a phenomenon called *quantum entanglement.* This happens when a pair of entangled particles is separated by a vast distance, and yet when one spins clockwise, the other spins counter-clockwise. Scientists assume that there are explanations for this odd behavior. Neil deGrasse Tyson said, "The universe is under no obligation to make sense to us."

Such is the scientific method. We observe. We question. We make testable hypotheses based on our observations. We experiment. We analyze the results, make conclusions, and these suggest new experiments. So the cycle of observation and experimentation continues to expand human understanding. We leave religion and superstition and miracles out of our investigations. For example, on the subject of rivers, scientists do not ruminate on what possible theological reasons a God or gods had to create them, or whether they're perfect or not, or how to pray to keep them flowing. Instead, science seeks to understand them and to predict their behavior, so we know how to prevent floods, whether they're safe to swim in or drink from, and so forth.

Everything can be questioned. Everything we learn is subject to further review and experimentation. We record precisely how we did experiments so other scientists can try to replicate our results. We share what we learn. Science can't prove what is true, but rather it can disprove what isn't true, according to Karl Popper's *Falsification Principle*. If a given proposition is to be considered to be scientific, we must be able to imagine an experiment that could prove that the proposition was false. We don't have to do the experiment. But if we could design such an experiment, then our proposition is scientific. A problem with religious propositions is that they're not falsifiable.

The scientist Carl Sagan gave an example of an unscientific not-falsifiable proposition. Suppose somebody said that *there is a dragon in my garage.* That's the proposition. When we inspected the garage, we saw only empty paint cans and an old tricycle, so where is it? We are told that *it's an invisible dragon.* So we propose putting flour on the floor to detect footprints. *But it floats in the air.* Let's get an infrared sensor to check its fiery breath. *Sorry it's a cold-blooded dragon.* This back-and-forth could continue indefinitely, such that every possible suggestion of an experiment will be met with an explanation of why it won't find anything. So the proposition is not falsifiable. It's not scientific. There may indeed be a dragon in the garage, in the same way that there may indeed be a God or gods, but since we can't design an experiment to disprove it, we're wasting our time thinking about it.

Luckily the scientific method does not require people to be geniuses in order to advance human understanding. It enables ordinary investigators to plod along at a slow pace, provided that they adhere to the scientific method, and over time they're likely to learn new things. Alternatively, a genius who doesn't follow the scientific method will likely not get anywhere. So science became a cumulative, cooperative and systematic human enterprise. It can proceed in a slow and plodding manner as long as it follows the right path of the scientific method.

The goal isn't just understanding, but understanding in ways that help us make new inventions that help us survive and thrive. To investigate scientifically requires a sort of collective humility to admit that we don't know everything, and from this starting point, we can learn how the human body fights disease, how to improve crop yields by adding ingredients to the soil, how to harness steam power, and how to forge steel. We try to figure out what causes what. When Einstein pondered the frontiers of human intellectual exploration, he felt like a five year old child in a library, with huge books written in different languages that he didn't yet understand, with an order to the whole system, and a feeling that it would be possible to understand everything someday in the distant future.

While the result of trial-and-error experimentation is experience-based knowledge, such knowledge is uncertain. As Bertrand Russell explained, "Science is at no moment quite right, but it is seldom quite wrong, and has, as a rule, a better chance of being right than the theories of the unscientific. It is, therefore, rational to accept it hypothetically." There are neither final determinations nor ultimate answers since any idea or theory or fact can be overturned upon later inspection. An exception is mathematical knowledge, which is true in itself. Two plus two will always equal four, and the length of the hypotenuse of a right triangle will always equal the square root of the sum of the squares of the two shorter sides, and no experiment can disprove these truths. The application of mathematics to experimentation led to the discovery of universal laws regarding motion and gravity. Isaac Newton's *Principia Mathematica* in 1687 was a huge stride forward for human understanding. He showed mathematically how an apple falling from a tree was guided by the same gravitational force as the moon circling the Earth.

So human progress in the last few hundred years has been phenomenal. It has brought a whirlwind of new sources of power from the burning of fossil fuels, atomic energy, solar and wind power. Scientific investigation has accelerated with new and better tools for measurement and observation, such as telescopes, microscopes, X-rays and magnetic resonance imaging technologies. There are increasingly efficient and cost-effective ways to store the vastly expanding sets of knowledge. First, there was Diderot's encyclopedia, then the Encyclopedia Britannica, and today there is Wikipedia with millions of articles on a huge range of subjects. Humans can send an entire book across the planet in a nanosecond. We've built powerful new machines for transportation such as the train and the car and jet liners and rockets and submarines. At the time of this writing, new technologies such as artificial intelligence are just beginning to revolutionize our capabilities.

Humans today are the recipients of numerous advancements in medicine and technology and transportation and communication. Since 1700, the average human lifespan has increased from about forty years to about seventy years. Our longer lives were not brought about by mystics contemplating visions in the desert, by priests chanting on the plains, by gurus kneeling before statues of gods, by sacrificing animals or the daughters of kings, or by murdering persons suspected of being witches, but rather by scientists and inventors and business leaders and researchers using reason and rationality. They follow Bacon's scientific method. The goal is to endow human life with new discoveries and resources.

The pace of scientific investigation is speeding up exponentially. Today there are more scientists studying problems than all of the scientists in human history, and they know more, and they have better tools, than at any other era. Our quality of life has vastly improved. We have better protections against disease in the form of vaccines and medicines and treatment regimens. Science is real, solid, practical stuff that helps all of us.

Economy

Estimating value

Estimating value is applying the *Basic Principle of Ethics* quantitatively. Good is what is good for us, in wider spaces and longer time frames, as best that we can determine *something's future value to us*. We compare options. Perhaps we might buy an apple for X dollars or a quart of milk for Y dollars or maybe we'll keep our cash. Which choice is best? We try to quantify something's future goodness.

Value depends on the context. A dessert after a three course meal is not as valuable as when the person first sat down to dinner. A glass of water is less valuable at a wedding feast but highly valuable in the desert. Labor adds value to things, to make them more useful to humans in a given context, so the labor of bringing water to the desert makes it more valuable.

Most things that we value as individuals can be valued by other people. So when we extend our scope to examining humans in groups, it is not just what one human values, but what other people value. So there is a group assessment of what something is worth, and this assessment is of course reflected in its price, which depends on scarcity and demand. Gold has a high price because it is scarce and people want it. Air has a low price because it is not scarce although of course people need it to survive.

Our personal assessment of value can vary considerably from the group's consensus. A parent might value a finger painting made by their child, but most other people would not value it. But a painting such as the *Mona Lisa* will have an extremely high price because there is only one original and its extreme scarcity and the fact that it has attracted millions of viewers makes it highly valuable.

Energy that humans use for life originates mostly from light and heat from the sun as well as from thermal energy from the inner Earth. While the sun is projected to keep shining for another four billion years, if it stopped today, life on Earth would almost certainly cease. We utilize fossil fuel energy such as oil and natural gas and coal. According to several estimates, about 25% to 40% of the sun's energy that reaches the Earth is harnessed by humans.

Energy cycles through our human projects. When a contractor builds a skyscraper, it is paid millions of dollars which it uses to pay employees, who use the money to buy bread which is digested to become glucose. So the construction brings money, money buys bread, bread enables glucose, and glucose enables adenosine triphosphate energy molecules. At different levels of complexity, the terms are different but the functions are roughly the same. Energy at the cellular level is adenosine triphosphate; energy at the bodily level is glucose; energy at the human level is money in the bank; energy at the business level is stocks and bonds; energy at the national level is the gross domestic product.

A general rule is that a living entity must take in at least as much energy as it uses, over time, and preferably more. If an energy source stops, then stored energy is used, and if that runs out, the entity dies. This pattern holds at every level of complexity, from individual cells to humans to business firms to nations. The task of living things is to smooth out the delivery of energy so that there is a steady amount when and where it is needed. Our bodies can store energy as fat tissue, and the storage and release of fat is a subsystem in itself. Our hunter-gatherer ancestors relied on this mechanism when food was scarce, but in the modern world with abundant supplies of food, this mechanism has become problematic since it encourages obesity.

Families and firms and nations estimate future needs by thinking along the lines of the *Basic Principle of Ethics*, by trying to predict energy needs in the future. They store energy when it's abundant and release it when it's scarce. In the Biblical story, Joseph foresaw seven years of abundance followed by seven lean years, so he advised the Pharaoh to store grain to prevent starvation. Individuals apply similar planning by saving up with a so-called rainy day fund should they suffer an unexpected financial hardship. According to the Vedic tradition, we should spend about 90% on our current needs and save the remaining 10%. We try to use energy efficiently. We try to maximize value while minimizing cost. We spend on things we need and try not to overspend. There's an old proverb that a person who spends too much on a wallet won't have anything to put in it.

Fair transactions

The *Basic Principle of Ethics* can be applied to the concept of an economic exchange in that there are good exchanges and bad exchanges.

A good exchange is when a buyer and a seller agree, voluntarily, to swap goods or services. This exchange almost always leaves both parties better off, since both think that they will gain from the free exchange, and they're usually both right in their determinations. A hungry woman needs an apple, an orchard owner has a surplus of apples, so the woman buys the apple. She is better off with the apple and the seller is better off with the money. Each party is estimating that it will be good for them to do the exchange, in wider spaces and longer time frames, as best that they can determine. It is possible in a good exchange, even when both parties agree, that one party may be relatively better off while the other party is relatively worse off, even though both parties would be better off because of the exchange. They guess about what might benefit them in the future, and guesses can be mistaken.

A bad exchange happens when one side benefits unfairly from the exchange, such as in cases of fraud or theft. In a coercive transfer of property, one party did not consent to the transfer or else they were tricked into the transfer. One party gains; the other party loses. Stealing is a bad exchange, not only for the party that is reduced, but for society as a whole, since the act of stealing undercuts a general faith in the marketplace. It dampens a general enthusiasm for working and investing and exchanging. Growers might worry that their future efforts may be undone. Investors would be reluctant to loan money to growers. Fewer apples for sale might bring higher prices. Stealing not only diminishes the wealth of the victim, essentially undermining their motivation to create further wealth, but it rewards the thief for not producing anything. Stealing distorts the social mechanisms of rewards and punishments. It is ultimately bad for the thief in the wider-longer sense since it almost always results in negative repercussions and punishments.

There may be exceptions when it is necessary for a person to steal, if there is a greater evil that will result by failing to steal. Still, stealing should be a temporary measure only, and repayment made as soon as possible. For example, a poor man starving, who has tried without success to beg or borrow, who will die without bread, may steal a loaf of bread, but as he regains health and wealth, then he should compensate the grocer.

Creating value

Work usually means being part of a coordinated effort undertaken with other humans in which the human is a subsystem in a larger system such as a business enterprise. Creating value requires know-how: knowing how things work, what people want, how to build things, how to use a tool, and how to learn about using that tool. Sometimes it means learning the established way of doing something, and then simply repeating that established way. Other times it means figuring out a more efficient method. Aristotle explained: "First, have a definite, clear practical ideal, a goal, an objective; second, have the necessary means to achieve your ends, such as wisdom, money, materials, and methods; third, adjust all your means to that end." A lesson in the Bhagavad Gita and echoed by Stoic philosophy is that we should focus our full attention on working, and not on what rewards we might receive afterward. If we think too much while working about how we'll spend our upcoming paycheck, our activity will be less focused and less enjoyable and prone to errors, reducing our chance that we will actually get that paycheck.

Martin Luther King Jr. said, "Whatever your life's work is, do it well; if it falls on your lot to be a street sweeper, sweep streets like Michelangelo painted pictures." To achieve excellence, analyst Geoff Colvin noted how top performers isolated necessary skills that they weren't good at, and then practiced them rigorously with intense concentration, often with the help of a coach or a teacher, getting continuous feedback. Tiger Woods would spend hours each day practicing how to knock a golf ball out of a sand trap. Great performers practice so intently that the hard stuff becomes automatic. By working, the result hopefully will be greater energy, more food, better resources, a more efficient tool, a helpful service or a better alternative.

It is important to have basic financial literacy. We should have a common sense understanding of how to calculate interest payments, how a mortgage works, how to invest money in stocks and bonds and real estate, the logic of diversification, how time changes the value of money through inflation, how to save for the future, how to avoid unnecessary taxes and so forth. So a worker can keep more of what they earn and become self-sufficient.

A question that most workers face is whether to become a generalist or a specialist. A generalist has more opportunities for work but their rate of pay is not usually as high as that of a specialist. Adviser Pat Flynn thinks it is better to be pretty good at many tasks rather than being superior at one skill. To straddle the generalist-specialist divide, he recommends getting good at several relevant skills and then combining them in a winning package. For example, rather than focusing exclusively on the specialist task of becoming the best solo lead guitarist, it is better to cultivate generalist skills such as songwriting and singing and guitar playing, and then to combine them to build a successful career in music.

It is important to be where the action is. To be a filmmaker, move to Hollywood or Bollywood. A country singer? Nashville. A painter? Paris. A computer chip designer? Taiwan.

Creating value almost always requires higher level thinking. It requires combining idea-chains into longer and longer ordered cause-and-effect sequences which reflect reality, which solve a problem, which help a person or a firm reach a goal. Sometimes this requires imagining a better way of doing something, trying it, seeing if it works, and then working with it to make it better. It doesn't always require high-level thinking. A worker or a firm may try something different, and if it works, they'll keep doing it, or if it doesn't, they'll try something else. Hockey player Wayne Gretzky said "You miss 100% of the shots you don't take." It is possible to discover a more efficient method while not understanding why it is better.

We try more efficient arrangements. In 1965 Frederick W. Smith imagined a more efficient overnight package delivery system. Instead of the logistical complexity of scheduling hundreds of direct flights between dozens of cities, packages would be flown into a hub city, sorted by destination, and then flown to their destination cities. For example, packages from Boston would fly to Memphis, get sorted overnight, and then flown to New York. Each package would fly farther than a direct flight, but the system as a whole was more efficient.

As a general pattern, jobs that create more value, pay more. These jobs take longer to learn. They are riskier not only in terms of safety but in terms of the likelihood of success. They require greater skill and talent and education. People who can do these types of jobs are few in number so their ability to command a higher wage is greater. It isn't always fair; some jobs pay huge amounts for not really creating much value, and other jobs pay little for creating much value. It depends partly on what a society values and how rewards are structured. A society which values war will have the best-paying jobs going to weapons makers and generals and soldiers; a society which values agriculture will have the best-paying jobs going to agronomists and farmers; a society which values entertainment will have the best-paying jobs going to filmmakers and actors.

A formula for a successful career is to unite human agency with a worthwhile goal. Eleanor Roosevelt said "The future belongs to those who believe in the beauty of their dreams." We prioritize important tasks. According to the *Pareto Principle,* we should direct our energy toward the 20% of tasks which yield 80% of the results. While striving to make something as good as we can is a good thing, perfectionism can be problematic if it causes too much effort to be focused on only one part of a project to the detriment of the whole, or if it brings about a paralysis of action.

To have a successful career often requires straddling trade-offs. According to the *Four Burners Theory*, there are four primary areas of our lives: family, friends, health and work, and each aspect is like a burner of a stove. To have all four burners going prevents success in one area, so the advice is to turn off one or two burners to direct our energies to what's important. For example, to succeed as a business entrepreneur might require spending less time with family and friends. A way to manage trade-offs is to shift one's focus during different stages of life, perhaps by raising a family when younger and then focusing on a career when older. The general consensus from religious and philosophical thinking, however, is that we should lead a balanced life, enjoying all four areas, devoting time to family and friends, working and being productive, and never sacrificing health for ambition.

Ralph Waldo Emerson offered his prescription for success: "When you do a thing, do it with all your might, put your whole soul into it, stamp it with your own personality, be active, be energetic, be enthusiastic and faithful, and you will accomplish your object." Colin Powell said "There are no secrets to success; it is the result of preparation, hard work, and learning from failure."

Good work habits are helpful. According to Buddhist teaching, good habits bring great achievements, and it is drop by drop that the water bottle is filled. We get restful sleep. Benjamin Franklin said "Early to bed, early to rise, makes a man healthy, wealthy and wise."

There is consensus among successful people that hard work, persistence, and not giving up are vital for success. Nelson Mandela said "The greatest glory in living lies not in never falling, but in rising every time we fall." Maya Angelou said "You will face many defeats in life, but never let yourself be defeated." Thomas Edison wrote that "Many of life's failures are people who did not realize how close they were to success when they gave up." Winston Churchill said "Success is not final; failure is not fatal; it is the courage to continue that counts." Steve Jobs said "If you really look closely, most overnight successes took a long time." In our striving, when we confront obstacles, we find ways to overcome them or bypass them or negate them to keep moving forward. According to Confucius, our ultimate success depends on how we bounce back from temporary failures. Winston Churchill put it somewhat differently, saying that "Success is walking from failure to failure with no loss of enthusiasm." It's important to set high goals; James Cameron said "If you set your goals ridiculously high and it's a failure, you will fail above everyone else's success." Marcus Aurelius suggested that we should ask ourselves if what we're doing is essential, and if not, we should not do it; we should only do what's important, and that we should live life as if today was our last.

Many humans have a predisposition to delay doing necessary tasks. Procrastination is when we knowingly delay doing something, and we're aware that our inaction will hurt us later on. When this happens, our calculations of the *Basic Principle of Ethics* are somewhat off, as if we are weighing whether it's better to work now for a future benefit, or enjoy a present distraction. We choose the short-term distraction rather than the long-term benefit. It seems more fun to play a video game now rather than begin to write that term paper that is due in three weeks. One cause of procrastination is perfectionism, that happens when we delay an activity out of an anxiety of not doing it perfectly right. Another cause is the mistaken belief that our work will improve under the pressure of the deadline.

General strategies to fight procrastination include trying to visualize what steps need to be done to complete a multi-step project, thus breaking down a seemingly intimidating project into easier-to-do steps. It is easier to write two hundred words than to write an entire novel. We can eliminate distractions such as turning off the television. Perhaps the hardest part of working is simply starting, since once we're working, we enjoy the activity and we are likely to keep working on it. A Daoist saying is that the journey of a thousand steps starts with the first step. Amelia Earhart said "The most difficult thing is the decision to act, the rest is merely tenacity." The actor Hugh Laurie said "It's a terrible thing, I think, in life to wait until you're ready... There is almost no such thing as ready. There is only now. And you may as well do it now."

The variety of jobs has expanded exponentially in modern times. In the Middle Ages, there were just a few types of people: farmers and fighters and clergy, plus a few specialists such as the makers of tools and clothing and buildings. Today there is a smorgasbord of types of jobs of all kinds. There are professional bridesmaids who are paid to assist with weddings. Online dating ghostwriters help single people write personal descriptions on dating apps. Full time movie watchers critique films. Professional ethical hackers try to break into computer networks to search for weak points to improve online security. Body part models feature in advertisements for skin care products. A hundred years ago, there were doctors; today there are cardiologists and nephrologists and ophthalmologists and orthopedic surgeons and a slew of expanding medical specialties. There is an ever-wider choice of possible occupations.

Systems of employment

Generally the strategies for becoming a better human identified so far can be applied to workplace success. The *Basic Principle of Ethics* can serve as an algorithm to help us make career-related decisions. To the extent that we have good characters, tell the truth consistently, know how things work and have human agency, we are better able to mesh constructively with fellow workers in larger systems of employment. Colleagues know that they can count on us to keep our promises. We avoid emotional entanglements. We're good thinkers who understand how everything is fated so we're loath to blame people and wag fingers or feel guilty about stuff that happens. We're accountable for what we do. We're able to form constructive bonds with friends and colleagues and bosses and clients. We don't take ourselves too seriously, as Epicureans advise. According to Hiram Crespo, "Laughter is a healthy way to deal with tribulations and difficult, shameful, or uncomfortable situations" and it helps to "soften criticism, encourage authenticity, deflate empty pretensions, and to clear the air."

Accordingly, to be productive, we try to get a flexible clearheaded frame of mind that is ready to work. We figure out what is important to us and what we want to accomplish, perhaps by looking inwardly into our deepest desires. We should not choose a career path based on the expectations of others, or what our parents want or what society in general wants from us, but rather what we, ourselves, want. We orient our educational pursuits accordingly. We try to forecast how our career path might progress, and we make imperfect decisions based on our best guesses. Barbara Walters suggested that we should choose something that we love to do even if we didn't get paid, then get a job in that industry or business, starting at any level, and be there first in the morning and be the last to leave at night. It helps to cultivate a circle of colleagues who respect what we do, who can hire us and recommend us to possible employers and who can alert us to new job opportunities.

Preparation is important. We set things up beforehand so we have what we need before working, so we can begin our project without having to hunt down supplies. If we're a writer, we have a distraction-free room with a lamp and a computer. If we're an office worker, we have clothes laid out in advance, pressed and clean, along with train tickets and a raincoat and such. We learn to do our chores efficiently, so we can free up our schedule for work.

We seek employers with a similar sense of agency. Such firms appreciate talent, are open-minded and flexible, and operate like a healthy individual but on a larger scale. Their goals are consistent with our own goals. They play fair, keep their commitments, and create valuable products and services. They have a good grasp of reality. They have excellent internal deliberation so that they're not afraid to explore new markets or to experiment with new arrangements. They understand the rhythms of financial markets, saving during the bullish years, so they can meet the payroll during the bearish years. They mesh well with the regulatory environment. They tolerate and encourage different viewpoints. They are skilled at motivating employees to work productively.

The principles that apply to an individual human apply to a firm. It's at a higher level of complexity. Like a human, a firm seeks what's best for itself in wider spaces and longer time frames, as best that it can determine. A healthy firm gets things done. It has know-how in the form of accumulated knowledge about how to succeed in its industry. Firms often have a lifespan longer than a solitary human. While a human may live on average about seventy years, a firm can last longer, although there are no guarantees that a firm will do so.

The collective "mind" of a firm is the interconnected minds of its managers and employees. Its deliberations should mirror the internal mental processes of a healthy mind, drawing ideas from a variety of views, reflecting on past decisions, not getting stuck, avoiding obsessions or preoccupations with irrelevant issues, heeding feedback from customers, making intelligent plans and so forth. It is not good if a firm's decision-making is emotional in nature or characterized by departures from reality.

How nations create value

A nation is like a living entity such as an individual human but it's obviously bigger and more complex. Since it shares many of the same properties of living things, we can apply the rules of life to its operation, including of course the *Basic Principle of Ethics*. Good is what is good for the *nation*, in wider spaces and longer time frames, as best that it can determine.

We should have a basic understanding of the national economy because we're a part of it. We work. We buy things. We live in it. To a small extent, we influence what happens by our economic and political participation. We should be able to distinguish good economic policies from bad ones. Some of us may become government officials.

A national economy is a vast network of interconnected subsystems that includes individuals, households, farms, businesses, colleges, nonprofit organizations, banks, military and police forces, artists, retailers, local officials, and so forth. Government's task is to order activity among these subsystems so that the internal energy flows are predictable and stable. The system should be balanced so that each subsystem keeps to its proper size and proportion. Each subsystem should have a clearly defined function, so that colleges educate students, farms grow corn, restaurants feed truck drivers, police prevent crime, the military defends the nation, and so on. The government manages these interactions.

What primarily keeps these various subsystems within bounds is competition. Individuals compete. Firms compete. They struggle for efficiency. They're constantly striving to improve. Every subsystem tries to make good products and to provide useful services, and if they don't, they go out of business. This mirrors what happens in life, in that unfit creatures die out. It is built on inequalities, in that some are richer and some are poorer, some are talented and some are less talented, and it is by straddling these inequalities that exchanges happen. Diversity is good and necessary but it brings about internal stress.

A way to think about the government's role in a complex economy is as follows. Suppose we're the government. We're like referees at a giant sporting arena. But it's not just one game that we're refereeing, but countless games that are happening simultaneously in different places. We don't play in the games. Rather, we make and enforce the rules.

Various teams play. They compete. When teams score goals, they get points. That's how they're rewarded. The drive to win points motivates the players. By analogy, the drive to win profits is the basic motivating force for a nation's subsystems.

So our job as referees is to make sure that the games are fair, that points are awarded as expected, and that the system of rewards continues to motivate the players. For this end, it is best to have a direct relation between goals scored and points awarded, so that one goal equals one point, for example. In a national economy, there should be a direct relation between constructive work that creates value, and profits, so that each lamp built earns X dollars, for example. Players know that excellent play will bring points, and firms know that hard work will bring profits, and this awareness motivates them to keep playing and to keep making lamps.

Sometimes a team will get negative points, perhaps because of penalties, and they'll have to disband, such as when a business firm goes bankrupt. That happens sometimes. Our job as referees is to let such teams disband. Similarly, the government has to let some firms go out of business. Some teams will do better than other teams. That is the nature of fair competition. As referees, our job is to ensure that no team has an artificial advantage, and that teams win or lose because of their effort and not because of arbitrary reasons. When gameplay is fair, players are motivated.

Our job as referees is to make sure that the rules are clear and simple enough to be easily understood. For example, in basketball, everybody understands the rule against double dribbling, and in European football, players know not to touch the ball with their hands. We should not change the rules to benefit some teams at the expense of other teams. Our job as referees is not to counsel players how to play or what shots to take but rather it should be limited to explaining and enforcing the rules. Similarly, the government should not tell Mary to buy broccoli or tell widget makers how to price their widgets. Governments that dictate prices subvert the basic motivations that underlie economic activity, resulting in shortages and famines.

Before a particular game begins, players join teams. Our job as referees is to ensure that players are free to join whatever team they choose. We should not allow existing teams to prevent new teams from forming. Similarly, the government's task is to prevent established firms from blocking start-up competitors.

Teams have diverse players. Their talents vary. Some are highly skilled. Others are less skilled. As referees, we can't insist that all starting players show up with identical skills. We must not try to rectify these imbalances by handicapping the better players during the game because their opponents showed up with shortcomings. We can't control what happens *before* the game. But we can insist that once the games are underway, that players and teams follow the same fair rules. In a national economy, the corresponding principle is called *equal opportunity* in that the same fair rules apply equally to all players and firms.

When we begin our careers as referees, the games have been underway for years. Players know what the existing rules are. These rules are well established. In most cases, we should assume that these existing rules are fair and good. Maintaining the consistency of rules is highly beneficial. If we change the rules, it's a big deal. We risk upsetting established patterns of play. We might make things worse or we might make things better. So we should have good reasons for any adjustments. Perhaps some rules are inadequate or favor some teams or are detrimental to the nation. Perhaps emerging technologies require changes to the existing order.

The system of penalties should be consistent and simple and fair and well understood. If a player violates a rule, then the penalty should be proportional to the offense. So if a player is offside, the other team will get the ball. If a player intentionally injures another player, then the offender is booted from the game. But a player should not be booted for being offside.

As referees, players and teams may question our decisions. Sometimes they'll want us to rule in ways that make it easier for them to win. We are in constant danger of being pressured or bribed. Some of our family members and friends and colleagues play on those teams, and we can abuse our authority to unfairly help them win points. If unrewarded teams discover the unfair advantage, they may complain and not want to play any more. We need to be responsible and fair and impartial lest we subvert the motivation to play and therein weaken the entire nation. Biased rulings violate the *Basic Principle of Ethics* by sacrificing long term economic health for short term profits.

If a player follows the rules and scores a goal, then they get points. They've earned it. We can't arbitrarily take their points away. By analogy, the government must protect property rights. The idea that what an individual works for, and earns, is theirs, is central to motivating everybody to keep creating more value. If property can be seized, arbitrarily, without recourse to law or due process, then that possibility kills off the spirit of work throughout society. The protection of private property is a mainstay for a healthy economic sphere.

A related idea is that governments facilitate economic activity by enforcing contracts. This is vital. A contract is a meeting of the minds between two or more parties about what will be done and for how much compensation. A contract is essentially the idea of a right in economic form in the sense of a shared understanding before an exchange happens, which binds parties together, about what will be exchanged for what. It is how economic players bind and unbind for mutual betterment.

To illustrate, suppose a player agrees to play for an entire season. They sign a contract to this effect. They'll be paid. The team can plan accordingly. It spends money to advertise this association. Then, midway through the season, the player switches to play for a rival. The first team loses a key player. It is injured because the contract was breached. In such a case, the government should intervene. It must examine who promised what to whom, and hold the contract breakers accountable. When people and businesses know that their contracts are indeed binding, then they can plan accordingly. Contracts are freeing. They enable constructive economic activity.

As referees, we can manipulate the system of points. We can

decide that each goal is worth one point, or that each goal is worth two points, or that each goal is worth only a quarter point, or that each goal on Sundays is worth three quarters of a point. Similarly, government officials can manipulate the money supply. We can decide how many units of currency to make, in effect controlling its relative scarcity and its relative value. We should strive to print just the right amount of money so there is enough for exchange while stabilizing its value. If we print too much money, the resulting *inflation* dilutes its value. It is a bit like stealing from the public since the purchasing power of the money that they've worked hard to earn begins to shrink in their pockets. If we print too little, the resulting *deflation* makes money scarce, increasing its value and discouraging buying. It is like putting a wet rag on the entire marketplace. So as referees, we should seek that Goldilocks level of making just the right amount of money, so that neither inflation nor deflation skews the economy.

As referees, we're paid in points just like the players. It is how we pay our bills, buy food and pay our mortgages. So while the games are underway, we extract a fraction of the accrued points for ourselves called taxes. We must resist the temptation to enrich ourselves to the detriment of economic activity. If we tax too heavily, workers and businesses lose their inner fire for play. If we tax too lightly, we won't be able to pay ourselves sufficiently or be able to buy referee uniforms and scoreboards and cameras. It is one more Goldilocks situation in that we should neither tax too heavily nor too lightly but just the right amount, and it is difficult to determine that right amount.

To complicate matters, games are always changing. New types of balls and hoops and goals emerge. A skateboard with improved wheels enables a new looping trick. A flying plastic disk enables a new sport. Composite flexible materials in baseball bats propel balls farther. Pickleball becomes fashionable. The world of economic competition is always changing, and our task as referees is to adjust to these changing dynamics as best that we can.

As referees our task is to manage the system as an integrated whole. It might happen that a game interferes with an adjacent game. Perhaps a noisy basketball game is next to a quiet tennis stadium. We must separate those playfields. Similarly, the activity of one industry can hurt another industry. For example, offshore oil drilling may hamper tourism, and as referees, we must find a way to balance competing interests.

Some games nobody wants to play. There are other games that players are unqualified to play by virtue of their status as players, or which are impractical for people to play because of the competitive format. Nevertheless, these games must be played. So the government must play these games. Scoreboards must be built. Security must be hired for crowd control.

Accordingly, the government runs the judicial system, hires police and firefighters, pays judges, builds courthouses, builds road networks, hires air traffic controllers, manages utilities such as water and electricity, and so forth. It does not make sense to have firms competing to distribute electricity to an entire region. The overhead wiring would be impractical and inefficient. Sometimes the government funds speculative scientific research that the private sector is unsuited for subsidizing, but which could be highly beneficial for future generations. The government is well suited to gathering information about economic activity, such as what people are buying, what things cost, what resources are available, and so forth; with such data, businesses and firms can make better decisions. Nevertheless, there are temptations for the government to intrude into the private sector unnecessarily. When this happens, corruption can fester.

A key task of economic management is maintaining motivation. As an economy grows richer, the incentive for hard work can lessen. Players don't need huge salaries. They've played the game and won the points, so it's not like the prospect of risking new business ventures is as appealing as it once was. So, how does a nation keep its workers and firms motivated? This is a general problem with no easy answers.

Inequality is a vital precondition for life. The unequal distribution of particles and energy is how life formed. Inequality spurs activity. It enables greater complexity. But it can cause problems. In a market-based economy, some will prosper while others lag behind. Since the government protects property rights, it must protect the rights of people who worked to earn what they have. With their newly earned wealth, it is possible for them to simply reinvest their earnings to generate even greater wealth. It is as if the rich are not really earning their additional profits, but rather their previous profits are earning the additional profits. Accumulated wealth can have a corrosive effect. It can make people lazy.

Too much inequality can be detrimental. It is not good for a nation if vast swaths of its citizens live in poverty or lack education or health care while a few bask in luxury. To deal with inequality, a government might consider redistribution, usually through tax policy. If the government transfers resources from one group to another, there are risks as well. It violates the idea of having a level playing field. Since the recipients didn't earn these transfer payments by working and creating value, it is possible for them to convert this transferred wealth into political power. It could be misused to bribe referees or to corrupt public officials to keep the transfer payments flowing even when they are no longer needed. Is there a right level of inequality, which is enough to sustain the needy without prompting corruptions of the system? It is a thorny calculus with no easy answers.

The point of this analogy is to try to demonstrate how *governing is extremely difficult*. A vast economy with interacting subsystems on multiple levels is a tough problem for managers. Most nations throughout history have struggled with the task of creating and maintaining a business-friendly climate. So it is somewhat miraculous when nations begin to get it right.

Humans as creators

The artist

Artistic creation is an important human activity. It is how we adapt to changing conditions. It is how we can enjoy life to its fullest. It is how we add to the beauty of nature. We create beauty. We write the *Epic of Gilgamesh* and sculpt the *Venus de Milo* and compose Beethoven's *Fifth Symphony*.

Humans are created beings. We are the product of countless iterations of the engine of creation, from quarks to carbon atoms to amino acids to single celled creatures to mammals to us. As created beings, when we make things, *we* become the creators. *We* do the creating. We create not just children but paintings and poems, books and businesses and sculptures and skyscrapers. Some of our creations are unique. They never existed in the universe, ever, anywhere, as if they emerged by magic.

Consider the *Mona Lisa*. In 1503, Leonardo da Vinci was commissioned to do a portrait of a wealthy Florentine businessman's wife, Lisa del Giocondo. Da Vinci focused his lifelong experience on this project, gained through years of intense curiosity and study and experimentation. From studying the dissections of human cadavers, he knew which facial muscles made a smile. He was familiar with optics, after having read a book on the subject by the Islamic physicist Alhazen.

Da Vinci used his human agency to make deliberate choices, in effect linking together his thoughts into longer and longer cause-and-effect idea chains. He chose to accept the assignment of a relatively obscure non-aristocrat, so that he didn't have a powerful patron looking over his shoulder to limit his decision-making. Free from such oversight, he chose to omit distracting elements like jewelry and fancy apparel. He began with a white underlayment and added layer after layer of thin glazes, so light would reflect back to the viewer from the lower layer. This rendered a glow as if her face was lit by moonlight. He painted the imaginary landscape behind her with a blurrier focus to foster the illusion of distance. He used the technique of chiaroscuro to contrast dark and light areas to foster a three dimensional feeling. By not aligning the background horizon line on the left and right sides of her face, it gave a viewer the sense that her shoulders were moving. He blended the edges between different colors into smooth transitions for a smoky effect, so when we look at her eyes, she seems to smile, and when we look at her mouth, she seems to smirk. This gave the *Mona Lisa* a beguiling quality: Was she smiling or laughing?

Da Vinci's masterpiece has bewitched viewers for centuries, including French kings, Napoleon, an Italian art thief, and millions of visitors to the Louvre.

What is instructive is to see the parallels between a star's creation and the painting. Both began with a concentrated 'hot' spot: the gaseous cloud of hydrogen and helium in the case of the star, and Da Vinci's lifelong accumulation of scientific knowledge and artistic skill in the case of the painting. Forces of attraction were at work. The gravitational attractions pulled together hydrogen and helium atoms to make the star, and Da Vinci's intense curiosity pulled together the information and skill to enable his artistic agency. Then each burst forth. A supernova created carbon. Da Vinci created the *Mona Lisa*. These created things had *never existed before*.

Then the newly created things became springboards for even more complex creations. Exploding stars helped create planets, our sun, the Earth, and eventually life including humans. The *Mona Lisa* inspired poems and books and films and later artists, as if the painting, itself, became like a star in its own right to spur even more creations.

To be an artist, we start with human agency, as if that's the primary prerequisite. But we need something more. We need a desire to create something new. Our human agency should be supercharged with a drive for creation. We strive to have what Da Vinci had: experience, concentrated knowledge of how things work, new insights and ideas, and exploratory painting techniques. We pull together disparate thoughts and facts and skills in the same way that a star pulls together its fuel. It helps to not only have an intense curiosity about the world, but to have traveled widely and to have a robust circle of relevant friends who themselves have good characters and have human agency. Concentrating these skills and knowledge takes time, sometimes months, sometimes years, sometimes decades. It might require studying with a mentor or working as an apprentice. An aspiring painter might learn about perspective theory and vanishing points. Knowing the rules, the artist is then free to start breaking them.

It helps to be healthy physically. A painter needs good hand-to-eye coordination and stamina and eyesight. An artist should not be stuck with imprisoning emotions. It helps to have sufficient resources. A painter needs paints and an easel and a canvas. An architect needs flat surfaces for drawing sketches and a computer. An entrepreneur needs venture capital. Creating usually requires a surplus of some sort, such as free time or money or supplies. It is difficult for a laborer earning minimum wage and working long hours to have the resources for creation.

Education is often vital. Painters learn perspective in art school. Entrepreneurs learn accounting in business school.

The process of creation

Creating demands mental concentration, a focus, and thinking in a rigorous and sustained way to imagine something new. We have an idea in our minds of something that does not yet exist, but could exist, and we have a strategy in our minds for the specific steps that we should take and in what order to create our imagined thing.

If we set out to solve a problem, it requires seeing, first, that there is a problem, and making such a realization is not always easy. For example, in the United States in the 1960s, many women felt a simmering resentment and unfulfilled longing about being second-class citizens. But they did not realize it until Betty Friedan wrote *The Feminine Mystique,* calling public attention to the "problem that has no name." By identifying the problem, it spurred rethinking and helped spark an expansion of rights for women.

With the problem identified and the question formulated, then thinking can proceed toward an answer. The mental state when an artist is actively creating is sometimes called *flow* which describes a heightened state of intense concentration and deep enjoyment. Their whole being seems immersed in the creative activity. They lose focus on distractions. The Italian inventor Tesla could imagine entire constructions in his head and even operate the imagined device as if it was physically in his hands. Flow happens when the carpenter mind and manager mind are fully engaged toward the same goal. The composer Mozart said "When I am completely myself, entirely alone, or during the night when I cannot sleep, my ideas flow best and most abundantly; whence and how these ideas come I know not, nor can I force them." Indeed, many artists can not explain how they went about creating something.

The act of creating almost always involves putting two or more things together in a new and unexpected way. Robert and Michele Root-Bernstein wrote that "Great ideas arrive in the strangest ways and are blended from the oddest ingredients." Creativity can mean figuring out a puzzle. The scientist Alfred Wegener noticed that the shapes of continents fit together like a jigsaw puzzle, and this led geologists to understand plate tectonics and continental drift. Graham Wallas said that insights can happen when we're not actively thinking about it, and then we have a flash, an "aha moment" when "happy ideas come unexpectedly without effort." When the illumination comes, it's certain, it's sure, it's an unexpected shift to a better story, and it happens to a mind that is ready to receive new thinking. For example, Darwin's mind was ready. He knew about the diversity of species, about how human breeders created variation in dogs and horses, and about Malthus' ideas on the competition for scarce resources. Then the aha moment came. He deciphered the puzzle of evolution.

Creativity may mean changing the frame or context in which something is thought about, by using the tools of thinking, such as exaggeration, contrast, logic, comparison, abstraction, pattern recognition, empathizing, thinking by analogy, building a model, synthesizing, transforming, and playing. It can be seeing what is missing. If the artist sees a gap in the path of a cause-and-effect relation, then that can suggest an insight into how to bridge that gap. If games are playful activities with rules, the process of creating art often breaks those rules. Flashes of insight can happen at unexpected times when the mind is distracted or resting or focused on an unrelated problem. There have been cases in which a solution to a scientific problem comes when the thinker is showering or waking up in the morning or doing a crossword puzzle.

Artists help us to celebrate beauty. They extend our sense of beauty beyond an appreciation of the human body, beyond our enjoyment of flowers and sunsets, to new things. Artists seek to make the world more beautiful. Emerson said that "to satisfy the love of beauty", poets and painters and sculptors and musicians and architects "concentrate the radiance of the world on one point." Kurt Vonnegut said that the arts were a "very human way of making life more bearable."

Art is not routine. It is about breaking habits and journeying to a new place. It often brings risk, since there is no guarantee that the time and effort expended will yield anything of value. The artist is like an explorer but there is no clearly marked path toward the goal, no road signs pointing to the destination. This could mean months and years and decades of wandering and going nowhere. While the artist may feel that their effort is worthwhile in a personal sense, the creation may not benefit anybody. It could all be wasted effort if the new technology doesn't work or if the scientific discovery doesn't happen. In the acting world, only a few hundred actors make enough to support themselves financially, while the vast majority labor year after year, hoping to be discovered, without success. Yet there is the chance that something wonderful might emerge, something valuable and fresh that lifts humanity to a higher plateau, like Da Vinci's *Mona Lisa*.

A random factor is luck. Sometimes an artist is in the right place and the right time for their creation to be observed and valued.

The place of creation can be important, such as a quiet desk for a writer, a warm studio for a painter, a lounge with nervous people for a comedian, or a lab with bubbling test-tubes for a scientist. The right environment can help an artist work creatively.

In business, product development teams sometimes engage in brainstorming. This is a free-wheeling discussion in which members bounce ideas back and forth, not criticizing any idea, encouraging more ideas to emerge. There are no bosses to please, no participants to inhibit the free flow of discussion, no premature judgments of the usefulness of the suggestions. The discussion is recorded while a facilitator keeps the group focused on the topic. Later, the group goes into a sort of editing mode, winnowing down the ideas to those few that are practicable. The group tries to mimic the mental processes that happen within a creative human mind.

In the artistic process, an artist takes diverse things or objects or story elements or facts or ideas, and plays with them, rearranges them, putting them into new patterns to explore new configurations. Yet at this point it is merely an assemblage of diverse elements. At some point, however, the materials coalesce into something new that has meaning and a structure that makes sense. The artist brings these materials to life. The work crosses a threshold of sorts to coalesce into art. It can still be honed and refined at this point but the essence of the creation is there.

Creations

If the created product is successful, it will have a transformative power in that it can take a listener or viewer or reader or audience member or consumer from a lesser state to a greater state. The recipient is better off. They know something new. They have a new insight or a deeper perception. They can travel to more places with greater comfort. The transformation makes life better, richer, deeper, more beautiful and more meaningful, and in this sense, art helps humans become unstuck, to have a greater imagination, and to be freer and happier. Leonard Bernstein said "Music can name the unnameable and know the unknowable." Art can help humans develop a state of serenity and wonder.

Since art is in the mind of the beholder, it can mean different things to different people. What is considered valuable varies considerably across cultures. However, there is an objective value of art in that other people may enjoy the creation and may feel empowered by it. While a child's crayon drawing might be appreciated by the child and the parent, it is unlikely to affect others, whereas the *Mona Lisa* often has a powerful effect on the viewer.

The something-the-same something-different formula often applies. This formula is another way of describing gradual Goldilocks-type transformations that are neither too abrupt nor too slight. If the created product is so radical that people can not relate to it, then it will be hard for them to be transformed in a positive way. If the created product is too similar to established products, it's boring. The something-the-same part is a necessary and familiar starting point which the recipient understands and feels comfortable with, and the something-different part takes them to a new place that may be initially uncomfortable but is fresh and invigorating. Both are needed. If it's only the same, it's routine and boring. If it's only different, people can not latch on. But having both means that the artist can grab a person at their current state and then lift them to a higher level of awareness.

In a song, an initial chord is pleasant to hear, with the individual notes resonating delightfully. We hear the harmony and enjoy it during that moment. It is a positive transition from the lesser state of not hearing the harmony to the greater state of hearing the harmony. Then the song progresses to a second chord, slightly different from the first chord, but similar enough so that we not only enjoy the new chord but remember the harmony of the previous chord. So pleasure is amplified. The enjoyment resonates upon itself, combining delightful sounds and memories, with the second chord, the memory of the first chord, the similarity of the two chords, and the mind's power to distinguish the change of chords, so that all of these impressions work together to enhance the effect. Our minds experience our powers of auditory perception. Music is enjoyment in motion, like manufactured happiness that combines past pleasure with present pleasure. It echoes the past in that we enjoy past transitions while experiencing new ones at the same time.

That might help to explain why art often references the past, not just in music, but in most forms of art. A new novel might reference characters from past novels, such as James Joyce's *Ulysses* referencing Homer's *Odyssey*. A romantic comedy like *Sleepless in Seattle* references the earlier film *An Affair to Remember*. Some video games reference Magritte's surrealist painting *Treachery of Images*, which shows a painting of a brown pipe along with the phrase "This is not a pipe." Raphael's fresco *The School of Athens* contrasts the eternal viewpoint of Plato with the practical viewpoint of Aristotle. The idea is to amplify pleasure.

Authenticity in a creation is important. A copy or a derivation of something previously created is relatively routine and does not advance the human experience, so that the something-different part is not included with the something-the-same part. Herman Melville said that "It is better to fail in originality than to succeed in imitation."

The best art is original and fresh and somewhat radical and captures some underlying truth about something. An abstract painting of a horse might not resemble an actual physical horse but the brush marks might capture the feeling of what a horse is about. The Bhagavad Gita advises against creating imitations of perfect works, and recommends creating original works even if they are imperfect. Emerson advised artists to "Be yourself, no base imitator of another, but your best self."

A HUMAN WITH OTHER HUMANS

Art has structure. If one is playing tennis, then the structure is the court, the rackets, the net, the lines on the court, the rules, and the game happens within that structure. If a player tried to play tennis without a net, it would not be tennis but two people hitting a ball on a solid surface. Art could be about breaking down the structure, or reacting to it in some new way, but regardless, the structural aspect factors into its value. A novel's structure is the sequence of cause-and-effect relations that make up the plot; a story with only random elements is not art except if it is trying to make the point that everything is random.

Art has a beginning and a middle and an end, a story, a delineation or boundary such as the frame around a painting. It is similar in some respects to a living entity, such as having an inside and an outside, and a lifespan. A completed artwork is like an organic whole with its various parts working together in harmony in patterns of causal relations that make sense, such that one couldn't remove a part of the artwork without lessening the whole. It has a focus. It means something. We can make sense of what it is about, even if the message of the artwork is that nothing is comprehensible. It often has a certain efficiency such as when a songwriter creates an ethereal melody by using as few musical notes as possible, or when a poet creates vivid images with only a few choice words.

Artwork benefits us. We learn something new. We grow. We expand our powers of perception. This is particularly true of literature which can help us understand the inner lives of other people. In a story, whether it is fiction or nonfiction, we can explore the minds of the characters. The exercise of studying the constraints and habits of constructed characters can help us develop the key skill of empathy. We can get a sense of why people think as they think. This can help to break down barriers of prejudice, although it can also reinforce negative stereotypes, depending on the content.

The human mind is predisposed to following stories. It is hardwired to follow the plot points of a story and to remember it, while it is more difficult to remember a series of random unconnected events. It is easy to retell a simple story to another person. Stories are not only enjoyable to listen to but they can teach us something. They often have a moral lesson of what to do or how to behave or what to avoid. They allow people to explore new places and to understand created fictional people in a safe way. They can expand our sense of what people are about. The novelist Willa Cather, when writing, described that she felt a "unique and marvelous experience of entering into the very skin of another human being", and her novels helped readers develop empathy for different people. The novelist George Eliot said that she did her best writing when she became someone, "not herself", that took possession of her, enabling her to identify totally with the feelings of her imagined characters. A good story takes us somewhere new, leads us on, teases us into wanting to know what happens next.

Fighting

Fighting, unfortunately, is part of our human nature. We hunted animals for food, so it was not much of a stretch to hunt other humans if they trespassed into our territory. We evolved from creatures which fought each other for mates and territory by inflicting deadly harm. While our evolutionary background predisposes us to sometimes act violently, fighting is a regressive act returning us to our primal roots, and it is not the best way for civilized humans to resolve disputes.

Fighting is not necessarily bad. The *Basic Principle of Ethics* can be interpreted to mean that fighting may be required in some situations. What is good, in wider spaces and longer time frames, as best that can be determined, may be to fight. What is vital is making the correct determination about whether to fight, and this can be a difficult calculation. To add to the difficulty, sometimes the decision must be made within seconds. It is a difficult transition to go from a peaceful state to a bellicose state, like going from bright daylight to darkest night in a nanosecond.

A HUMAN WITH OTHER HUMANS

Accordingly, it is important to know how to fight, and armed with such knowledge, one will be less likely to ever have to fight.

At every level of life, from molecules to cells to humans to nations, fighting means breaking apart, slicing through, chopping up, identifying a target and applying hard parts to soft parts, splintering and dividing, for the purpose of rendering the attacker unable to keep fighting. A cell fights a virus by hurling chemicals at the invader in an attempt to break it apart. A soldier kills by firing a bullet into an enemy. An army fights by invading the enemy's territory. All living things are organized systems, so fighting involves disrupting those systems.

The goal of fighting is to lessen, thwart, impede and cripple, with the end goal being to cause the fighting to cease, whether by running away or by struggling and winning. Fighting is rarely an end-in-itself because of the risk and the destruction involved, except perhaps in cases of professional sports such as boxing. In such sports, the goal of the fighting is to win without killing.

Fighting takes energy and consumes resources. When it happens, people and things are hurt and destroyed. The battling is a struggle to deprive the opponent of energy and resources. It is also a struggle to manage time more efficiently than the enemy. For example, in a war, one army will occupy a strategic hill to force the enemy to waste time maneuvering around the hill.

Fighting often involves reducing the complexity level of the living being from a higher to a lower level. For example, a human spearing a tiger to death causes the complexity level of the tiger to be reduced from a complex living animal to an assemblage of complex living cells; the tiger dies but its cells live on for a while later. Fighting is a dangerous and uncertain activity which brings a risk of losing or the promise of winning. There is a desperate urgency when fighting because the stakes can be life or death.

The activity of fighting should involve the entire organism. It should not have two minds or waffle indecisively but have a coordinated effort to subdue the enemy. For thinking beings, the manager-mind and the carpenter-mind should work in internal harmony to execute the fighting, and they should not be distracted or unfocused, with parts of the organism working at cross purposes from other parts. The degree of an organism's internal cohesion can decide the outcome.

Fighting is binary. It involves only two opposing combatants or groups of combatants, not three or more. In a situation with multiple combatants, with each of them hostile to the others, the combatants will take sides until only two sides are left. They fight. One side wins. If hostile feelings remain among the winners, the coalition may break apart into two sides to resume fighting. The logic, of course, is that *my enemy's enemy is my friend* since both are working for the common purpose of reducing their mutual enemy and, as a result, they side together. In the rare situation of an all-against-all fight, such as an out-of-control barroom brawl, there is usually another factor at work, such as confusion or inebriation or mistaken identities.

Fighting is a battle between opposing systems. Each system tries to disrupt the opponent, to break its boundary, to block its internal and external energy flows, to starve or suffocate it, or to confound its internal organization. Each tries to exert overwhelming force against a weak link, to find a choke hold, to apply pressure to block the enemy's system so that the enemy can not wriggle free. Fighting reduces both systems, but the one which prevails is the one which is reduced less.

Size matters. Numbers matter. Advantages such as these can determine the outcome. In most fights, big wins over small, many wins over the few, stronger wins over the weaker, youth wins over the aged, healthier wins over the sicker, smarter wins over the dumber, energetic wins over the tired, and nimble wins over the clumsy. A small creature such as bacteria can only kill a large one such as a human by invading and multiplying in such numbers by consuming the body's resources until the host is overcome. In battles between different species, each organism has evolved structures for

A HUMAN WITH OTHER HUMANS

attack or defense; for example, foxes have strong teeth and jaws, and rabbits have strong legs for hopping away.

Simple creatures have simple structures for attack and defense which evolved from the continuing trial-and-error of evolution. The microscopic hydra, for example, captures and kills food by paralyzing it with its poison-laced nematocysts and brings it to its mouth by tentacles, but it does not have a brain or muscles.

But creatures which can think add an entirely new level of complexity to their ability to fight. Planning is involved. There is guesswork about what the enemy might do, and how to counter it. It is as if both fighters have networks of cause-and-effect ideas in their heads which they are constantly adjusting as new information is learned.

So the fighting becomes in part a struggle between the thought processes of the two creatures, such that the ability to correctly guess what the other is thinking and planning becomes a strategic advantage. It can be a psychological battle to plant false ideas in the enemy's mind. The intent is to confuse or befuddle or becloud the enemy's understanding, or to make them afraid or overconfident. If one fighter can lodge an idea in the enemy's mind that fighting is fruitless or that victory is impossible, then that idea might win the fight.

Thinking clearly and correctly are important when thinking beings fight, since the mind must coordinate a variety of tasks, such as executing physical instructions to the body, perceiving what the enemy is doing, understanding the space where battling happens, planning possible responses to possible enemy actions, and trying to guess what the enemy is thinking and planning. A side task is recalculating from time to time the *Basic Principle of Ethics* in determining whether to keep fighting, whether to surrender or to flee or to claim victory.

For these reasons, it is easy for the mind to become overwhelmed. This is why disciplines that teach people to fight, ahead of time, through practice and repetition and study, such as judo and karate, can be helpful, since they lessen the amount of time needed to think through possible moves and reactions. The moves are rehearsed so responses will be speedy and sure. The mind is prepared and ready. The study of fighting technique is a way to concentrate time to maximize mental efficiency.

Good strategy in fighting often means taking gradual steps while forcing the enemy to take extreme steps. One walks down the stairs while forcing the adversary to jump down an entire flight.

Fighting is based on deception. So a fighter, when weak, appears strong; when alone, appears to be with friends; when weaponless, appears armed; when ready, appears disorganized. Sometimes a threat of doing something is better than really doing it, to deceive an opponent with false expectations. To enable a deception to work effectively, it may help to mix in some accurate yet irrelevant information along with the deceptive untrue content, so that the target will have more difficulty figuring out which is which.

That is a general sense of fighting, but fighting between two humans in a society brings complications. Society seeks to preserve the health and well-being of its members. While many societies encourage peaceful competition as a spur to action, disputes between competitors can escalate into violence. There are judicial structures such as courts to resolve disputes.

Humans are less likely to succumb to needless fighting when they have their act together and they have human agency. They are less likely to be insulted and are more likely to be forgiving and generous and to have better relations with others in society.

Nevertheless, such persons still need to know how to fight, since they are likely to come into contact with persons who don't have their act together. Misunderstandings can happen. A joke might be misperceived as an insult. When this happens, if there is time, then every effort should be made to clarify the misunderstanding, to apologize if that is warranted, and to try to use words and reason to de-escalate the conflict. If that is not possible, then physical distance can prevent fighting. If that is not possible, then attempts should be made to get the authorities to intervene, such as summoning police, or asking friends and family and fellow humans for assistance. If none of these options are possible, and if the other person starts the fight, then one must fight. There are no rules when fighting. As the saying goes, all is fair in love and war.

For the person of reason and virtue, fighting should be a last resort when all other options have been exhausted and when time and circumstances leave no other choice. It is right for a person to defend themselves. If, during the fighting, there are opportunities to de-escalate the conflict, or to avoid causing further damage, then these should be chosen.

Except in specific circumstances when the law can not intervene on a person's behalf, people cede the right of self-defense to the authorities. The state becomes the rightful entity to exercise force and justice and punishment. It is the task of individuals to follow the law, to honor the judgments of courts as they resolve disputes, and to respect the rights of others and those of the state.

Wisdom

Humans should strive for wisdom. It is not only how our species improves but how we can better our own lives. Wisdom is like a marriage of reason and emotion which combines the best of both. It is so bound up with goodness that it is hard to imagine a wise person committing evil acts knowingly and willingly. It is a key to life but it is not the whole of life; it is a good thing but it is not the only good thing. It happens when human-type understanding begins to approach god-type understanding, and it is not easy to get. We can describe the character of a hypothetical wise person, how they gained their wisdom, and how they make wise decisions.

A wise person is patient and calm, healthy with a hungry curiosity, highly intelligent, and a good listener. Zeno of Citium wrote "We have two ears and one mouth, so we should listen more than we say." They are often older; Benjamin Franklin observed that "Life's tragedy is that we get old too soon and wise too late."

Wise persons are keen explorers and competent communicators. They love learning. They try to learn from everybody. Ralph Waldo Emerson wrote "In my walks, every man I meet is my superior in some way, and in that I learn from him." Ben Zoma agreed, saying "Who is wise? The one who learns from every person." They have discretion. Benjamin Franklin wrote "He that would live in peace and at ease, must not speak all he knows or judge all he sees."

Wise persons have extensive knowledge of systems, and they understand how people fit into these systems. They have a good grasp of reality. They have a skeptical frame of mind. Gandhi said "It is unwise to be too sure of one's own wisdom." They know what they know, and they know what they don't know, and they understand their limitations. They study a subject from every possible angle, and try to learn about it from "persons of every variety of opinion", according to John Stuart Mill.

As Einstein observed, the more that is learned, the more exposure there is to what is not known. A wise person has self-discipline in that they can delay gratification, which gives them time to think before making a decision. They have self-mastery. Siddhartha said "Irrigators channel waters; fletchers straighten arrows; carpenters bend wood; the wise master themselves." They have a realistic assessment of who they are and what their place is in society. They are not proud. They have friends. They are tolerant of human weakness. They usually have a sunny outlook. They have reflective intelligence in the sense that they can remember their past thinking and behavior and use that to enlighten their understanding of a specific problem. They are smart and knowledgeable, and they strive to act ethically and to base their thinking on what they consider to be the wider-space and longer-term considerations of a particular situation. They try to see the big picture. They are willing to admit to their past mistakes; for example, the American financial guru Warren Buffett admitted in a letter to shareholders that he made a $3.5 billion mistake by purchasing a worthless shoe business in 1993.

A HUMAN WITH OTHER HUMANS

We can contrast a smart person with a wise person in the following way. A smart human has lots of mental connections, so that their brains can perform calculations quickly such as recognizing patterns and seeing analogies. They think quickly. But they may or may not act ethically. If they act ethically and make good decisions, then they may become wise over time. Intelligence is perhaps one of many prerequisites for attaining wisdom.

But perhaps the most important characteristic is that a wise person understands humans. They have empathy. It is almost like they can see within the head of another human and disentangle the knots in their thinking. They know how people succumb to emotions. Since they know that everything is determined, they are less likely to pass judgment and to find fault, and they are more likely to be helpful. They have an ability to see what's best for themselves and what's best for others and what's best for the community as a whole, pretty far into the future, so that their knowledge of people and things and systems has the effect of informing their decision-making.

If a wise person and an ignorant person were together, with both of them trying to understand something, the wise person could explain not only what the ignorant person got wrong, but *why* they had made an incorrect determination. But the ignorant person could not explain why the wise person thought as they did.

There may have been moments in their intellectual development when they grappled with a confusing set of circumstances and observations that didn't make any sense. Abigail Adams said that "The habits of a vigorous mind are formed in contending with difficulties." Persons find themselves confused by random-seeming aspects about something important for them at the time, and it bothered them that they could not figure out what was going on. Then they thought about it, applied logic and common sense, and then they had an *aha moment* when they figured out the underlying pattern. Instantly everything made sense. They felt joy in their realization. They learned to appreciate the power of their own mind and learned to trust it to figure out what's what. They developed a taste for learning, and they wanted to repeat their experience by finding out new truths.

As an example, suppose a young child learns that Santa Claus delivers presents worldwide on Christmas Eve by a flying reindeer-pulled sleigh. Naturally the child develops an intense curiosity about how this happens, while their knowledge grows about matters such as chimney widths and forest animals and the climate of the North Pole. How can reindeer fly without wings? Sooner or later the child will have that *aha moment* and figure out the real source of the shiny presents. Suddenly, everything becomes clear. The bedazzling complexity of the Santa story gets replaced by a simple and elegant explanation. Children who figure it out, without help from friends or siblings, learn to trust their own mind to figure out things, and they'll hunger for more such experiences.

In human history, wise people often came from affluent families. They were the sons and daughters of royalty and wealthy merchants, so that early in life, they got a solid education. But in their youth or early adulthood, they faced situations that forced them to see things differently. Perhaps they were homosexuals in a heterosexual world, or women in a male-dominated world, or fat persons in a thin world, or dark-skinned persons in a light-skinned world, or single people in a married world, or provincials in a colonial world, or members of the in-group shunted to the out-group. These situations radicalized them, allowed them to peer into hidden parts of society, so they could see through popular misconceptions. The Chinese sage Confucius lost his father at three years old and grew up hungry and poor. They often had unconventional approaches to living. They traveled. Abigail Adams said that "Wisdom and penetration are the fruit of experience, not the lessons of retirement and leisure."

During their lives, they sometimes made serious mistakes which brought considerable pain but not death, that spurred them to re-evaluate their flawed thinking. As the saying goes, good judgment comes from experience, and most of that experience comes from bad judgment. According to an ancient proverb, the wise learn from adversity, the foolish repeat it. Not only did they learn not to repeat their mistake, but they studied how their internal deliberations had caused them to make their mistake, and out of such experiences grew a respect for good thinking. Perhaps they isolated themselves for stretches of time to think, but not permanently; wisdom does not come to hermits meditating in a desert. Rather, wisdom comes from interactions with people.

A wise person is like a free human on steroids. Their passions are mostly controlled with no excessive love or hate. They are rarely beset with sadness. They are much less troubled by hopes and fears. Their focus is not on death but on life. They are free to attach themselves to things and people that benefit themselves and others, and they are free to break these attachments when necessary. They pursue their self-interest and the interests of society in a harmonious way. They have human agency. They understand how everything is determined and how they can get a greater share of the determining by informed wider-longer thinking. But compared to a regular free human, they know more, their thinking runs deeper, they can see around corners, they can see through false facades, and they have an enhanced ability to predict future outcomes.

While wise people can emerge from any activity, some professions tend to foster its development, such as military commanders in wartime, movie directors and entrepreneurs, judges, public intellectuals, heads of corporations and nonprofit organizations and large churches, and other positions of leadership. People in these posts tend to be smart, which is how they got there in the first place, and they are put in the position of having to make substantive decisions regularly for which they get feedback. If they decide wisely, they are rewarded; if not, they are blamed or fired or punished. Their jobs require them to become good decision makers, but it is not a guarantee that they will gain wisdom.

One arrangement can impair wisdom. Power, and more

precisely political power in the form of control over large numbers of people and vast resources, can have a corrosive effect on wisdom. Knowledge and intelligence can lift people into positions of power, but once they're in power, their earlier ethical constraints can fade in importance. They may find themselves surrounded by yes-men and sycophants who are unwilling or afraid to tell them the truth, and they may begin to live in an intellectual bubble of their own making. They may place too much faith in their own 'genius' and lose basic common sense and a respect for reality. They may become blind to the greater good. If they can keep their internal wisdom, then they can benefit humankind, and there have been cases when wise leaders rose to power and brought about good things. But in many cases, power brought out a ruler's negative underlying character. Perhaps the most dangerous humans throughout time have been smart men with human agency who lacked a moral compass, and who had disturbed and prejudicial ideas in their heads. They inflicted mass misery. People like Hilter and Stalin and Pol Pot caused millions of deaths and sent humanity backwards in horrific ways.

We can study how a wise person goes about making a decision. When a problem appears, they determine rather quickly whether it is a problem solvable by thinking. If so, the first order of business is to allot time for thinking. It is as if they hit the pause button while the movie of their life has been playing, in effect postponing the act of choosing. They stretch out the time between problem definition and action, as if they tell themselves, *let's think before deciding*.

An important initial task is framing the problem correctly: what, exactly, *is* the problem? This is where experience is vital. A wise person tries to identify the players and obstacles and variables and goals, as if they were mapping out the cause-and-effect sequences to locate the point where the flow of arrows is interrupted.

A tough problem involves uncertainty, but a wise person can manage working with unknowns by intelligent guessing, and seeking out further information. They have a sense of balance and proportionality, so they can use imperfect data to make educated guesses. They hedge their bets and weigh probabilities and apply common sense logic. They find workarounds when parts of the puzzle are too time consuming. They can handle the anxiety that sometimes accompanies uncertainty. They stay focused. They listen. They think through the problem.

Then, a decision is made. The manager-mind says *enough* and orders the carpenter-mind to *wrap up the thinking and choose.* There is a keen sense that the decision-making process can not go on indefinitely. The choice can be X or Y or Z, or to postpone the decision to a later time, to gather further information, or to do nothing. It may be wrong or right but it's the best that they can do.

If this seems abstract, an example might bring clarification.

Siddhartha was approached by a distraught mother carrying her dead baby who sought assistance to treat her baby's 'sickness'. From this story from the Buddhist tradition, we can examine Siddhartha's thinking process. He didn't tell the lady *hey your baby is dead, bury the corpse and get on with your life*. Rather, he paused to think. He used empathy to see the mother's mindset: *baby sick, find cure, baby healthy*. He saw how the mother's extreme attachment to her child prevented her from coping with its death. From experience, he knew that trying to reason with her would not work. He figured that the best way for her to cope with her grief was for her to have heart-to-heart talks with others who have grieved. He knew her mindset was ready for an easy-to-understand cure, and it was not ready for a complex explanation of why people die. So he told the mother to find mustard seeds from a household in which nobody had died. This focused her mind: *get seeds, cure baby*. Her quest would bring her face to face with others who had experienced tragedy, so she might begin to understand her own grief through conversations with others.

In another story, a wise teacher of ten year old girls dealt with a theft in her classroom. One student had swiped a calculator from another student. So she instructed the girls to form a circle with their purses behind them, and to keep their eyes closed. She walked around, feeling inside every purse, found the missing calculator, and kept hunting in every purse. When the students opened their eyes, there was the missing calculator on her desk. It was returned to its owner. The girls wanted to know who the thief was, but the teacher would not say, because she, too, had had her eyes closed. She fixed the problem without embarrassing anybody.

A wise person knows that our ability to help others is limited. If we give our meager resources to help another, then we may become needy. There is a risk that gifts may cause recipients to become lazy or dependent and in that sense giving may have a harmful side-effect. It is particularly difficult to help self-destructive people or to persuade them to stop harming themselves. A suicidal person is like an enemy unto themselves, which means that the two 'enemies' can not be separated physically. Efforts to keep a suicidal person alive can be expensive, and it puts society in a weird dilemma: Any restraints put upon them to try to keep them from hurting themselves essentially shackles their freedom.

The trajectory of humankind is toward greater knowledge and wealth. The quality of education today is much better than during Siddhartha's time. We know much more. We live longer. The general trend is for humanity to generate more and more wise people. Back in ancient times, when most people couldn't read, when education was severely limited, and when there was not much to know, there were perhaps a handful of wise people. Today, however, with mass literacy and extensive knowledge and formal education that continues from youth into young adulthood and then is further fortified with continuing education and digital communication technology, the numbers of wise humans will grow exponentially.

Humans and the environment

We are Earthlings. We evolved over billions of years to be who we are and what we are at *this* time and on *this* planet. This is *our* planet. This is our *only* planet. We are not fit to live on any other planet. The only possible way that we could live on another planet is if our bodies changed substantially to suit its environment, or we changed the other planet's environment to suit us, and neither option seems realistic given our present state of technology. To enable even a small outpost on the moon or Mars, humans would have to bring Earth-type materials along, such as air and water and energy, to fabricate an Earth-type environment there, and even then it would be a precarious existence.

Since Earth is our home, we need to take care of it. We depend on its air and water and lands and forests for our existence. If we pollute it, destroy it, heat it up or freeze it down, then we will have no other place to live.

By happenstance, by the inevitable workings of fate and time, humans have become the dominant species on the Earth. Our species won the genetic lottery. Our numbers are staggering, currently in the billions. We inhabit every continent. We have repurposed entire species of plants and animals to serve our needs for food and clothing and building materials. We breed dogs for companionship, sheep for wool, cows for food, and trees for lumber. Our activity makes entire species flourish or perish. With our brainpower and technology, we have invented weapons which can destroy cities. We can literally move mountains, tunnel through them, build submarines to explore the oceans and spaceships to explore the solar system.

While humans reign supreme in the animal kingdom, we are one type of creature amidst billions of other creatures, and we interact with them in exceedingly intricate ways. We eat some creatures and some creatures eat us. Living creatures depend on other living creatures. Plants harvest sunlight, some animals eat plants, and some animals eat other animals in vast networks which recycle energy. A change in one system can have numerous effects on other systems. If human activity causes one species to become extinct, then other species that depended on that species might become extinct as well, including species that humans depend on for food and materials and medicines. There could be a ripple effect of cascading problems. It is probably the case that the planet is better off with a wide diversity of species, and that less variety makes human existence more fragile. We are a link in vast interconnected food chains in which elements like nitrogen and carbon are constantly being recycled to support life.

Human influence is so powerful that it is easy for our activity, whether intentional or unintentional, to disrupt these systems, and to render the environment inhospitable. What we do or don't do today could boomerang negatively on future generations. If we cut down all the trees, then we can not build boats for fishing or fires for cooking, as the humans on Easter Island learned long ago. If we heat up the atmosphere by burning fossil fuels, the oceans might expand and flood coastal areas.

Human understanding of these interconnected systems of life is meager. We need to study them with intellectual rigor to understand what consequences our actions or inactions might have. It behooves humans to become responsible caretakers of our planet. The actor William Shatner played the role of a starship captain cruising the galaxy at the fictional faster-than-light warp speed, mingling with aliens. When, at age 90, he finally rocketed to space, his perspective changed. He felt that we were living on a "tiny oasis of life, surrounded by an immensity of death", that space was the "deepest darkness I could have ever imagined" and not the "welcoming warmth of our nurturing home planet", and he added that "Earth is and will stay our only home."

A human in a state

Political structures

The political structures that we belong to, such as our cities and states and nations, exist at a higher level of complexity than ourselves as individuals. Our ability to influence them is limited. Nevertheless, these structures can have a substantial impact on our well-being. Unlike a human's membership in smaller structures such as the family, membership in a nation has more of an official character.

It is important, then, to understand political systems, how they work, whether they're good, and to know how to interact with them. Sometimes the only way of coping with a bad political system is to leave it, although emigrating presents challenges. It is like cliff diving into the ocean because it requires exquisite timing and it could result in tragedy, but those who leap successfully can have a better life.

Generally the principles that apply to humans as individuals apply to the nation, such as the *Basic Principle of Ethics*. Good is what is good for the *nation*, in wider spaces and longer time frames, as best that can be determined. Its determinations, of course, are made by government officials. It functions best when officials engage in healthy thinking, and when their deliberations are fluid, open to diverse viewpoints, rational, not stuck, based on reality, not afraid, unemotional, and so forth.

Nations evolve. They learn from their predecessors. A nation is best suited for dealing with other nations at their same level of complexity, according to the *Principle of Similar Scale*. Nations prefer not-too-abrupt not-too-slow Goldilocks transitions. According

A HUMAN IN A STATE

to the *Principle of Accountability*, they're accountable to other nations. They try to exercise their national free will. They should strive to have a good character. Their foreign policy should usually entail telling the truth and keeping promises.

Political structures have evolved considerably since our ancestors began as hunter-gatherer bands about 250,000 years ago. Back then, tribes were usually led by a chief or group of elders. When humans invented agriculture about 10,000 years ago, everything changed.

The default political arrangement in agrarian civilizations was for a single human, almost always a man, to occupy the top leadership position. His rule was law. There was an underlying bargain in effect: people provide sustenance in exchange for protection. The arrangement could be symbiotic, in which both ruler and ruled benefit, or parasitic, in which the ruler benefits to the detriment of the ruled.

In ancient Greece about 2500 years ago, a new political structure emerged. Since the geography around the Mediterranean was mostly mountainous, various small city-states formed in small flatter enclaves. They traded with each other, exchanged ideas, and sometimes fought using a battle formation known as the phalanx. Each soldier's shield would protect the soldier to his left. The result was a powerful rectangular block of fighters who could knock a disorganized enemy off of the field. But the phalanx required tight cohesion. To motivate soldiers to fight cooperatively as a unit, men became *citizens*. They had a say in public affairs. States such as Athens that adopted democratic arrangements tended to thrive. Democracy established itself as a viable competitor to rival monarchical and aristocratic systems, although it wasn't perfect; women had few rights, and these systems tended to foster slavery.

Accordingly, out of random experimentation, gradually, by cause-and-effect, by further iterations of the engine of creation, humans began to figure out how to govern ourselves. They learned to resolve disputes with words instead of spears. They developed law as a fixed code applicable to everybody. Sometimes the best political thinking happened when rival powers competed, such as China during the warring states period, Greece during the Peloponesian war, and Italy during the Renaissance. Political ideas emerged about the benefits of representative government, constitutions, voting, elections, majority rule, jury trials, rights and citizenship.

The major political development of the past few hundred years has been the empowerment of the individual. Industrial age machines replaced serfs and slaves, rendering slavery as unnecessary. Humans developed new technologies and tools. Unlike the most powerful kings of the past, a person today can fly above the clouds, have a video call with a friend on the other side of the planet, and fight off diseases like tuberculosis and malaria and syphilis and cholera. We live longer with greater health and well-being. While there is more wealth overall, the fruits of human labor are distributed unevenly. Like everything, the solutions of the past bring new problems to the present.

It is perhaps a fair assessment that humans will continue to struggle with governing ourselves, and that it is likely that this will always be the case.

Political structures are complex, but we can break them down into essentially six types, while acknowledging of course that most structures are a blend of these types.

The six underlying structures include three good ones …

- A monarchy is rule by one person
- An aristocracy is rule by a minority
- A democracy is rule by a majority

… and three bad ones …

- A tyranny is rule by one person
- An oligarchy is rule by a minority
- An anarchy is rule by a majority

What distinguishes the good from the bad structures is whether rulers follow the *rules of ruling* and whether the ruled follow the *rules of being ruled*. Good structures enable a symbiotic relationship in which both rulers and ruled benefit. Each does its job. Rulers lead the nation, keep order, and manage defense. The ruled create sustenance and obey good laws. Both the rulers and the ruled support each other. There is harmony and balance and proportionality. They don't corrupt the operation of the other. Each follows the many principles of good living set forth previously. The *Principle of Accountability* is in effect: each is accountable to the other. If rulers fail at ruling, they can be replaced. If the ruled fail to obey good laws, they can be punished. Transparency is necessary so that each can judge whether the other is behaving properly.

Good rulers are farsighted. They focus on the long-term good, for themselves as rulers, for their nation, and for the public, as best that can be determined. They pursue the general welfare. They foster a framework in which people can make themselves healthier and wealthier and stronger and wiser. They do not waste the national treasury on fruitless projects. Monarchs do not imprison critics or behead wives for failing to produce a male heir or start ego-inspired wars. Aristocrats do not enrich themselves while starving the public. Good citizens do not pilfer public property or turn minority persons into their servants.

Bad rulers are nearsighted. They violate the rules of ruling. They elevate their personal interests above the national interest. They are not accountable to the public. They lie. They break their promises. Their nations are like a body in which organs, such as the heart or lungs or kidneys, are deprived of necessary nutrients, while the brain is flooded with extra resources. Such corruption weakens nations. If two nations are identical in every way except that one nation has a legitimate monarch while the other has a tyrant, the monarch-ruled nation will probably prevail in a conflict. Bad governments tend to be unstable and short-lived and fraught with violence and itchy for war. They are poorly positioned to cope with earthquakes and floods and plagues and invasions. While they exist, they are a nuisance for humanity.

Autocrats and dictators

Perhaps the most common political arrangement is rule by a single human. This is usually a man with a team of underlings to carry out his orders. Why has this been humanity's default political arrangement? Perhaps it's because it is so easy to happen. It doesn't require much thinking. People don't need to be educated. They don't need to understand concepts such as rights or fair play or majority rule or the law. Rather, it is as simple as a ruler pointing a finger and saying *do this or else*. So people obey. It is better than getting beaten up or fined or thrown in jail. To disobey an order is akin to challenging the ruler, in effect saying *I want to rule instead of you*. So people fall in line. There are no easy ways to hold the autocrat accountable for what they do.

For would-be autocrats, there is fierce competition for the top spot. The allure of ruling is so powerful that humans will resort to all manner of tricks and artifice and violence to win the throne. They kill their brothers, cheat their friends, and lie to the public.

In 1979 Saddam Hussein came to power in Iraq through a coup. He summoned Ba'ath party members to an auditorium. He claimed there was a conspiracy. Sixty-six names were read while Hussein calmly smoked a Cuban cigar. Each named person was removed; a third of them were later executed. He then congratulated the remaining members for their loyalty. They were grateful that their lives were spared. They pledged loyalty to Hussein. There is a video recording of the proceeding. The purge is a nasty example of the brutality of dictators, how they rule by fear, and how they diminish the collective brainpower of their own government by reducing any opposition.

When an autocrat is in power, they may revert to goodness, or cloak over their previous misdeeds with a veneer of propriety, and they may follow the rules of ruling to make good decisions in the wider-longer sense. But probably they won't. According to Confucius, good rulers elicit cooperation through ethical charisma, while bad rulers rule by fear. People rarely get to influence the character of their ruler.

A dictatorship has built in weaknesses. It is like a two-handed bully with one hand hitting itself. It is often the case that many people within such a society are exploited, forced to work against their will, so rulers need a second class of enforcers who don't really contribute much to the national effort. They are like prison guards, not making anything, with their primary job being to instill fear and mete out punishments. The workers probably contribute suboptimally since they never chose their jobs. They have few incentives to improve efficiency or invent new things. In comparison, a healthy well-ordered democratic-republican state has pretty much everybody contributing to the national effort, making things and growing, and so it is likely to be stronger.

It is especially dangerous in a dictatorship to speak truth to power. Any statement or gesture with a whiff of criticism can get the speaker killed. So communications should be avoided, or if they must be made, couched in indirect language. Political protests rarely work against an evil regime which controls the courts and the police and the law. An exception is when the regime has a moral conscience; for example, the nonviolent protest movements of Mahatma Gandhi and Martin Luther King Jr. were effective in improving their societies. Protesting can be scary. The American civil rights activist Rosa Parks confronted discrimination by refusing to obey a law about seating on buses; she said "I have learned over the years that when one's mind is made up, this diminishes fear." Tokugawa Yoshimune, a Japanese shogun, understood how people were reluctant to criticize, so he started an anonymous suggestion box so people could offer ideas, without fear of reprisal, to expose corruption and incompetence.

What is particularly dangerous is when all power is held by only one person who is the lawmaker, judge, jury and executioner, embodying both the secular and the religious authority. There are no moral restraints on their behavior. They can murder millions with the flimsiest of excuses. There have been few examples of bad leaders turning good, with a possible exception of Ashoka, the ruler of the Mauryan Empire about twenty three centuries ago. He was particularly brutal. His conquest of the state of Kalinga caused horrific loss of life, with body counts in the hundreds of thousands, causing the river Daya to run red with blood. But when Ashoka saw the destruction, he grieved, and he spent his remaining years trying to atone for the destruction.

Perhaps the deadliest regimes in human history were fascist or communist, in which a single bad ruler did the "thinking" for the entire nation, imposing their distorted and paranoiac views on national policy by their control of mass propaganda, as if to foist an unquestioning religious mindset into the political realm. This arrangement violates the principles of good thinking because it stifles dissent and internal debate which might have prevented wrongheaded ideas from festering. Things seem easy at first. There's less mental friction when everybody is forced to think one way. It is easier to prepare for war with an artificial uniformity of purpose. But things get hard soon thereafter. Such nations are dangerous in the short term but weak in the long term. Recent examples include fascist leaders such as Hitler and communist leaders such as Stalin and Pol Pot. The rule of evil men rarely lasts for generations, but when in power, they wreak havoc on humankind.

When rulers are good, even if imperfect, people should obey their commands, as if the ruler is the wind, and the people are like grass bending when the wind blows, according to Confucius. Rituals that encourage rulers to be good should be respected.

Hybrid structures

While the three good forms are better than the three bad forms, each of the good forms has strengths and weaknesses.

A monarchy is limited by the wisdom and resourcefulness of the monarch. If the monarch is a shrewd military leader and a skillful economic manager, then the state is blessed with good fortune. Much depends on the monarch's health; when the monarch dies, there is a risk of incompetent successors. When a government is ruled by a single person, there is a unity of command that enables nimble reactions to changing situations. Lengthy discussions and votes are not required for action, but quick decision-making can lead to mistakes.

An aristocracy solves the problem of the short life-span of a monarch. Since it is a body of rulers, when some die off, replacements can be added, so the body as a whole preserves continuity as incoming members learn from older ones. An aristocracy is like a "wise man who never dies", to use Tocqueville's description. Its institutional memory enables a realistic understanding of world affairs. Decision-making benefits from diverse views. How it deliberates is important; decisions will be better if they mirror the internal thought processes of a healthy mind, with thoughtful and reasoned discussions from multiple perspectives. Such a body is less prone to vacillation like a king or a fickle despot or a democracy. It can keep long-term commitments to allies. It can follow through on plans which take decades to implement. It suffers somewhat during a crisis when unity of action is required. It has a strong tendency to concentrate wealth within its own class while impoverishing the public, which can hamstring economic growth.

Democracies are good at advancing the needs of the majority. They foster a business climate that favors innovation and trade and personal growth. But they suffer in a crisis when quick action is vital. They require citizens to be educated and knowledgeable and capable of governing themselves. In war, citizens will be motivated to fight since it was their decision. There is the problem of the tyranny of the majority that can happen if the majority abuses its power to turn minorities into second class citizens, or if it stifles debate by imposing its worldview into the public sphere. Democracies work best in small nations or city-states when issues are simple and when people are well-informed. Even in a populous democracy with representatives, the problem of slow decision-making remains. In foreign policy, democracies can be short-sighted.

Accordingly, as civilization progresses, human societies continue to experiment with hybrid structures. The best hybrids combine the monarchic and aristocratic and democratic elements into a system so that the strengths of each type can offset the weaknesses of the other types. Each type should have its own sphere of influence. If each type, by itself, is brittle and weak, with glaring deficiencies, then a hybrid can bring flexibility and overall stability by balancing the flaws. If one power center becomes too powerful, the others can rein in the excess. This usually requires a constitution, usually written as a fixed general-purpose document, although it can be a shared understanding based on custom. It should be vague enough to cover a variety of problems, yet be specific enough to guide decision making in particular circumstances. Numerous hybrid forms are possible. As civilization progresses, whatever arrangements evolve should help rulers follow the rules of ruling, and help the ruled follow the rules of being ruled.

In an effort to identify an ideal political structure, let's start with a general statement. The greatest protection for a person is to live with virtuous persons in a state that is strong and well-ordered and good. Citizens make decisions based on reason and ethics. They are productive and skilled and focused on the long-term health of their fellow citizens and of their nation. The people and the government follow the *Basic Principle of Ethics*.

The standard by which we should evaluate a political system is what is good for us as an individual within that system. Structures which focus on the needs of the nation as a whole, while disregarding the needs of individuals, almost always benefit a ruler or a ruling elite. Systems such as fascism, communism, authoritarianism, dictatorships, and oligarchies are often based on altruism in the sense of one-way giving. Rulers in such states try to justify their power with the presumption that they know what's best for the nation as a whole, but they are human, and their personal needs are often entangled with those of the state. The result is corruption. To varying extents, such political structures are bad, particularly for people excluded from power.

Rights and laws and freedom and liberty

Good political structures empower individuals. They do this by supporting individual rights. While most people understand this concept intuitively, a definition may clarify it further.

A right is a power of an individual to act in the future which is understood and acknowledged beforehand by others.

First, there is a time element involved. The right exists in the present moment about something that might or might not happen in the future.

Second, a right is a shared understanding in the minds of people. It is a general acknowledgement in the minds of the person and others and the authorities that the contemplated future action is permitted. A person won't be prevented from doing it, and if they do it, they won't be punished afterwards for having done it.

Third, rights are powers in the sense that they are limited to what an individual might or might not do in the future. If a person has the physical power to jump up and down, then one could say that they may have a right to jump up and down if others permit it. But people can not jump unassisted above the clouds. They don't have the power to do so. So to claim that people have a right to jump that high does not make sense.

To illustrate, suppose a person wants to walk on the sidewalk. At the present moment, they plan to walk on the sidewalk. They have the physical capability of walking. At the present moment, as well, there are other people who have the idea in their minds that walking on the sidewalk is permitted. There is general agreement about this. The person won't be blocked or fined or tripped or otherwise punished afterwards if they walk on the sidewalk. So, one could say that such a person has a *right* to walk on the sidewalk.

They may decide not to walk on the sidewalk, but nevertheless, they have such a right.

Related to the concept of rights are the concepts of freedom and liberty.

Freedom is a mental state in which a person can think flexibly, usually in an organized fashion, linking cause-and-effect ideas into longer and longer idea-chains, usually with an aim of solving a specific problem or responding to some external situation for the person's betterment. It is the looseness of an unstuck mind, marked by openness and fluidity, like an uncluttered desk. To the extent that people identify freedom with God-type uncaused-by-the-past free will, the concept is confused; rather, freedom is better understood as the ability to make choices.

Liberty, in contrast, is a lack of restraint in a social or political context. It can be a physical restraint such as handcuffs or the bars of a jail. It can be a psychological restraint such as if a person is rationally afraid of doing something because of the threat of violence or repercussions from authorities. For instance, people who are detained by police do not have liberty.

Mostly freedom and liberty reinforce each other. A person with a free mind, who can go anywhere and read anything and talk with others of their choosing, who is not afraid to think, is more likely to have liberty. And a person with liberty has more opportunities to get accurate information about living, so they're more likely to have a free mind. Conversely, a person who has lost their liberty, such as a jailed convict, may find it harder to think freely because of the stress of confinement, since their ability to learn new things is diminished. Nevertheless it is possible for a prisoner to be mentally free while lacking liberty, such as the writer Aleksandr Solzhenitsyn, who wrote brilliantly while in prison. It is also possible to have liberty but not freedom, such as a mentally challenged person who has the liberty to walk about society but who has trouble thinking. If one had to choose between having either freedom or liberty, but not both, then having freedom is better because one can use one's mind to try to regain one's liberty, but a person who lacks freedom often lives a wretched life.

Generally, rights enable the liberty of free-minded people. A right clarifies possible future action, and that expands liberty. Rights are a fundamental building block of a good political system.

Rights in a general sense are intrinsically good to the extent that they permit future action, although specific rights can be good or bad, depending on the circumstances. For instance, one can think of a right to vote as being good in an intrinsic way, but the exercise of such a right could be bad if it results in unthinking voters bringing a cruel autocrat to power. One could think of a right to kill as being good only in limited circumstances, such as a police officer killing a violent criminal to prevent further bloodshed.

This is a simplistic understanding of rights, but of course the topic can become complex. Some rights depend on other rights. For example, one can buy a ticket to ride in an airplane, but being able to ride in that airplane depends on the person being suitably dressed and not being intoxicated and following rules about luggage and so forth. Further, the airline company may have a right to refuse service if the weather is inclement. Rights can depend on the context. For example, a person might have a general right to raise their hand, but if they are in a classroom, they may have to answer the teacher's question, or if they are at an auction, they may have to buy something. A right of jumping may not apply if one is on the ledge of a skyscraper. Some political rights such as voting depend on other political rights such as citizenship. There can be misunderstandings of which behaviors are permitted and which are not, such as what clothing one has a right to wear at a specific location such as at an office or at a beach. Other rights are contingent on other rights; for example, a stock option permits a buyer to buy a stock during a specific time for a specific price, but if the firm goes out of business, then that right may be lost.

To visualize the essence of rights, one can think of rights as a zone of future action that surrounds a person, like a bubble of permitted behaviors. A good society tries to expand these bubbles of future action as far as possible, which broadens liberty. Not only individuals have rights, but the state has rights as well. The rights of the state are its powers to act in the future that are understood and acknowledged beforehand by society.

The problem comes when these bubbles bump into each other that happens when rights conflict. For example, on a road, some cars wish to travel west and others east. Each driver has a right to drive but the road has limited space. The rights of westbound and eastbound drivers can bump into each other.

One can think of a law as a boundary between rights. It is the space between one person's rights and another person's rights. A person has the right to do whatever they want within their own sphere of permitted future action but they must not transgress into another's sphere. If this happens, then either one of the persons, or perhaps both, may be hurt in some way, perhaps physically or financially or psychologically. Their freedom to do something in the future is diminished. Since a law was broken, punishment might ensue. For the system of rights to work properly, people should respect these boundaries.

There are boundaries as well between the rights of a person and the rights of the state, and these boundaries are defined and clarified by the state's constitution and specified with statute law. Individual people can buy and sell things, travel, join volunteer groups, but they can't do other things such as park their car in a spot designated for public officials. Knowing these boundaries is freeing.

A common misconception confuses rights with transfer payments. A right allows activity that an individual can do for themselves, using their own initiative and resources, with the understanding that they will not be punished afterward for exercising their power. The idea of a free society is to expand these rights as far as possible, provided that they do not intrude on the rights of others. But some senses are confused, such as a *right to a job* or a *right to welfare payments.* The problem is that others must provide that job or that money, which reduces them to servitude and fosters an inequality of getters and givers. The underlying spirit of rights is that everybody should be treated equally and that the same rules should apply to everybody. While policies that redistribute wealth from one group to another can be good, even necessary, in some circumstances, they are more properly described not as rights but as transfer payments.

Generally, since laws clarify the boundaries of rights, they are good in an overall sense, although specific laws can be helpful or harmful, depending on the context, so the next section will try to describe the criteria for good laws.

Criteria for good laws

Good laws serve as boundaries between rights. If the *Basic Principle of Ethics* is a subjective assessment of what one person thinks is right, then law is more of a generalized assessment of what everybody thinks is right. The idea is to codify goodness, to maximize utility, to preserve the well-being of everybody, and to ensure fair and equal treatment. Equality is a key idea in the religion of Sikhism, which discourages legal preferences based on class or gender or race.

Good laws have the following characteristics. They are made indirectly by the citizens via constructive political participation, and are formalized by their elected representatives in the legislature. Good laws …

- help us plan
- are simple
- are clear
- are logical
- are easy to understand
- are easy to explain to others
- are consistent over time and space

- treat people equally and fairly
- help preserve peace
- keep people alive
- keep the nation alive
- expand personal liberty as much as possible

An example of a good law is the double yellow line down the middle of the road. It is clear and simple and easy to understand, that drivers should stick to their side to avoid an accident. It is easy to explain to people. There is a clear-cut logic of how it helps everybody, since it prevents collisions. It is consistent over time and place. It is fair that the road is divided equally. It helps preserve the peace since there are fewer fights after accidents. It helps to keep people alive.

An example of a bad law is daylight savings time. In some countries there is a seasonal adjustment made to the clocks, usually by an hour, to compensate for fewer hours of daylight during the winter. The law works against planning, since people have to change their habits. It would be simpler to keep the time schedules uniform and consistent. Moving clocks backward or forward twice a year introduces uncertainty. Most people can not explain the supposed rationale behind the law. The law might benefit school teachers who like to wake up earlier, while hurting teenage students who have trouble being fully awake on winter mornings, so in this sense, the law does not treat people equally. It does not expand freedom; rather, it is more of a lateral move, helping some while hampering others. Overall, it violates many of the characteristics of a good law.

So-called retroactive laws are almost always bad. Suppose a certain activity in the past was legal. But in the present it is declared to have been illegal in the past, so that people who did that thing, back when it was legal, "broke" the law. This is how autocrats operate, as if they mock the spirit of the law. When they don't like what someone did, they declare it to have been illegal, and punish them, and in such an environment, people don't know how to act safely.

What complicates matters is that the law itself is evolving, as if it is a living entity adapting to changing circumstances. The legal code should follow the principle that gradual change is preferred to radical change. A good way for it to evolve gradually is when past decisions are consulted before making new ones. A respect for past legal rulings, called *stare decisis*, promotes the gradual evolution of the law, fostering predictability, so that it is easier for lawyers and judges to guess correctly about how to assess an ambiguous dispute. It also gives judges the freedom to tweak the law when new circumstances arise, thereby keeping it in tune with changing times.

Accordingly there is a slight lag between the present reality and past legal decisions. For example, suppose there is a rule against wearing headphones while crossing streets, because they hamper the ability to hear oncoming traffic. Then smartphones become prevalent. It is a new technology. People text while crossing streets. Some get hurt. But there is no written rule prohibiting texting while crossing. With stare decisis, a judge can apply the old rule about headphones to smartphones as well, and thereby maintain the underlying consistency of the code.

Principles of a good state
Attention will now focus on the principles underlying a good state.

The basic idea of a good state is that it expands our sphere of possible future action as far as possible, by clarifying rights with good laws, and it protects people from each other, from the government and from foreign violence.

A good state has elements of a republic and a democracy, with both liberal and conservative aspects, united in a hybrid form in which the strengths of its monarchic and aristocratic and democratic elements counteract the weaknesses. The government is structured into separate spheres of influence so that there is not one power center, but competing power centers which check each other, allowing each center to contribute to the structure by doing what it is best suited at doing. Each power center has its particular function.

A good state has characteristics such as the following.

- A good state is based on the rule of law and not on the rule of persons, so that everybody, including public officials, are subject to the law.
- People hold power collectively with popular sovereignty. They are educated. They have virtue. They respect the rules of ruling and the rules of being ruled. They understand the privileges and responsibilities of citizenship. They have equal political power with the principle being one-person one-vote. They understand the wider-longer benefits of liberty and they will fight to keep that liberty.
- Branches of government are separate and distinct with clearly defined functions and zones of influence. One branch should make the law, another should interpret the law, and another should enforce the law. One branch should make domestic policy and another should make foreign policy. The branches should check each other to keep the system balanced. The legislature meets regularly. When policy preferences are debated publicly, no substantive viewpoints are excluded.
- Elections are competitive with no candidate having an unfair advantage such as incumbency. Elections are free from coercion and fraud and violence. They happen regularly. Candidates are elected by the principle of majority rule.
- The state has national agency, which is like human agency but on the national level. National agency entails the consistent and regular application of human-type free will to strive toward its foreign policy goals by the systematic linking of longer and longer cause-and-effect idea chains. The

state pursues its objectives with steady consistency. While everything that happens internationally is determined by past events, a state with national agency grabs a greater share of that determining for its own betterment. For example, a state with national agency does not let foreigners manipulate its elections.
- The nation is strong militarily or has powerful allies.
- The nation is a fierce protector of individual rights. It is skilled at catching and prosecuting criminals and upholding the law.
- The government is a competent manager of the economy.

A good state has a sensible judicial system. The essential purpose is to describe and clarify the boundaries between rights. Laws are generally agreed upon by the entire society, and written in a fixed format so that they can't be changed arbitrarily based on a whim. It helps if people respect the laws, and they're likely to have this respect if they feel that the laws are fair and just. They require good people, acting fairly, who have reason and common sense, to participate. People should not clog up the courts with frivolous lawsuits.

A good judicial system embraces the adversarial system. In the competitive battling between opposing views, truth is more likely to emerge, so courtroom deliberations should be like the thinking that happens within a healthy mind. Lawyers argue before hopefully impartial jurors while a judge oversees the process. Each disputing party has a chance to state their case. Rules guide the process; for example, there are rules for what types of evidence can be used. Defendants are assumed to be innocent until proven guilty. There are ways to appeal a decision. If defendants are found guilty, they are separated from society. Ideally incarceration should try to reform the behavior of convicted criminals.

Generally the death penalty is not a good choice, since everything is fated, so in a real sense, nobody is at fault. However, capital punishment may be necessary to punish violence that targets the state. If a criminal kills police officers or assassinates government officials or causes substantial loss of life or property damage, so that the state sees itself as the victim, then the death penalty may deter future violence. Every state has the right of self defense. So a justification for capital punishment is national self preservation.

There is a danger identified by thinkers such as Alexis de Tocqueville and John Stuart Mill called the tyranny of the majority. The majority controls public opinion. It controls the government. It has the power to impose its somewhat narrow ideas on behavior and thought. It can enable a majority race to disadvantage a minority race. It can enable one sex to disadvantage the other sex. A good state should respect that all individuals are unique and worthwhile, and not punish people whose ideas differ from that of the majority. It should establish legal protections for minorities. John Stuart Mill wrote that "Mankind are greater gainers by suffering each other to live as seems good to themselves, than by compelling each to live as seems good to the rest."

There are sad examples from history when states punished people for thinking differently. Athenians killed Socrates on judicial grounds for "impiety and immorality". Romans killed Jesus as a "blasphemer". Any government that thinks that it knows what is best, and uses its coercive political power to enforce its thinking, is illegitimate, according to John Stuart Mill. It deprives itself of contrary opinions which, if they're right, can help everybody, and which, if they're wrong, are helpful still because they prompt a reevaluation of why the good ideas are indeed good. It's as if bad ideas *test* the good ones, and in the testing, good ideas emerge stronger because of the testing. Accordingly, a good state should try to protect the views of individuals, and it should permit free speech as much as possible.

These are some characteristics of an ideal state. To the extent that a nation has these characteristics, it is good, and life is better for those individuals within them. Like any arrangement, an ideal state has strengths and weaknesses.

Strengths of a good state are as follows:

- It enables human flourishing. Since a good state encourages economic opportunity, people can find good jobs and have time for art and the enjoyment of life. It fosters intellectual growth and expertise. People have better health care and they can live longer and better.
- It is likely to be strong militarily. Its affluence allows it to buy effective weapons. Its soldiers are motivated to fight for their liberty. In contrast, soldiers of an autocracy are less motivated to keep the ruling party in power.
- It has moral force. Such a nation is likely to be kinder to people everywhere. By emphasizing human rights, it can steer world opinion in a positive direction.

Weaknesses of a good state are as follows:

- Complexity. A good state depends on complex subsystems working in harmony, which is difficult to maintain. With diverse moving parts, more things can go wrong.
- It depends on people being good, and people are not always good.
- There is a risk of corruption. There is a continuing temptation for elected leaders to heap unfair advantages for themselves. Citizens can be distracted from their civic responsibilities. Wealth can have a corrosive influence, making people lazy.
- The transition from peacetime to wartime can be difficult. It requires a society-wide shift from an individual rights orientation to a group rights orientation, from personal betterment to fighting. It is easier for states which don't value individual rights to shift to a wartime orientation, since people have been accustomed to obeying orders without question.

- A policy of tolerating diverse views allows bad ideas to enter the political discourse. These are ideas which advocate an end to all free speech or the violent overthrow of the legitimate government, or that claim falsely that elections have been rigged. It is not always an easy calculation; for example, speech advocating the violent overthrow can be good if the government is indeed bad and should be overthrown.

That such a state is a nation of laws and not of people is both a strength and a weakness. It is a strength in that it may check the power of ambitious malcontents who seek to subvert the system, since if they break the law, they can be punished. But it is a weakness in that the law is a complex concept, easily misinterpreted. Sometimes the law seems like only words on a page that don't gel into actionable ideas. It is easier to be loyal to a human giving easy-to-follow commands who can reduce the complexity of legal understanding to simple statements such as *do this and do that*. So confused humans, seeking to know what to do, with an incomplete understanding of the law, may find it easier to choose the simpler yet more dangerous course of obeying the autocrat.

A vexing problem confronting every state is how to keep officials honest. Officials are emotional beings like everybody else, with personal needs and illusions and limited intelligence. Ideally there should be a harmony of purposes so that officials focus on the betterment of the nation as well as on their own personal betterment. According to Abigail Adams, "Among all the causes which degrade and demoralize men, power is the most constant and most active."

A way to keep officials honest is to have competing power centers. So if one branch of the government becomes too powerful, the others can rein in its officials. Transparency is helpful. Public officials should be subjected to an intense level of scrutiny of their financial dealings. Term limits and the periodic shuffling of officials into different posts can forestall corruption that festers from entrenched positions of authority.

Citizenship

A good state connects the people with the government. People listen to leaders, and leaders listen to the people. This two-way connection underpins popular sovereignty and allows the public to control their destiny collectively through human-type free will. It is analogous to a healthy human in which the body and the brain sense each other's needs.

A successful state needs virtuous citizens. Without them, democratic self-rule doesn't work well. The ideal citizens are rational thinkers with human agency who understand and respect their roles as citizens, and who work collectively to preserve the virtue of their fellow citizens. Since knowledgeable citizens are better able to see the wider-sphere longer-term consequences of their decisions, the state should encourage public education, including civics.

Citizenship is a relation between a human and the state. It is like glue which binds them together. Citizenship entails:

- Active political participation. Citizenship should be more than a badge of national membership. It is a commitment that requires time and effort. Citizens meet periodically with representatives, stay informed about current events, subscribe to legitimate news media, and vote.
- Military service. A citizen promises to serve in the armed forces if summoned. Having liberty means being ready to fight to defend that liberty. Linking citizenship with military service strengthens the government, since it knows that it can count on citizens to serve if necessary. The nation can respond to external threats as a unified entity rather than as competing factions.
- Acceptance of the core values of good government. Citizens value the peaceful resolution of disputes with words and arguments rather than fisticuffs. They tolerate opposing views. They believe in individual rights and equality and

free and fair elections. They serve as fair and impartial jurors. They respect the law. They pay taxes.
- Citizens hold the government accountable if it misbehaves. If it makes bad decisions, citizens must protest them.
- Citizens protect fellow citizens. If the government becomes abusive, perhaps by neglecting due process, overtaxing people, making unjust decisions, or appropriating private property without justification, then citizens have a duty to protest such decisions, particularly when the government focuses its firepower on a single individual or a small group of individuals. Since the government has a monopoly of armed force and controls the justice system, the only real defense against an abusive government is the vigilance of fellow citizens.
- If citizens become public officials, they must serve responsibly. They must try to make choices which benefit the entire nation, not just their friends or family members or a particular group.

The state has duties as well:

- The state must protect the individual rights of citizens. It must defend people from external attack, protect their property, and punish lawbreakers. This duty extends to protecting private citizens who visit foreign nations, as well as protecting law-abiding visitors from foreign nations.
- The state must treat all citizens equally in terms of due process.
- The state must recognize the right of citizens to protest peacefully.
- The state must respect the rules of ruling by holding free and fair elections periodically, following the constitution, enforcing justice, and so forth.

It is important that citizens pay for subscriptions to legitimate news sources because it sets up a financial obligation for journalists to tell their subscribers the truth. With funds from subscribers, journalists have the financial means to investigate politicians and governments. There should be rival newspapers competing to find the best information.

Since citizenship entails commitments, some may choose not to be citizens, and there should be a place in society for them. But non-citizens should not be able to vote or hold public office or serve on juries. The proper arrangement is to link privileges with duties, so that the privilege of voting is linked to the duty of possible military service. It is not fair for citizens, who bear the risk of having to fight in a war, to have their nation's policies influenced by non-citizens who do not bear such a burden. Still, non-citizens should be treated as fairly as possible. It may happen that a person at some time in their life may be a citizen, and at other times not a citizen. Their status can alternate based on circumstances. People should have opportunities to petition to be either citizens or non-citizens, with formal procedures governing such transitions.

In every society, forces push people away from political participation. People tend to avoid debate since it can entail a conflict of ideas, and people tend to avoid conflict. There is a continuing temptation to let others do the work of citizenship while one enjoys the common good of a functioning political system. Therefore, it is an important responsibility of citizens to monitor the commitment of other citizens. If fellow citizens are not staying informed, not meeting with representatives, not voting, or shirking jury duty, then their citizenship status could be challenged. It should be possible for one citizen to challenge the citizenship of another citizen in a legal forum if their commitment lapses.

Public debate between private citizens, between citizens and officials, and between public officials is how a nation thinks. It is good in a general way. In the Jewish tradition, differences of opinion are appreciated and encouraged. There are exceptions such as when fast action is needed during an emergency, or when the debate itself becomes nonsensical pollution with a devious purpose, distracting attention away from serious matters. A debate for the purpose of ending all public debate can be bad. Healthy debate begins with persons who have rational-critical discussions within their own minds. They are free people with human-type agency. They care about public life. They can express themselves by speaking and writing. They are good listeners. They have a tolerant mindset in that they know that they don't know everything and have an open-minded appreciation of what they don't know. They are willing to learn. They are able to handle uncertainty. They understand their roles as citizens. They have the ability to persuade others to adopt their point of view, with calm, reasoned arguments. As Charles Martin once wrote, words that soak into one's ears are whispered, not yelled.

The idea of the public sphere is a space between the government and private citizens where people can meet, exchange ideas, and discuss public policy. It is not only a physical space such as coffee houses or public streets or town meeting halls, but an intellectual space where people write letters on the Internet or answer public opinion polls or post comments on social media. It allows people to criticize government policy and to organize peaceful protests. There are temptations for business interests to invade the public sphere for commercial purposes, such as using political polls to tout skin rejuvenating products. The public sphere is a fragile zone which needs legal protection from such encroachments.

It is particularly important that constructive debate happens in more formal settings such as in legislatures. Healthy public discussion should mirror what happens within a healthy human mind. There should be flexibility and a diversity of views and a rational-critical assessment of facts. It should happen at a place conducive to communication with no loud interruptions or visual distractions, and at a convenient time. There should be a respect for alternative views. People should be able to separate the view from the person holding the view, so that when debating, the views are criticized but not the person holding the views. So-called *ad hominem* attacks do not belong in healthy discussions. There is a risk that egos may be hurt if people are proved wrong; as much as possible, people should try to see participants and their views as separate. Participants should have a sense of each other, such as who they are and how they relate to the discussion. There should be no hidden agendas. People should not present a false front about their motives. For example, a speaker should not advocate a public construction project while disguising the fact that they are a contractor who might benefit from such a project.

The discussion should be characterized by give-and-take. It should keep moving forward so that as it progresses, issues become clearer. While there may be setbacks and distractions, the general direction should be toward greater understanding. The discussion should not get stuck. If the same idea is presented again and again, or if one or more participants latch on to one idea and refuse to consider others, then progress may stall. Discussion is healthier if diverse views are presented, including contrary ones, since this improves the chances that the best ideas will emerge.

Participants should become competent at persuasion. They should know how to craft arguments that are clear and concise and follow the rules of thinking based on cause-and-effect, logic, analogy, comparisons and so forth.

A parallel between a healthy mind and a healthy discussion is that in both processes there is a controller function to keep the thinking focused. Instead of a manager-mind to regulate the carpenter-mind, the discussion might have a moderator, such as a parliamentarian in a legislature or a judge in a courtroom. Their task is to keep the discussion moving forward in an orderly, disciplined way, making sure that what is said stays relevant to the subject. They try to prevent individuals from dominating or derailing the discussion. A way to record the discussion could be as informal as people remembering what was said, or more formal with a secretary summarizing major points in a transcript. There should be agreement about how a decision might be reached, whether by a vote, a consensus, or a third party judgment.

In a formal meeting, such as in Congress or Parliament or in local government, the topic should be important enough to merit discussion and yet be ambiguous in the sense that there is a lack of clarity about what to do. The topic should not be trivial in nature or be an easily answerable matter of fact. It should be about a subject that affects people and that can be addressed or fixed by human action.

Arguments can be constructed from parts to a whole, or from the whole to a part. An example of a parts-to-whole argument is (1) trees prevent soil erosion (2) trees provide shade (3) trees are aesthetically pleasing (4) trees require minimal upkeep (5) trees are inexpensive to plant, so, in conclusion, the town should plant more trees. An example of a whole-to-parts argument is that trees are good, so, in conclusion, let's plant ten trees at this park and fifteen at that park. Arguments can be made using probabilities, correlations, syllogisms, categorical statements, associations, definitions, logical subsets, and other types of reasoning in which premises lead to conclusions. It helps if points are made in an orderly manner so that listeners can follow them. Evidence may include facts which support claims, eyewitness testimony, statistics, and opinions from experts. It helps to bring in credible sources when issues are complex; these include unbiased persons considered to be trustworthy who know about a given issue, and who have provided reliable evidence in past deliberations.

Bad arguments should be avoided. These include arguments that confuse a surface symptom with an underlying cause, or ones that ignore contrary facts and evidence. Arguments should not confuse correlations with cause-and-effect relations. Vague terminology should be avoided, along with *non sequitur* claims in which there is no connection between the claim and the evidence. Irrelevant distractions or so-called *red herring* arguments waste everybody's time. Arguments that appeal to authority, when it is not the authority's area of expertise, should be avoided. Arguments that assert that because everybody does something, that it's the right thing to do, sometimes called the *bandwagon effect*, should be avoided as well. Emotion-laden appeals do not belong on issues when rational-critical reasoning is needed. So-called *false dilemma* arguments claim that there are only two options, when there are more options. A *straw man* argument sets up an artificially weak version of an opposing point, making it too easy to refute. *Circular reasoning* or *begging the question* arguments involve simply assuming what one is trying to prove, like restating the conclusion as if it was the evidence for the conclusion.

Arguments should be settled in such a way that the participants view the decision as legitimate. Maybe there is a vote, or a judgment from a jury or from an administrator. One position may be adopted, or not adopted, or maybe a decision is postponed for later review. All decisions are imperfect since they are made by humans who have incomplete information. So a difficult aspect of any decision-making process is knowing how much information to get before deciding. Deliberations can not go on endlessly. It may be necessary to review a decision at a later time when more information becomes available.

The competition of ideas creates tension which wants to resolve itself to a less-tense state. Something similar happens in music when an odd chord wants to resolve itself back to a harmonious one. Humans can handle tension in short bursts, for brief stretches, but it becomes more difficult if tension persists. It is natural for people to avoid tension or seek ways to prevent it from arising. There is a risk that people in a political discussion will skirt around an issue or subvert discussion or walk out of a meeting as a counterproductive way to resolve this tension. In courtroom battling there is an undercurrent of wanting a trial to be resolved soon, along with an unstated resentment of having to judge something that one is not interested in judging. Such forces can push courts to end trials prematurely, and they can push people away from politics. So a good state should manage these tensions and encourage participation.

Public discussion requires many things to go right for it to work properly. It is a complex system with many vulnerabilities. It is good when it works right. If a nation can get into a habit of constructive discussion, then people can govern themselves. The process can be self-reinforcing if it continually teaches people how to do it right.

The rights of states

States have rights just like people. The state has a right to exist and to do those things that preserve its existence, and these rights are an understanding now, in the "minds" of other states and in the minds of people, about what it might possibly do in the future. It is a bubble-like sphere of possible future action in which it is acknowledged, beforehand, by citizens and officials and visitors and foreign officials, what the state can do and what it can't do. What is generally good for all living entities, including humans as well as states, is for these spheres of possible future activity to be as wide as possible, and yet delineated by clearly drawn boundaries.

Boundary lines vary:

- The boundaries between two private individuals are **laws.**
- The boundary between an individual and the nation is a **constitution.**
- The boundaries between nations are **treaties and international law**.

It is customary, in the chain of complexity, for higher-up entities to draw the boundaries between lower-down entities. So a higher-up government makes the laws governing relations between lower-down citizens, such as making rules about highway driving. An international governing body such as the United Nations makes international law between nations. A measure of a government's authority is the extent to which it can enforce respect for the boundary lines that it draws.

It is good when a nation and its internal subsystems have shared values. The nation wants to live. The people within the nation want to live and they want their nation to live, and both the nation and the people are in agreement about how to do this. People respect the rights of the nation, and the nation respects the rights of the people, and there is wide freedom for each to act within its proper sphere of influence, fostering harmony and productivity.

In a vibrant economy in which citizens engage in peaceful competition to make goods and provide services, activity can sometimes devolve into violence. Humans are tempted to exploit other humans by fraud or slavery or serfdom, and it is the state's task to prevent abuse. In the true nature of things, everything is fated to happen so that nobody is ultimately at fault, but in the practical world, people are accountable for their actions, and it is the task of the state to assign blame and punish lawbreakers.

Regulatory issues

While the state is supposed to maintain law and order, prevent violence, preserve itself, and protect the lives and property of its citizens, there are issues which can confound how it goes about these tasks.

Since the human brain has neurochemical circuitry which regulates pain and pleasure by using chemicals such as dopamine and cortisol, it is possible to tamper with these systems with drugs. In some situations, they can be helpful by relieving pain and heightening pleasure. Morphine can minimize pain during surgery. Other drugs can help artists expand their powers of creativity and perception.

But some addictive drugs rewire the neural circuitry so drastically that the user becomes enslaved by the drug almost instantaneously. The brain is reprogrammed to want only the drug.

According to Roger Scruton, "Addiction is a function of easy rewards – the addict is someone who presses again and again on the pleasure switch, whose pleasures bypass thought and judgment to settle in the realm of need" that causes a "short-circuiting of the pleasure network." Such persons no longer enjoy eating or sleeping or watching a sunset or making love but they only want the drug. Other drugs present an escalating risk of an overdose, as if taking the drug for the first time brought about one's eventual suicide.

Drugs present a nagging regulatory dilemma. If the state restricts drugs too tightly, it lessens freedom by excluding their positive uses; if it restricts them too narrowly, people can become addicted. Banning popular and mostly safe drugs makes them scarce, raising their price twentyfold, enabling a criminal industry to fester to satisfy demand.

The key test for where to draw the line between whether drugs should be legal or illegal is whether their use leads to violence. If that happens, the state has a rightful duty to prohibit cultivation and manufacture and sale and distribution and use, since prohibition is an attempt to prevent a predictable future crime. Conversely, if a drug does not lead to violence, it should be permitted. The state should encourage education about drugs, and it should treat addiction as a public health issue rather than as a criminal issue. It makes sense to avoid blaming addicts for their condition, and to help them cope as efficiently and painlessly and inexpensively as possible.

A good state protects people. That should be its primary concern. It prevents violence. It keeps people alive. A state needs to be excellent at this task. A secondary task is expanding freedom by empowering people, expanding their rights, and defining and clarifying the limits of their rights through law. So people are free from fear and anxiety, knowing that where they go, what they do, what they say and who they meet, how they make money and so forth will not cause them physical or financial harm.

Problems arise if a state goes beyond these primary duties and takes on tasks for which it is ill-equipped to do. A state should not legislate morality. It should allow a wide range of nonviolent behaviors and attitudes. It should allow people to believe whatever religion they wish, including of course atheism. It should allow most forms of sexual expression, including infidelity and homosexuality and gender switching, and it should allow diverse unions between consenting adults. It should allow unconventional forms of art and music and dance, as well as most forms of political expression. If a state tries to enforce a particular code of behavior or criminalizes nonviolent rituals or jails people who engage in bizarre yet harmless sexual practices, then it stifles freedom and liberty.

The only reasonable boundary between permitted and prohibited activity is whether it leads to violence. That is where the state must draw the line. It should prohibit violence in every form, including murder, theft, and rape, as well as threats to commit such actions. As John Stuart Mill wrote in *On Liberty,* "The only purpose for which power can be rightfully exercised over any member of a civilised community, against his will, is to prevent harm to others. His own good, either physical or moral, is not a sufficient warrant." A good state should not impose its peculiar ideas of what is good on individuals. When violence happens, the state must determine what happened, catch and punish the perpetrators, and try to undo the damage as much as it can. It does this by physically separating violent people from peaceful people.

The state must have a monopoly on the use of force within its borders. It needs this power to do its job of preventing violence and keeping order and protecting against invasion. Without this power, it isn't really a state but is more accurately described as a disorganized political entity. The implicit bargain is that we give up most of our rights of self-defense in exchange for safety.

A state that allows private citizens to own guns is a confused arrangement. Gun ownership allows a private citizen to become, in effect, a police officer and a prosecutor and a judge and a juror and an executioner, all bundled in one dangerous alternative mini-government. A good state separates these functions, so that a police officer is one person, a prosecutor is somebody else, and so on, and the different people can check each other and administer justice from different perspectives. By separating these tasks, a good state brings more people and more thinking into the various stages of justice, from identifying a criminal act, to apprehending the perpetrator, to proving a legal case, and to assigning punishment. But a single armed private citizen can speed through the judicial process with a quick squeeze of a trigger. They can impose a death penalty on somebody that they don't like. Gun ownership fractures the state. It complicates the job of legitimate police officers. It enables mass killing. It is bad.

Gun ownership is not really a right because it violates the right of the state to protect people and administer justice, and it violates the rights of other citizens to life.

The proper way for people to protect themselves from nasty neighbors is a state skilled in violence prevention. The proper protection from government abuse is by fellow citizens exercising political power for mutual self-protection. This is one more reason why it is vital for citizens to control the government. Every individual is vulnerable to government predation. An arbitrary attack against one citizen is an attack against everyone. So we must watch the government and keep a vigil on its actions.

A good state manages two conflicting responsibilities: protecting people while safeguarding their privacy.

To protect people, the state has a duty to monitor public places. The state should be able to see what people do outside of their homes, such as who they are, what they buy, where they go, who they meet, what they send through the mail, what they own, and so forth. The state needs this information to prevent fraud and violence as well as to punish transgressors. When it can't monitor internal activity, people get hurt, property gets stolen, justice is stymied, and the innocent are sometimes punished by mistake.

At the same time, people need privacy. It is a bulwark of personal freedom. There are nonviolent and legal actions that a person might do but which may elicit public disapproval, and the fear of exposure might prevent them from doing those things, in effect limiting their freedom. A planned activity may be acceptable in one context but not in another; for example, employees who party with friends after hours may not want their employers to know about this activity, and the fear of exposure might inhibit their partying.

A good state, accordingly, must harmonize safety and privacy. One arrangement is if the state gathers information about public activity but locks this information behind a secure privacy fence. Investigators need this information. But nosy neighbors, friends, employers, journalists, medical insurers and others do not need this information. So what people do in public can be tracked and recorded by impersonal cameras and computers, but access to this information would require permission from a judge. So if violence happened, investigators could get permission to query the databases to learn what happened. To prevent abuse by investigators, their searches of the databases would be tracked and recorded as well. So breaches of privacy by officials could be exposed and punished. A society-wide security system could drastically reduce crime and make it safe for people to travel virtually anywhere in public, at any time of day or night, without fear, secure in the knowledge that their public activity would remain private. To bring legitimacy to such a system, citizens must have political power so they can ensure that it serves the dual functions of preventing crime and protecting privacy.

Violence
Violence is an attack on individual rights.

Violence is trespassing from one's permitted zone of possible future action into another's permitted zone of possible future action. It is breaking a law. It causes injury. It is a threat not only to the victim but to everybody's safety, so it can not be left unpunished. Simply, violence is bad, and force used to counter violence, is good.

If we look into the mind of a violent person, there is a form of stuckness, a rigid non-thinking behavior as if their rational mind is no longer working, or as if their manager-mind has crashed like a computer in an infinite loop. It thinks, by mistake, that all legitimate options have been exhausted. A human wants something, wants it badly and wants it now, but they can not see how to get it by working or persuading or saving or begging or negotiating or trading. They violate the *Basic Principle of Ethics*. They feel forced to go to the extreme: to kill, to maim, to steal, to blow things up. It feels to them as if time has squeezed itself into a crevice of opportunity that spurs them to act badly and without much thinking. They have a confused understanding, a mental deficiency, like an electrical grid with a short circuit. A spurned suitor in a love triangle might be overcome by jealousy. A greedy person might think that a theft will go unnoticed. An ambitious politician might bribe voters. The violent person can not see the wider-area longer-term benefits of playing by the rules. The unfortunate reality is that some humans will become violent regardless of how we structure society.

In a physical sense, violence is bumping. It is one human bumping into another, not accidentally but deliberately in the sense of human-type free will, in the mind of at least one of the combatants. When people don't like each other, they separate in opposite directions like magnets pushing each other apart, but with violence, in the case of at least one of the antagonists, the inclination is to close in on the other. The idea of distance seems to be insufficient to resolve the antagonism. Violence is like an unfortunate return to our primitive roots.

While violence, like everything that happens, is totally determined by the past, so that nobody is blameworthy from the god-type perspective, yet from our human-type perspectives, blame must be assigned. Somebody transgressed the bubble boundary between one person's rights and another person's rights. In an escalating verbal dispute between two people, name-calling and finger gestures may be acceptable, but throwing the first punch is not, so humans label the puncher as violent and the recipient of the punch as the victim, even though nobody is blameworthy from the god-type perspective.

It is the state's duty to prevent violence and to punish transgressors. A person in a civilized society essentially surrenders their right of self-defense to the state with the understanding that the state will be an impartial judge in any disputes. The state is like a bundle of the accumulated power of all persons inside it, and therefore it exerts great force. There are numerous advantages for individuals with this arrangement since the state is clearly more powerful than any single person within it, and it is much better equipped to make and enforce the law. It is better able to render impartial verdicts because its fortunes are not linked to one person or group of persons, but because of its higher-level position in the chain of complexity, it should seek what is best for everybody, assuming of course that the state and its laws are good.

In a state that is strong and well-ordered and good and that respects individual rights, then people would not need to worry much about violence because the state would protect everybody. But we don't live in an ideal state. So it is important for us as individuals to understand violence and to know how to deal with it if it happens.

Violence begins in the confused mind of a would-be criminal. Their ideas are bad. Their attempts to link longer and longer idea-chains into correct sequences are clumsy and riddled with error and don't reflect reality. Their desires overpower them. They can not see the wider-longer picture of how to get what they want. So they risk a long-term benefit for a short-term payout.

Violators usually have the initiative. They can choose when and where to attack. They usually choose a location where police can not intervene quickly and where their attack is obscured from view. That is why a good state should try to monitor public movement everywhere to discourage violence. A would-be violator usually has greater resources than their intended victim, such as a weapon or better information.

The unfortunate reality is that to confront a violent person, nonviolent persons may have to fight back using physical force. The stuck person begins the fight, but the unstuck person must end it. The victim struggles to figure out what is happening. This is why it is good to rehearse self-defense strategies, so there is less thinking involved, and the response to the attacker can be fast and sure.

If the victim and the attacker are alone, then the outcome depends on circumstances. There are no rules. Any act or gesture or idea that works to subdue the attacker is good. It is an intellectual battle to find the weak points in the attacker's strategy, and to guard one's own weak points. The idea is to interrupt or block the attacker's idea-chains of cause-and-effect, to persuade them that violence will backfire against them. It is an attempt to unglue the attacker's stuck mind, so whatever helps this to happen is good. If a critical advantage is secured so that the victim can either escape or neutralize the attacker, then it becomes a matter of containing the problem until police arrive. In other words, the extent of a victim's response should be limited to what is necessary to stop the violence.

Violence transforms rights instantly. When an attack begins, individual rights vanish. Poof, they're gone, not just for the victim but for people nearby. Rights are fragile. They depend on everybody respecting them. All it takes is for one person to disrespect them with an attack, and they disappear. A thug has the power to instantly transform a civilized area of the world, governed by law, into a lawless and uncivilized state of nature.

It is in the long-term best interests of the bystanders, as well as the victim, to not simply stand by and do nothing, but to work actively to restore individual rights. The attacker doesn't threaten just the victim, but threatens everybody indirectly. If the attacker kills the victim, then the bystanders could become their next victim.

So it behooves them to act. So a victim, under attack, should try to communicate what is happening to people nearby, and to elicit their help to contact the police or to help subdue the attacker.

How to fight violence
The basic formula for fighting violence is as follows.

Individuals form a group, subdue the violator, and then disband.

This is the common sense approach which humans know intuitively. The formula works at various levels of complexity. It works for individual humans coping with a thug: They bunch together to overpower the thug, then disband. It works for citizens coping with an abusive government: They band together, protest to oust the bad officials, then disband. It is how free nations deal with a rogue nation: They form an alliance, subdue the rogue, then disband.

Rights undergo a transformation during violence. The best wider-area longer-term response for everybody is to bind themselves together into a group which is united for the purpose of defeating the attacker, and for this end, it is the group that has rights, not individuals. A group is a more powerful entity than an assembly of uncoordinated persons. Individuals band together to form their own temporary "state".

A group properly constituted is much more likely to prevail in the conflict. When the group fights the violator, it may win or lose, and factors which decide the outcome include coordination, leadership, weapons, resources, intelligence and so forth. But if the group fails to coalesce, and people continue to operate as isolated individuals, so that the transformation from the rights of individuals to the rights of the group does not happen, then their prospects are worse.

A real world example might illustrate this dynamic. In 2001, the 9/11 hijackers on United Flight 93 killed the pilots and took control of the airliner, with the intention of crashing it into the Pentagon or the White House. At the moment of the attack, the individual rights of the passengers vanished. The passengers could have continued to act as isolated persons, as if their individual rights continued to exist, but they did not do this. Rather, some of them banded together into a group and rammed a food cart into the cockpit to try to retake control. While their efforts did not save their lives, they were partially successful by diverting the plane from its intended target to crash into a field in Pennsylvania.

It is better for each individual in the wider-space longer-time sense to unite as a group when violence threatens. The group is stronger to the extent that each person gives themselves totally to its operation. People become like soldiers and do what the group wills. It is not a democratic-republican entity by any stretch but more of a mini-totalitarian state tasked with the limited mission of defeating the violator. After it prevails, then it disbands, and rights return back to individuals.

There are limits to group action. Its power is temporary in that its duration is limited to the time when violence threatens. It is limited geographically, so that violence in one location does not curtail rights elsewhere.

While specific situations such as the airplane hijacking happen rarely, it is important to understand this essential dynamic, and to be ready to fight if such a situation presents itself. It entails an obligation to act: to side with the victim, to contact the police, or to serve as witnesses at a subsequent court trial. It is the duty of free people to commit fully to individual rights, and to fight to restore those rights when necessary.

Preventing violence

If we see things from the state's perspective, violence prevention is a systems problem. Violence can be committed by individuals, by groups of individuals, or by foreign governments, and it can be both internal and external, with the perpetrators inside or outside the nation, or both. It is possible that the government, itself, commits violence against its own people, which is a form of tyranny.

What is common to all types of violence is the attack on the rights of individuals. It is characterized by the breaking of rules and the temporary enslavement of people, often accompanied by lying and other distortions of the truth, and the creation of fear. It goes against the *Basic Principle of Ethics*. It reduces people. It is a short-term way of dealing with long-term problems. It is some people turning other people into tools.

We can classify violators by what rules they violate. Neighbors who don't obey laws we call *criminals*. Government officials who don't obey their constitutions we might call *tyrants*. Foreign leaders or powerful foreign groups who don't obey international law we might call *foreign terrorists*. What is common to each of these violators is that they don't do what's good for themselves, in wider spaces and longer time frames. Their determinations of what is good are seriously flawed. Things go badly for them as time passes. Criminals go to jail. Tyrants get exiled. Foreign terrorist leaders lose the wars that they start.

The key to preventing violence is an umbrella concept which, for lack of a better term, might be called *light*, which describes how information and knowledge and ideas and reason can prevent violence.

One type of light is inserting correct cause-and-effect idea chains into the mind of a would-be violator to persuade them to think through the longer-term consequences of a planned future act of violence. They'll understand that if they do the crime, they'll do the time, and such an inserted idea may prevent them from following through with their aggression.

To illustrate, in the movie *Witness*, near the end, a bad guy with a gun is holding a little boy hostage, and they are surrounded by the good guy and the boy's mother and a dozen farmers in a tense standoff. Only the bad guy had a gun, but there was only one bad guy. But the bad guy surrendered. Why? It was because of an idea which shone like light within the bad guy's mind. Most likely, the idea was that *the number of bullets in the gun is less than the number of witnesses.* This idea suggested that it was impossible for him to kill every witness and flee with impunity. The cause-and-effect idea chain, in the bad guy's mind, might have gone something like this: *If I kill the boy, and maybe one or two farmers, then I will have no more bullets, and then there will be more witnesses to my additional murders, and I could get into even more trouble with the law.* Light entered his mind so the bad guy surrendered. While this story is fictional, it gives a general sense of how correct thinking can enter the mind of a would-be aggressor and dissuade them from committing violence.

Here is another example of how light can prevent crime. Decades ago when somebody received a telephone call on a landline, it was impossible to know the identity of the caller. We never knew for sure who was calling. This anonymity permitted anonymous threats as well as crank calls and scams. Later, the technology of caller identification came along, so people could identify the caller's phone number. Caller identification was a form of light. Abuses stopped. There were no more anonymous death threats. It acted like an antiseptic, like sunlight, killing off bacteria. It helped to make people accountable to each other. Unfortunately new technologies are emerging that enable a caller to disguise their identities.

Light can prevent most forms of violence at different levels of complexity. Light might be a picture of a license plate, a mental image of the face of a rapist, an expense report of a public official, or eyewitness testimony. It can be a written treaty, a contract, a constitution or rules of courtroom procedure, or a citizenship document. It can be a system of identifying movement in public while preserving privacy.

If citizens are clear-thinking and informed and participate constructively in the political process, then tyranny in the form of a single autocrat coming to power is extremely unlikely. A free press and widespread respect for the rule of law would make it difficult for a would-be tyrant to insinuate themselves into a position of authority. One way that a tyrant or a malevolent faction might slip into power is by exploiting flaws in the constitutional architecture. A more likely scenario is when an extended crisis stresses the nation, such as a natural disaster or a war or an economic depression, and a leader promises to save the republic but fails to relinquish power after the danger has passed. Once a despot becomes entrenched in power, they are difficult to dislodge, although their rule, like that of all tyrants, will be fraught with tension and strife.

War

In the Bhagavad Gita, the mythical warrior Arjuna hesitates before battle. He sees some of his friends and family on the opposing side. He fears being called a coward. He says "My members fail, my tongue dries in my mouth, a shudder thrills my body, and my hair bristles with horror." He doubts that any good can come from mutual slaughter. But he is persuaded to fight by thinking that the wider-longer goal of sustained peace was worth the struggle, even if it entails sacrifice, as if he had applied the *Basic Principle of Ethics* to the decision.

War, unfortunately, is part of the human condition. Struggling over land or food or wealth or mates or respect has a long history like crumpled litter along a highway. Since nations have rights in the sense of zones of possible future action that are accepted beforehand, war is trespassing into these zones. It often springs from an imbalance of military power, either real or perceived, coupled with a greed to have something that the other side has. The miscalculation is that the best way to get what is wanted is by violence, since diplomacy and trade and bargaining and hard work seem fruitless. Each side thinks that what is bad for its adversary is good for itself. Usually the stronger side attacks the weaker one, and it usually wins. We love our countries, but feelings of patriotism can devolve into a prejudicial nationalism that confuses us, and leads us to war.

Wars are often started by leaders who lack virtue. They can't see what's best for themselves and their nation in the wider-longer sense. So they latch on to war as a slapdash solution to their political problems. What happens is bad not only for people on both sides but for the environment, since it usually involves destruction, fire, pollution, the death of animals and the depletion of resources, and opportunities for dangerous pathogens to breed.

Our warlike tendencies seem to be baked into our human nature. Our human predisposition is unlikely to change because of technological progress or greater understanding or education or spiritual enlightenment or instruction in ethics. The unfortunate reality is that some of our weapons have become so powerful that we risk unthinkable destruction if they are used.

In war, the survival of the entire nation is at stake. If it loses, citizens and soldiers and officials and visitors may lose their property and freedom and lives.

The onset of war demands an abrupt transformation from a peacetime to a wartime orientation. Factories shift from making cars to tanks. Citizens shift from workers to soldiers. This transformation can be difficult for a democratic-republican nation, but it must be done quickly and efficiently. People who had been accustomed to doing what they liked, going where they pleased, and saying what they wanted, may resent new restrictions such as rationing and price controls as well as military service. Speech criticizing the war effort or dampening enthusiasm for it may be censored. Travel may be restricted and elections postponed.

The transition requires a shift of rights from the individual to the group, with the group in this case being the nation. The nation makes decisions. It acts. It exerts great control over citizens and the economy. The predominant mode for everybody is short-term sacrifice for long-term benefit.

During wartime, it is the role of the sovereign, whether a king or a legislative body or the head of state, to declare war or peace. It is the role of civilians to serve as soldiers or to supply the military effort. It is the role of the general to create and execute military strategy, for officers to implement that strategy, and for soldiers to fight. It is vital for everybody to have a shared sense of mission and a sense that their cause is just. There need not be agreement about the morality of the methods used to subdue the enemy for, as the saying goes, all is fair in love and war, although adhering to wartime guidelines set by treaties is usually a good choice. The war effort should involve the entire society, not merely a part.

Being a soldier is a tough task. It means becoming an expendable tool and obeying commands without question. It requires a clear-headed mind focused on reality that is not disabled by fear or anxiety. Officers have the responsibility of protecting those under their command while carrying out orders.

The principles of war are like those for fighting, except on a higher level. It is a struggle between rival systems at a higher level of complexity. The struggle happens not just between two sides, but within the minds of all participants. Both sides try to preserve their human-type free will and to thwart their enemy's human-type free will.

Strategy is an extended linking of cause-and-effect relations reflecting many players and resources. It should be constantly updated and revised as the war continues. It is an active search for weak places within the enemy's strategy where a little force can have a devastating impact and where a tiny effort can interrupt entire chains of the enemy's ideas of cause-and-effect.

The essence of war is to attack the enemy's strategy. It means guessing correctly what that strategy is, and then countering that strategy. It might be planting false ideas into the enemy's mind to short-circuit their thinking. It might mean limiting enemy movement through fear. If one army can successfully encircle the other, the concentrated velocity of firepower into a single cramped space can lead to victory. In the best scenario, this means getting the enemy to submit without fighting.

Since the enemy is similarly trying to cripple one's own strategy, plans and resources and capabilities and weapons must be disguised. War is based on subterfuge, with an intent to confuse the enemy, to appear strong when weak, dispersed when concentrated, energized when tired, far away when up close. Like fighting, war is binary. Only two sides fight. At no time in history has there been a war with each of three sides fighting the other two sides simultaneously.

What often decides the outcome is the skill of the general. His or her mind should be healthy and flexible and fluid, free from crippling emotions so that they are neither cowardly nor reckless nor egotistical. It should not have a delicacy of honor which leads to shame. It should not vacillate on decision-making but make good decisions in a timely manner. It should listen to skilled advisers to benefit from their differing views and collective learning. It should be able to merge innovative technologies and people into dynamic new combinations. It should be knowledgeable about weapons, logistics, terrain, timetables, equipment, resources, morale, and soldiers of their own army and those of their enemy. While a general may feel self-doubt and uncertainty, they should communicate confidence and steadfast resolve to the soldiers. They should be able to see through the enemy's deceptions to correctly guess their plans. Since war requires vast expenditures of energy, economic management is important. A general might split the army into two divisions, such as one large but slow force, and another small but mobile force. Military discipline should be consistent and rigorous, with a constancy of rewards and punishment, so that soldiers obey commands without hesitation. Moral force is vital. If the enemy can be persuaded that their cause is morally wrong, they might surrender. So it makes sense for a democratic-republican state to nourish and educate its military officers to turn them into highly competent commanders, so that their skills are never needed.

Meaning in our lives

Thinkers throughout history have wondered about what our lives mean. "The mystery of human existence lies not in just staying alive, but in finding something to live for", said Dostoyevsky. But how do we find what to live for? It is a tough question. The mythological character Gilgamesh, wrestling with grief after his best friend Enkidu died, struggled to live a meaningful life. This brings us to the subject of what our lives mean, and perhaps it is best to begin in a roundabout fashion.

Consider that when we examine something, we take in so much information that it would flood our capacity to think about it. So we distill the torrent of data to a core pattern. We figure out what is important and ignore the rest. If billions of photons enter our eyes, we pick out the figure of an object such as a chair. It is the pattern that makes sense to us. It is what the billions of photons *means*.

A computer can not do this, as far as we know. Computers take in data, manipulate it, and send data back out. But it doesn't mean anything to a computer. It is simply a machine.

What humans do to individual objects such as a chair, we do to our whole lives. We look for patterns which explain to us what our lives are all about. We try to make sense of the billions of experiences and insights and friendships and lessons that we remember. What does our life mean? We reflect on past events, such as what we learned as a child, in school, from our families and friends and lovers, and from our imagination, and then we try to assemble these disparate tidbits into something meaningful.

We are like authors constructing a personal autobiography that we write in our minds for ourselves. We paint ourselves as the protagonist and give ourselves a purpose which is usually larger than us, such as a quest, a project, or a problem to solve. This goal is something in the distant future which usually involves other people and can be understood by us as an integral part of the ongoing human project. Our quest is something bigger than us, something that we see as important and worthy, and something that we think is good in and of itself.

Will Durant said that "To give life a meaning one must have a purpose larger than one's self, and more enduring than one's life." For Durant, meaningful pursuits could involve family and friends, a cause we care about, a movement, or "any endeavor to make life better for others." Durant found meaning in the joy of existence. He wrote "The simplest meaning of life then is joy—the exhilaration of experience itself, of physical well-being; sheer satisfaction of muscle and sense, of palate and ear and eye … Even if life had no meaning except for its moments of beauty … that would be enough; this plodding through the rain, or fighting the wind, or tramping the snow under sun, or watching the twilight turn into night, is reason a-plenty for loving life."

Our stories are more meaningful if they are internally consistent and if they make sense to us. Our stories link our past and present and future, so that our plans for the future are extensions of our past progress. Our efforts to explain ourselves to ourselves are not always rational and can be wrapped up with our emotional longings and biases. Naturally we focus on what is consistent within our story and ignore the inconsistent details. This is what good fiction writers do, and it is what we try to do in our own in-progress autobiography.

Our quest should not seem trivial but something that might occupy much of our lives. According to Confucian philosophy, choosing a goal that is practicable but difficult is a key to happiness. It should not be something easy such as making ourselves a sandwich. If the sandwich is made, then we're done. We won't imagine ourselves as earning a medal for the making-of-a-sandwich achievement and we won't ask our friends to hold a party in our honor. However, if one is a quadriplegic, then the sandwich-making quest might be meaningful because of the difficulty. We value goals that are harder to achieve.

While the goal might be difficult, we believe it to be achievable somehow, such as ending malaria or curing cancer or winning the Tour de France or having a family or writing a best-selling novel or building a pyramid. The goal is distant. Reinhold Niebuhr said "Nothing that is worth doing can be achieved in our lifetime." The goal is usually something concrete and simple enough so that we can communicate it to others, perhaps in a sentence or even a phrase. A lesson in the Bhagavad Gita is that we should choose worthy goals, and not be tempted by a clear path to a lesser goal.

As we go about living, we dangle our goal before us and orient our activity toward achieving it. We acquire helpful skills. A journalist might become an accurate typist. An architect might master computer design programs. An oceanographer might become a certified diver.

To the extent that we believe that our day-to-day activity is directed toward our way-in-the-distance larger-than-life goal, we are happier. Conversely, if we believe that we are distracted from our goal, then we are unhappier, adrift, bothered.

Our lives seem more meaningful if we see ourselves as choosing our goal rather than hitchhiking on to somebody else's goal. A pyramid builder in ancient Egypt might see their effort as more meaningful if they thought that they had chosen it out of their own human-type free will, or if they had had a critical role in its accomplishment. Unlike the pharaohs or chief engineers, it might be less meaningful to the workers lugging giant slabs up the pyramid's face. Essentially leadership is about communicating a vision of what's meaningful to others and persuading them that it's a good vision.

It seems as if the human experience is wrapped up in our quest for meaning. Like everything, it is a guess. We are looking for a pattern of meaningfulness, but we see what we want to see, and our vision is limited by time and circumstance, by what we know and by what we don't know, and by time and our limited mental capability.

As storytellers of our own story, it helps to be facile writers, skilled at narrative, creatively writing a story in which we see ourselves as good and important and advancing some key aspect of humanity. Hopefully our stories help us to be happy.

Our goals can be good or bad. Each of us usually thinks that our goal is good, but we have differing perspectives, and a goal that might be good for one person might be bad for another. A goal of building the best tree-logging firm might conflict with a goal of protecting the Earth's forests, for instance. We can get attached to our goals, emotional about them, even blinded by them. If by chance we succeed in our goal, then we are happy, and then we may choose a new goal.

It can help us in our quest if we are totally smitten with our goal, so that we become a firm and uncompromising believer in the rightness of our cause. Yet there is a benefit to being skeptical of its worthiness. Should we be doubt-free or skeptical? It is almost as if self-doubt wrecks the fun and dampens our inner fire. As a hero, it helps to be sure of ourselves, single-minded, with our entire being focused on achieving our goal, and yet, by really looking at things, it makes sense to be skeptical. That way, we can keep thinking and questioning and wondering and learning, with the benefit being that we can adjust our goal if we find out that it is bad or stupid or unachievable. Should we be cocksure or skeptical? There is no easy answer.

So it is up to each of us to decide what, if anything, our lives mean. It is not up to God or gods, to neighbors or bosses or politicians or the clergy or ideas planted in our heads from movies or parameters set forth by our parents. Rather, it is up to us. We choose. We choose what purpose we would like to direct our lives toward, and we choose what our lives mean to us. Life can only mean something to living creatures such as us, who puzzle about our existence and our purpose.

So, we, the living, live, for that is what we do, and our focus should not be on death or on dying but on life, as Spinoza insisted. We might follow the advice of the Buddha to "Live every day as if it's our last." Mark Twain wrote that "There isn't time for bickerings, apologies, heartburnings, callings to account, and there is only time for loving."

Loving. Living. That is what life is about. Time is short, so live well and smile.

Made in the USA
Middletown, DE
06 February 2025